TANGLED
vines

OTHER BOOKS BY DIANE NOBLE
(writing as Amanda MacLean)

Westward
Stonehaven
Everlasting
Promise Me the Dawn
Kingdom Come

Anthologies
A Christmas Joy
A Mother's Love
Heart's Delight

TANGLED
vines

DIANE NOBLE
ALSO KNOWN AS AMANDA MACLEAN

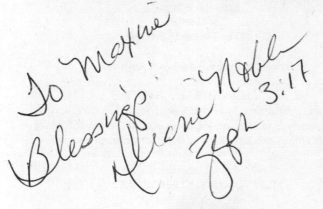

To Maxine
Blessing!
Diane Noble
Zep 3:17

ALABASTER

BOOKS

TANGLED VINES
published by Alabaster Books
a division of Multnomah Publishers, Inc.
and in association with the literary agency of Writer's House, Inc.

© 1998 by Diane Noble
International Standard Book Number: 1-57673-219-3

Cover illustration by Paul Bachem
Design by Brenda McGee

Scripture quotations are from:
The Holy Bible, New International Version
© 1973, 1984 by International Bible Society,
used by permission of Zondervan Publishing House

Epigraph is from:
The Message
© 1993 by Eugene H. Peterson

Printed in the United States of America

For information:
MULTNOMAH PUBLISHERS, INC.
POST OFFICE BOX 1720
SISTERS, OREGON 97759

98 99 00 01 02 03 04 — 10 9 8 7 6 5 4 3 2 1

To my brother Dennis

You were the first to teach me

the art of storytelling,

the skill of creating characters

who joyfully perform in the mind's theater.

Thank you.

I am the Vine, you are the branches.
When you're joined with me and I with you,
the relation intimate and organic,
the harvest is sure to be abundant.

(THE MESSAGE)

PROLOGUE

I t was early morning, and the slant of the sun created dapples of shadow and light through the cascading grape ivy on K.C. Keegan's condo patio. She settled into a chair, mug of coffee in one hand, laptop computer securely in the other. As soon as she had placed the laptop on a small white iron table, she turned it on and adjusted the screen.

She scrolled through her e-mail. Most days there were a few business-related posts, once in a while a message from a friend, or an update from her great-aunt Theodora, who was at her cabin working on her next mystery.

But this morning, there was only one message in K.C.'s mailbox. It was titled "Disappearances!" She didn't recognize the sender's screen name, BIZZYBEE. She clicked her mouse to open the letter and began to read:

TO: K.C. Keegan, Publisher, Pelican Journal

You MUST immediately investigate a series of disappearances from San Francisco north to our sweet Pelican Cove! Though I have no concrete proof, I KNOW lives are in danger! For more information, please hit "reply" and leave a message. I'll get back to you.

Have a nice day.

BIZZYBEE

P.S. A cult may be involved.

K.C. briefly wondered how BIZZYBEE had found her personal e-mail address, then dismissed it with a shrug. After all, the newspaper business, especially in a small town like Pelican Cove, attracted crackpots who loved nothing better than getting their names or pictures in the paper.

K.C. deleted the message.

~ ~ ~ ~ ~

One hundred miles inland, Rance Randolph watched his followers file through the tall double doors of the auditorium. They entered reverently, heads down, robes spilling around them in clouds of unbleached cotton, hoods draped around their faces.

When they were standing in rows before him, Randolph moved to the front of the platform and raised his arms heavenward. The Angels of Fellowship devotees imitated his action. In the rear of the room the drums began their rhythmic, pulsating beat, and Randolph closed his eyes and began to sway. His followers did the same.

"Atara-our-home-in-the-heavens." His followers' voices lifted as one as they repeated his words: "Angels of Atara. Come for us. Save us. Take us from this world. Take us to Atara. Atara-Atara-Atara."

He opened his eyes and watched his flock. As they swayed to the music, their faces were devoid of thought. Arms reaching upward, robes flowing and swinging. Drums beating. Voices chanting. Twirling and swaying, the devotees raised their voices in worship of the Atara deity, working themselves into the mild trance he knew would follow. "Atara-Atara-Atara."

The early morning sunlight streamed through the room's stained-glass windows and their resplendent depiction of angels, medieval and modern. A kaleidoscope of jeweled tones spilled over the robes in swirls of color as the Angels of Fellowship danced, over the massive pillars that seemed to stretch skyward as if to distant stars, planets, and other unknown universes. Eyes shut, the devotees lifted their arms, fingers grasping the air as if reaching for the Ataran Angels.

He allowed the drums to continue as his followers headed

into their mind-cleansing state. "Atara-Atara-Atara." When some of the older members fell silently to the floor, unconscious, he signaled for the chanting to halt.

"Atarans," he said when the drums had quit their throbbing. "Atarans, please give me your attention."

They halted abruptly, blinking, as if surprised to find themselves in the room. It was that way every morning and every evening. The ritual cleansed their minds of short-term memory. He fixed a reassuring look on his face and met their eyes with a solemn nod.

They were an obedient group. It hadn't taken him long to learn that followers were like children and longed to be told what to do. Lately, he'd also discovered that by adding a few simple rules he could draw them even closer to the childlike state in which he needed them to exist. No one was now allowed to use the pronoun *I*. Except himself, of course.

He was especially amused when they struggled to answer his staged questions without using the pronoun. Most of the time they ended up referring to themselves as *it,* which, of course, chiseled away at their humanity.

He lifted his arm dramatically. "The Atarans contacted me again last night." His words were followed by appreciative murmurs and words of wonder about his miraculous communication with the Ataran angels. He dropped his voice reverently. "Our time to join them is approaching sooner than I expected. Do you understand what this means?"

Childlike anticipation lit the devotees' faces.

"Brothers and sisters, they have described our journey in detail so that I may prepare you, their devoted followers. But I've been instructed to save this disclosure until just before we depart planet Earth.

"All in good time, my friends," he said. "For now, our mission is to continue to tell others of the fulfillment that will be theirs through following the doctrine of our Ataran angels. And it is a good life, is it not?

"Filled with clean living today, hope for the future..." He laughed heartily. "Well, maybe not for our dear, old planet Earth. But the coming holocaust doesn't concern us. And those few who pass through our gates will hear only our message of hope. Nothing more. Just as a taste of fine wine prepares the palate for more, so does a taste of our message to mankind.

"And speaking of fine wine, we are within days of harvest. This will prove to be one of the finest years ever for Angels Crest winery. Though our time to leave this earth draws nigh, our work here will continue just as if the vineyard will be here forever."

He paused, then continued earnestly. "Don't ever forget, brothers and sisters, it is through hard work and obedience that we are purified, made ready for the next life."

As usual, he went on to finish his talk with some additional instruction about the day's activities: The chosen of his flock would shed their robes so that the public would see only fresh-scrubbed, clean-cut people, young and old, sporting peppy logo-embroidered resort wear. Then they would take their places in the gift shop, wine-tasting cellars, video-viewing room, and, of course, his award-winning culinary arts center. Many of the others would head to the vineyards.

But before he dismissed them, one last mind-cleansing session was needed. He wanted to make sure they weren't influenced by those visitors who would later visit the chateau. The drums again began their rhythmic beating, and Randolph raised his arms and began to sway to the music.

Soon the room was filled with the sounds of praise. He imagined it was for himself. As always, the thought transported him to some distant place within his mind, a place where he could forget everything but the present glory.

"Angels of Atara. Come for us. Save us. Take us from this world. Take us to Atara."

Later that same morning, Theodora Whimple adjusted her wide-brimmed straw hat against the slant of the sun. She smiled to herself. She'd promised her grandniece, K.C., that she would get more exercise. But, lands, this climb was a bit more difficult than she'd expected.

She fanned herself with the straw hat and dabbed at her brow with a dainty handkerchief. Yes, this definitely would be a tale to tell her dear K.C. She'd already uncovered enough about this cult to cause quite a stir in her next book. No telling what else she'd unearth during her visit.

Her thoughts settled on K.C. They were as alike as two chipmunks in a woodpile. Nosy. Energetic. Insatiably curious. Stubborn as two redheads could possibly be. Well, one natural redhead; one, gray-helped-along-to-red. Though she preferred to think of the color as it was described on the bottle: Sunkissed Auburn.

She planned to be at the chateau just long enough to nose around. She had been away too long from Pelican Cove. Immediately following her visit to Angels Crest, she planned to return to the little cabin in Sugarloaf Ridge, then tomorrow, back home at last to K.C. and Max.

Dear Max. Even at Theodora's age, her heart did flip-flops when she thought of him, his kind blue eyes, the laugh lines that crinkled at their corners, his fringe of silver hair, his gentle yet powerful voice, a voice she knew spoke often and at great length with God. Oh, how she would love to have Max along for company this day.

Theodora let her gaze travel up the hillside beyond the terraced vineyards to the hill's summit. There, partially obscured by a canopy of live oaks, rose the rock-walled chateau in all its promised glory, turrets and all.

She started again up the dusty road, her hand looped through the leather thong of her walking stick. She reviewed what she knew about Angels Crest. Besides its proud role of an award-winning vineyard, it was the front for Angels of Fellowship, a cult that celebrated the cerebral, a keen self-awareness, a positive outlook, and the finer things in life—from Baccarat crystal to Johann Sebastian Bach. She'd discovered all this through the elusive Keb-Kaseko Rodolphe, world-renowned vintner and authority on Angels Crest, a man she'd met on the internet.

Still climbing upward, Theodora rounded one corner, then another, until she was close enough to see the scrolled silver gates with their Angels Crest insignia and the steel-railed electronic fence surrounding the compound.

In a guardhouse by the gate stood a figure draped in a hooded robe, and Theodora noticed the mounted surveillance cameras atop each high fence post, complete with spotlights bright enough when triggered, she was sure, to create a false daylight even in the darkest night.

Winded again, Theodora halted in the shade of a eucalyptus to rest before continuing up the steep incline. On the far side of the ridge hundreds of acres of lush, vine-covered terraced hills stretched for miles. More robed figures stooped low over the vines, sinister in their appearance, ivory robes with hoods drawn around their faces.

A sense of foreboding crept along Theodora's spine.

For the first time, she wondered whether she should have told someone where she was headed.

ONE

K C., I'm worried." Father Max Callahan leaned forward from where he was sitting on the far side of the young woman's desk at the *Pelican Journal*. "Theo didn't say a word about missing the ballet."

K.C. Keegan pushed up her tortoiseshell-framed eyeglasses on her nose—an act she was ever having to repeat since her nose was too small to keep them in place—and gave him what she hoped was a reassuring smile. The retired Episcopal priest, a widower, held a special place in her heart. He had been rector at K.C.'s church since before she was born, had officiated at her parents' wedding, had been the first to hear of their call to work in a Romanian orphanage after her father's retirement from the business world. And he had been her counselor during the darkest days of her life, three years ago, following her broken engagement.

Now, he was nearly part of the family because of his friendship with Aunt Theodora.

"I'm sure Aunt Theo's at the cabin writing," K.C. said, "away from telephones and people. She hasn't even been answering her e-mail lately. Or else she's off on one of her jaunts, soaking up atmosphere for a plot."

"We had tickets to the ballet," Father Max countered, "for last night's performance—in San Francisco. I saw her write it down. She was looking forward to it. She should have been back yesterday. She's never missed one of our dates before." His blue eyes were shaded with concern. "That's why I think we need to check on her."

"Aunt Theo gets caught up in new projects and loses all

track of time. Theo lets those characters take over her story—
and her life!"

Father Max managed a half-smile, and for a moment neither
one spoke as he seemed to be considering her reassurances. The
only sound came from K.C.'s friend and assistant editor,
Georgie O'Reilly, chatting on the phone in the outer office.

Finally, Father Max cleared his throat. "I think we should
drive up to the cabin. Something tells me things aren't quite
right."

K.C. glanced at the messy stacks of paper on her desk, the
pile of phone messages to answer. Only a couple days until her
sometimes serious, sometimes whimsical weekly, the *Pelican
Journal* had to be put to bed. And she and Georgie had inches
of ad space to fill, more stories to write; even K.C.'s own column, "Pelican Chat," was yet to be fleshed out.

"I really can't get away, Max. At least not today. Why don't
we wait another couple of days? Maybe by then we'll have
heard from Aunt Theo." Many times Theodora had disappeared for days on end, researching a book. K.C. usually didn't
worry. Her aunt was one of the most self-sufficient people she
knew.

Father Max still didn't look convinced. Maybe he was right
and they really should check on Theo. But again she surveyed
at the stacks of papers and phone messages on her desk and
made the decision to wait.

"I've got a newspaper to get out," she said regretfully. "As
much as I'd like to go, I really can't today. There are some
pressing matters...here at the paper. If you'll wait just a few
days, I'll go with you." She gave him another reassuring smile
as she adjusted her glasses.

On the other side of the desk, Father Max nodded slowly
and pushed himself to standing. The worry lines were still
deeply etched in his face. "I feel uneasy about waiting, K.C.,

16

but you're right. Theo's probably buried in another manuscript deadline. Maybe she just forgot about the ballet." But he didn't sound convinced.

K.C. rounded her desk and walked with him to the front door.

"I'll call you as soon as I can get away," she promised. "We'll make a day of it. Aunt Theo will probably laugh at the very idea we've been so worried."

As soon as Father Max had left her office, K.C. picked up the phone message at the top of the pile.

Suddenly the strange e-mail message she'd received earlier from BIZZYBEE made sense. Of course. It was from Marigold Green, the town's gadfly.

Georgie had already mentioned that Marigold had called twice, the first time alluding to a rumor about the disappearance of Ariel Tilman, an elderly and beloved long-time citizen of Pelican Cove. She'd added dramatically that she had it on good authority that shortly before leaving town several months ago, Ariel had announced she believed that people could be reincarnated as angels.

But Marigold's phone message the second time she called contained one sentence: *Why didn't you answer my e-mail?* And it was signed BIZZYBEE.

Marigold Green answered on the fourth ring. "I'm so glad to finally hear from you," she said breathlessly. "I've got more news about poor Ariel."

"Why didn't you leave your real name on the e-mail?"

There was a hesitation on the other end of the line. "I didn't think you'd act on information from me. The other seemed, well, more dramatic."

She was right; everyone knew that Marigold Green, a big-shouldered, spike-haired woman, exaggerated for the sake of attention. Most people gave little validity to anything she said.

17

K.C.'s voice was kinder when she spoke again. "Tell me what you've found out."

"It's not really anything substantial. Like a name or anything. It's just that, well,…"

K.C. tried to be patient. "Just tell me what you've heard, Marigold."

Marigold paused dramatically. "She joined a cult."

"You mentioned in the e-mail something about cults."

"Yes."

K.C. tapped her pencil on the notepad. "Do you have the cult's name?"

"I don't know where it is or what it's called."

"So you still can't substantiate anything about her disappearance?"

"No."

K.C. put down her pencil. "Do you know *anything* about the cult?"

"Only that she left everything to go there. She never returned. No one's heard from her since."

"I'll ask Aunt Theo," K.C. said. "I'm planning to drive up to see her in a few days." Her aunt had known Ariel Tilman since childhood, but she hadn't mentioned anything about her friend's disappearance. "I'll let you know what she says."

There was silence on the other end of the telephone.

"Are you still there?"

"Yes, yes. I'm here. It's just that I thought of the same thing. I drove up to Theo's cabin myself just yesterday."

"You did? How was Theo? We've been a bit worried—"

"She wasn't there. I looked in the front window. Saw her breakfast dishes on the table—like she'd just gone out for a stroll and would be back any minute."

Though rankled on behalf of her aunt, K.C. wasn't surprised at Marigold's snooping. She choked back a quick word of advice about the practice, letting the woman talk on.

"I waited around all afternoon, thinking she might be back anytime, but, well, no sign. So I drove back to Pelican Cove." She hesitated. "One more thing, K.C."

"What's that?"

"Just as I arrived at your aunt's house, the strangest thing happened."

Still tapping her pencil, K.C. waited for Marigold to go on.

"A white van pulled into the drive. Unmarked. I hid in the brush and watched while Theodora's big cat—what's-his-name—was catnapped."

"You mean Bubba?"

"Yes, I saw it with my own eyes."

"That is odd."

"And, well, K.C., I'm wondering if the same catnappers got Theodora."

K.C. swallowed a giggle. "I'm sure Aunt Theo's fine," she said. "If someone cat—I mean, kidnapped my aunt, why would they bother with the cat?"

"I thought, well, with all these disappearances, you just can't be sure..." Marigold's voice trailed off pointedly.

"It's quite a stretch to think that *one* disappearance, Ariel's, might have anything to do with Aunt Theo." She paused, letting her words sink in. "Now, when I see Aunt Theo tomorrow, I'll tell her of your concern. I'll also find out what happened to Bubba."

She hung up and turned to the stacks of papers on her desk, thumbing through them absently. For all her assurances to Father Max and Marigold Green, she couldn't push away her own nagging doubts about Aunt Theo's well-being.

Finally, she picked up the phone again and dialed.

When the deep, resonant voice answered, she said, "Father Max, I think we need to drive up to the cabin. Tomorrow. First thing."

The relief was evident in his voice. "I'll meet you at the office at sunup," he said.

"Just bring the coffee, Max," K.C. laughed. "And make it nine o'clock. I've still got a newspaper to run."

Rance Randolph headed across the compound to the chateau and climbed the wide spiral staircase to his tastefully decorated office on the third floor. He removed his hooded garment and brushed a piece of lint off the lapel of the custom-made business suit he had been wearing beneath the robe. Stretching his arms, he adjusted his cuffs and scrutinized his profile in a gold-leaf mirror across from his desk.

He walked to the long line of French doors on the far side of the room and stood looking out over the exquisitely manicured Angels Crest grounds. Just outside, a century oak, its trunk gnarled and twisted, leaned toward the chateau. It was said that a hundred years ago its deep roots had tapped into some underground wine barrels; that's why it had survived the decades with such obvious robust health, even with its precarious tilt.

A knock sounded at his door. Randolph turned. "Come in."

The door opened to reveal the round face and rotund robed body of Dakota Marshall.

"Brother Dakota," he said, crossing the room to shake the man's hand. "Please sit down." He nodded to a high-backed leather chair opposite his gleaming mahogany desk. He'd known Dakota Marshall, a San Francisco cop who was rumored to be on the take, since Haight-Ashbury days. But as Rance Randolph went on to gather more followers, Dakota Marshall headed deeper into a life of crime until he finally disappeared into the filthy underbelly of San Francisco's Chinatown.

He hadn't been surprised three years ago when Dakota showed up at Angels Crest looking for a job. Nor had he been reluctant to hire him. With his background, Dakota was the perfect choice to head up the estate's sophisticated security operation. Best of all, he knew the man to have no conscience; he would do anything necessary to keep the Angels of Fellowship members from leaving. He would also keep unwelcome guests from entering the premises.

"Thank you for being prompt," he said as Dakota settled into the plush, leather-fragrant chair. Randolph leaned forward, resting his forearms on his desk, steepling his fingertips in mock thoughtfulness. "I want to step up our schedule in the tasting room," he said.

"You mean for the *QmP?*"

"Yes." Randolph nodded. Dakota referred to the German designation for fine wines: *Quality Wine with Special Qualifications.* Special qualifications indeed. Starting tomorrow, mild tranquilizers would be discreetly added to some of the finer wines in the tasting cellar. The result would make the chateau's guests even more relaxed and thus more receptive to the ensuing film and presentation.

"Which do you want to start with?" Dakota asked.

"I think we'll use only the private reserve 1984 cabernet sauvignon and, of course, the chardonnay. They're very popular with our tourists."

Dakota smiled, an agreeable look on his round face. "Each bottle must be treated before it's poured," he said. "The formula

21

must be perfect, otherwise it might be detected. Sister Desirée and Sister Vesta are working Angels Repose tomorrow. Perhaps I—"

Randolph interrupted. "Perhaps *who?*" he asked.

Dakota stared at his leader silently, obviously unwilling to correct his mistake.

After a moment, Randolph went on, irritated he felt the need to fill the silence. "You must not leave your place at the security gate. You'll merely instruct Sister Vesta how to treat each bottle. It's too soon to trust Sister Desirée with such knowledge."

Dakota nodded then leaned forward with one hand on Randolph's desk, preparing to stand. "Is there anything else?"

"Actually there is." Randolph frowned. This would be his first disclosure of the next phase of his scheme. Dakota's villainous attributes would help in its implementation. "As more details are exposed about our…" he hesitated slightly, "…our departure to Atara, we'll need to be careful of any apostates—those who want out of the Fellowship. No one will leave this compound."

"You're telling me to tighten security."

Randolph narrowed his eyes and turned to gaze through the tall beveled window. "Yes," he said thoughtfully. "And to help me step up the program of indoctrination. We need to convince those who might be against us that there is a better way." He smiled. "Then we'll lead them back into our fold one step at a time—"

"Like sipping fine wine," Dakota interjected. "One sip leads to another…then another. Finally the whole glass is consumed."

"Then the bottle. And, of course, then one buys the whole case." He chuckled. "Yes. And as to our coming work with new seekers, we must convince them that no one can know their whereabouts. All contact with the outside world must be cut off.

"Once they've joined us, they'll not be allowed to leave the chateau's grounds. Ever."

Dakota nodded. "They will be saved when the end comes. That is the purpose." His voice was slightly mocking, or did Randolph imagine it?

"They will indeed," he agreed with a beatific smile. "There is another matter that I want you to be aware of."

"What is it?"

"Someone has been making inquiries about our Fellowship. In fact—" he glanced at his watch, "—if my powers of prediction are correct, she should be arriving sometime later this afternoon or evening." He did so enjoy the challenge of a potential new convert. He almost thought of them as quarry, for they provided the sport of guessing about everything, from the time of arrival to the time the seeker became a true believer, ready to do his bidding.

"Who is it?"

"It's someone who will not be allowed to leave from the first moment she sets foot inside our gates." He steepled his fingers again. "Her name is Theodora Whimple. She's a well-known mystery writer from Pelican Cove."

"Is she a seeker?"

"The best kind." He smiled. "She's pretending to be something she's not."

"She's not a mystery writer?"

Randolph let out a soft snort. "She's a writer, that's true. But she'll take some convincing to become a devotee. Until that epiphany in her life, she'll need to stay."

"How is that?"

"In our correspondence, she revealed her concerns about her friend Ariel Tilman. As you know, one can't always be sure

23

of the other party's true identity when corresponding electronically." He paused thoughtfully. "So I checked the records to be certain, and Sister Ariel listed Theodora Whimple as her emergency contact. Opposite the question asking about the relationship, Sister Ariel listed Theodora as 'my best friend since childhood.'"

"Good thing you keep records, even of the dead."

"I do more than that," he said. "I have other means of gathering information. Even without her disclosure, I would have known her surreptitious reasons for visiting Angels Crest." He didn't bother to elaborate.

"What about Sister Ariel's, er, unfortunate accident, then? Was Theodora Whimple notified?"

Randolph smiled. "There was really no need. Our sister merely departed this planet for Atara." When Dakota didn't reply, he continued. "You see, I personally invited Sister Theodora to visit Angels Crest."

"The invitation was from you, the vintner, or from you, our CEO?"

"What do you think?" Randolph smiled. "Ah, the convenience—and the gratification of anonymity—of these new modes of electronic communication."

"And—?"

"She agreed to come, of course."

"But you don't want her to leave once she's here."

"I have it on good authority she's here to investigate for entirely different reasons." He laughed at his own joke. "No, she will not leave."

Dakota stared hard at Randolph. "What about her family?" he said after a moment. "Or does she have family?"

"She revealed that she does indeed—a grandniece in Pelican Cove. A young woman named K.C. Keegan who runs a weekly newspaper. There's no one else. At least in this country."

He stood and again peered through the panes of glass in the French doors. Now the grounds were empty, as usual, during this time of the day. But by tomorrow morning, tourists would again be arriving by the dozens. They were expected; appointments were required at this exclusive vineyard. Most would have stopped at several wineries for tasting on their way to Angels Crest. He smiled. And, as usual, they would be even happier, and much better informed, by the time they left the chateau's grounds. Especially once they'd tasted those special wines with the *QmP* additive.

"What about the young woman? Won't she come looking for her great-aunt?" Dakota persisted.

"She'll provide a challenge all her own when that happens—and I'm betting it will," he said simply. He turned back to his robed brother. "I'm actually hoping she does follow her aunt into our hands.

"But back to the challenge before us. We could use someone of Theodora Whimple's stature." He chuckled. "If the Scientologists have their movie stars, why can't we have a famous mystery writer to promote our cause?" He pictured the media vans entering the compound to interview the woman.

He went on. "I believe we'll discover that our dear Sister Theodora Whimple will soon cut ties to family and friends—just as we convince all our followers to do. From the most delicate to the most stubborn of fruits, all eventually fall into our hands if we have them long enough."

After a moment Dakota pushed his heavy, round body to standing and straightened his robe, adjusting his hood over his bald head. "I'd better see to tomorrow's tasting," he said, turning to leave.

"*Who* will see to the wine?" He narrowed his eyes; this time he wouldn't let Dakota off the hook.

There was a moment of silence, and Dakota's eyes glinted

the color of gunmetal as they flicked across Randolph's face. "It will see to the wine," he finally said evenly. "It will."

"Yes, yes," Randolph said softly. "That's much better. And please, Brother Dakota, don't forget to watch for our beloved Sister Whimple's arrival."

"I will—" He stopped himself. "It will be a pleasure," he corrected with a flat voice as he let himself out of the room.

Randolph chuckled as he heard Dakota's solid footsteps thudding down the spiral staircase. How he enjoyed that latest edict. Kept everyone in their place. Even a tough old buzzard like Dakota.

How could he go deeper than the elimination of self? He frowned in concentration as he stood in front of his French doors, looking out at the ancient, twisted oak to one side of his balcony. The next obvious step was ridding his followers' hearts and minds of any thoughts of a personal God. He grimaced. Many still needed cleansing from their early childhood religious training, especially the idea of only one God existing in the universe. A God who loved them.

He considered the problem for a few minutes, his eyes resting on a distant water fountain.

Of course. The bronze statue he'd recently had installed by the water fountain at the entrance to the estate.

It was the likeness of the Keb-Kaseko Rodolphe, his alter ego. He'd already made the rule that Rodolphe's name was to be held in such reverence, it could not be spoken aloud, except by himself. Worshipping the image was a logical next step.

He imagined his followers bowing before the giant statue with its basket of grapes and bronzed face that so resembled his. After all, they would soon be worshipping Rodolphe on Atara. Or so they thought. They might as well become accustomed to the practice now.

TWO

Theodora halted in front of the chateau's ornate silver gates. She shivered, even though the sun now beat hot on her shoulders. The robed guard, a smallish, portly man, moved from within a small building, smiling as he approached Theodora. "Greetings, Sister!" he declared.

"Hello," Theodora replied in a friendly manner. "I've been invited to visit Angels Crest, have a guided tour, and hear a tad about your history."

"Do you have an appointment?"

"No, but I have an invitation to meet someone here—" She fished through her bag for the printout of her e-mail from Keb-Kaseko Rodolphe. "Here—" She held it toward the guard. "You'll see that it says I am welcome at any time."

The guard took the letter from her hands and scanned it quickly. "Well, well," he said, looking into her eyes as if he knew her. "So it does."

She nodded. "Then it's all right if I do visit—even without an appointment?" His expression troubled her. She considered telling him not to bother, that she would return another time. Return with Father Max or K.C. Maybe both.

But just as she wavered, the guard stepped into the guardhouse and triggered the release of the electronic gate. "The Fellowship will be pleased that you've come," he said as the gate swung open.

She turned, and started to say she had only come to visit, not to stay. But he once again walked toward her, this time in an almost aggressive manner, forcing her to move in the opposite direction...straight through the gate. "You will find your time here very interesting," he said. "Welcome to Angels Crest."

Theodora straightened her shoulders and tried to shake the dark thoughts from her mind. After all, what would it hurt to stay for only an hour or so, talk with Keb-Kaseko, take a quick tour, and, she hoped, have a chat with Ariel. Besides, she thought, looking up at the imposing chateau, what a wonderful backdrop for her next book. She would soak up every bit of atmosphere to use later.

She stepped through the gates, which quickly closed behind her. Seconds later the electronic lock clicked into place, unnaturally loud in the strange silence of the grounds. Theodora didn't look back but continued on the cobbled walkway until she reached a tall and brawny bronze statue in the center of a fountain and tiled pool.

She smiled, almost relieved when she saw the plaque beneath the statue: Keb-Kaseko Rodolphe. They'd corresponded by e-mail so often of late that she considered him a friend. He had disclosed to her that he was affiliated with Angels Crest, though he'd never given her details. She was a bit puzzled, however, that a vintner would merit a large bronze like this one.

Theodora continued on her way toward the chateau's wide portico. Moving up the steps toward the double pillars, she adjusted her straw hat, squared her shoulders, and reached for the brass knocker.

After drawing a deep breath, she rapped sharply. A moment later, she heard the sound of approaching footsteps from inside.

"Come in, come in." Rance Randolph stood to greet Theodora after she was ushered into his office on the third floor of the chateau. "I can't tell you how sorry I am that our dear Keb-

Kaseko Rodolphe is indisposed and cannot meet with you today." The vintner's name rolled off Randolph's tongue like music.

Theodora nodded, peering into Randolph's face. Was it her imagination that he so resembled the statue of Keb-Kaseko? "I was so looking forward to meeting him," she said, assessing him carefully. He was in his mid- to late fifties, she thought, though the smooth skin on his narrow face and longish nose had an ageless look to it. His dark hair was graying at the temples, and he sported a jaunty goatee. He was tall and thin, his neck sinewy, which made his habit of jaw clenching more noticeable. She decided the resemblance she'd noticed earlier must have been based on her always active novelist's imagination.

"Please, join me," he said, nodding across the room. "And I'll explain." She followed him across the room's polished oak floor to the pleasant-looking sitting area. A small floral sofa flanked by two striped high-back chairs had been arranged near a row of French doors overlooking the chateau's formal English gardens. A small antique table had been placed at the center of an oval Chinese rug in front of the sofa. She settled onto the sofa, and Randolph sat in the chair nearest her.

"You see," he said, getting right to the point, "Keb-Kaseko Rodolphe's services are in great demand—not only here at Angels Crest, but in other realms as well."

"I understand," Theodora said, though she was disappointed. "Do you know when he might be returning?"

"Not for some time."

"I had hoped to visit with him. We'd been corresponding. He invited me here."

"Yes, he told me."

She frowned, wondering how much the vintner had disclosed about her visit. She'd wanted to find Ariel and speak with her without raising any suspicions. "Primarily, I'm here to do research," she said finally. "I'm setting my next book in South Africa—in their new vineyards."

He nodded, his gaze never leaving her face. Theodora was bothered by his close scrutiny but went on as if not noticing. "I had hoped to have a tour, hear about your history."

"Ah yes," he said, brightening. "That's why Keb-Kaseko asked me to see you in his place. I can tell you every bit of information you'd ever want to know about the wine industry—and probably some you might not want to know."

Theodora pulled out her notepad and pen. "Then let's begin," she said. "I really can't stay long."

"I understand you walked to the chateau," he said, ignoring her words. "Brother Dakota said you arrived on foot." He then shook his head as if playfully chiding her. "You should have called. We could have sent one of our cars for you."

"Actually, I enjoyed the walk. I just didn't think it would be quite this far," Theodora said. "But that does remind me, could you have someone drive me back to town?" She glanced through the French doors. The sun was still high.

"Of course," he said smoothly, then frowned. "My dear, after your walk up the mountain, you must be exhausted. Would you care for some refreshment?"

Theodora held up a hand. "If you're thinking of a private wine tasting, no, thank you." She wrote the day's date on her pad, impatient to get started. "Now…" she began again, pen poised.

He ignored her pen and pad and leaned closer conspiratorially. "I don't blame you—about the wine tasting, I mean. And if you'll promise not to tell anyone, I'll let you in on a secret." He laughed again before continuing. "I get pretty tired of it all myself."

Theodora was becoming annoyed. "Now that I find difficult to believe!"

"I actually prefer tea," he said, stroking his goatee and sitting back to cross his leg. "Of course, I like the finest of teas served with watercress or caviar sandwiches. But nonetheless, give me a steaming pot of English tea any day—"

"Over a cabernet sauvignon?" she asked, incredulous.

"Let me demonstrate," he said with a wide smile. Before she could protest, he stepped outside the room. Theodora could hear him conferring with the same young woman who'd earlier escorted her to his office.

While he was gone, she glanced around the room beyond the sitting area. Dark wood beams set off ivory walls. Floor-to-ceiling French doors graced two walls, each opening onto a balcony that circled the third floor of the chateau. The office furniture was classic, lustrous, masculine. Fresh flowers filled large crystal vases on tabletops and Randolph's desk.

After a moment, Randolph reentered the room, closed the door, and flicked a switch near his desk that brought beautiful strains of Johann Sebastian Bach into the room through hidden speakers. Then he settled into his chair, leaning back as if he had all the time in the world.

"Our tea will be served momentarily," he said. "But while we wait, tell me more about your writing." His eyes narrowed almost imperceptibly. "What exactly is your book going to be about? That is, if you don't mind my asking."

Theodora laughed lightly. "Actually, I make it a rule never to talk about something before it's written. But please, don't take offense. It's merely because I have this strange idea that if I let the words leave my brain before I'm ready to write them, I'll never get them back again."

"Makes sense, dear. It makes sense." He frowned. "Obviously, you're planning to write about a vineyard such as ours, otherwise you wouldn't be here. But tell me, how can I be of assistance to you? What would you like to know about Angels Crest?"

She again took up her pad and pen. "I'd like to see the inner workings of the winery itself. Everything from the grape crusher to where the wine is aged in French oak barrels. And I'd like to take a tour, if we can fit it in."

"Of course, that can be arranged. But you might want to consider staying until tomorrow. We have a lovely lodge, you know. To see the place properly, you really need to spend longer than just a few hours."

Again she thought about no one knowing her whereabouts, and though Rance Randolph was being perfectly civil, there was something about him that bothered her. "Perhaps I could return another day for the tour," she said.

Just then there was a light tap on the door, and the young woman in the hooded robe entered with a sterling tray and ornate tea service and a crystal plate of dainty tea sandwiches.

"Thank you, Sister," Randolph said, taking the tray and setting it on the low antique table between them. He poured tea into a delicate bone-china cup and handed it on a saucer to Theodora. "Cream or sugar?" His manners were impeccable.

"No, thank you," she said, raising the cup to her lips. She savored her first sip. It was fragrant and delightful. She hadn't realized how thirsty and hungry she was after her morning's hike up the hillside. She reached for a small cucumber sandwich, with soft feta cheese and a sprig of cilantro, and took a bite. "Delicious," she murmured. A moment later she sampled the smoked salmon and caviar. It was even better than the first.

"These are addictive," she said with a smile.

"Yes, aren't they?" Randolph poured more tea into her cup. "These are made at our culinary arts school. They are quite unique." Though he raved about them, Theodora noticed he was not sampling even one.

"You must give your students my compliments," she said, beginning to feel more relaxed than she had all day. It must

32

have been the walk in the sun, she decided as her eyes fluttered closed for a moment.

She savored another few sips of tea. The sweet fragrance comforted her. The scents of peaches and mangoes and strawberries blended together, rising into her nostrils with the steam. Very appealing to the senses.

Yet, strangely, when she sipped the drink again, the taste seemed bitter. Perhaps she should have added sugar and cream.

Of course! She stifled a smile. She could have written this clichéd scene herself. The tea had been doctored. And she'd been expected to cover the taste with sugar. If she weren't feeling so pleasant and dreamy, she would be annoyed.

"Another sandwich?" Randolph asked, interrupting her thoughts.

Theodora lifted another cucumber sandwich from the plate and nibbled at its edge. No telling what he'd mixed with the feta. Without asking, Randolph poured more tea into her cup. She pretended to take another sip, smiling at him over the rim of the cup. He obviously wanted her relaxed, perhaps even unconscious. But why? Why would an elderly mystery writer be any threat to him? What did he not want her to find out? Now her curiosity was getting the best of her. No longer was she thinking only of leaving as quickly as possible. Instead, she hoped that whatever he'd doctored her tea with hadn't already dulled her senses.

"While you're enjoying your tea and sandwiches," Randolph said, his voice soothing, "let me tell you about our Angels of Fellowship."

Ah, maybe that was it. Indoctrination. "Please do," Theodora said. Two could play this game. She removed her straw hat, placed it primly on her lap, and settled back into the sofa. It did feel terribly cozy. She feigned another sip of the fragrant tea and sighed dramatically. "Tell me everything," she coaxed, ready to take mental notes. Her pad and pen had fallen to the floor.

"It will take me some time to get through the entire story...." he began, then let his voice drop expectantly.

She was intrigued. Of course, he was again going to invite her to stay. She knew his next question before he uttered the words. She couldn't have written his words better herself.

"...and I wouldn't want you to miss the last afternoon train. Would you like to stay as our guest in the chateau?" he asked. "As I mentioned, we have wonderful accommodations."

"That's such a nice idea," she murmured. Staying the night to discover the mystery behind this grand chateau and its owner began to make more sense. Besides, she'd come to visit Ariel. And Keb-Kaseko. "Yes, a very nice idea indeed."

"Wonderful." His voice dropped. "Now that it's settled, just relax and listen to what I'm about to tell you." The music filling the room was different now, dreamier. She recognized the Orpheus Chamber Orchestra performing Handel, one of his twelve concerti grossi, opus six, she thought sleepily.

Wrapped in a pleasant and dreamy cocoon, she drifted through the worlds he described...a planet called Atara and its population of angels...until he mentioned that he'd spoken with an angel just the night before, an angel named Abraham Lincoln, one of the forty-four he spoke with regularly. Some of the others were Winston Churchill and Socrates and Mark Twain.

What rubbish! She stifled a laugh.

Randolph's voice was hypnotic as he continued to describe Atara and the incomprehensible joys earthlings would know when they joined the forty-four Ataran Angels. Now and then he would pause, and though her eyes were closed, she sensed he was watching to see if she had yet lost consciousness.

Had the tea doctoring worked, this was when the room

would begin to fade to the deepest velvet black. At least, that's the way I would have written this scene, Theodora thought sleepily.

Sighing deeply, she tried to stay awake. But it was impossible, and at last the soft velvet darkness overtook her.

Theodora's breathing slowed, and Randolph felt certain she had indeed fallen into the stuporous sleep he'd intended. He moved silently to the door and called for the comely, young Sister Bastancherry who'd earlier brought tea.

"Yes, Brother Randolph?" she asked politely as she rose from her chair behind the desk in his outer office. She had been waiting patiently, as instructed.

"Sister, our novice has been quite overcome with weariness. I'll need you to prepare her quarters. Put her in the Mozart suite, and make sure there are fresh flowers for when she wakens from her nap. I'll need to speak with Sister Desirée. Please ask her to stop by and see me for instructions."

"Yes, Brother," Sister Bastancherry said. "I'll see to it immediately."

"Who will see to it, dear?"

She colored slightly. "It will see to Sister Theodora's accommodations," she corrected.

He beamed. "Yes, child. Thank you. Now you may go." He dismissed the young woman with a flutter of the fingertips.

Within a few minutes, the light fall of footsteps and the rustle of Sister Desirée's long robe could be heard as she climbed the stairs leading to the landing in front of his office. She was a beautiful and graceful woman, and he had been attracted to her from the first day he set eyes on her.

She was newly widowed, in her mid-fifties, and had come to him only a few months ago, first as a tourist interested in his award-winning vineyard, then gradually as a seeker, emotionally needy and searching for new meaning in her life. As he always did so successfully, he had cleansed her mind of the need for friends, family, and riches. She had finally realized they only served to entrap her in a dead-end life. A life that included the multimillion-dollar computer business she'd cofounded with her late husband.

He gazed at her now with a practiced look that she'd responded to many times, a look that was both compassionate and demanding. A look that caused her to flush as if it held a deeper meaning between them.

"I'm sorry to wake you, Sister Desirée," he said. "But I have an important mission that I believe you are called to carry out."

She had just completed classes instructing her how to lead tourists down the path of becoming seekers, how to be smiling, cheerful, and brimming with information about the historic winery and its beautiful grounds. She had learned just how to convince the Angels Crest visitors that they *must* view the film about the historic award-winning vineyard and how it had gained esteem under its current CEO, Rance Randolph. Only then would come the first mention of Angels of Fellowship, followed by literature handed out in a designer bag, complete with a complimentary bottle of Angels Crest private reserve estate chardonnay. The hook would be set.

But now, he had something else in mind for the beautiful woman.

"What is it, Brother Randolph?"

"We have a seeker among us, someone who needs the gentlest of nudgings into our Fellowship." He sighed, and circling his arm around Sister Desirée's shoulders, he turned her and walked slowly to a window. They stood looking out at the sweeping grounds, the lush gardens, the fountains. "You see, dear, just as you did when we first began talking, our dear Sister

Theodora has some questions, some doubts, about our beliefs."

He looked into Sister Desirée's clear eyes, giving her another of his practiced looks: piercing, caring, wise beyond comprehension. In return she gave him a trusting smile. Just as he knew she would. "What is it you require, Brother Randolph?" she asked.

"Be her friend," he said simply. "Let her trust you. Open your heart to her and let her see how being here has changed your life."

She smiled again. "That won't be difficult," she said.

He gently squeezed her shoulders. Again he let his gaze sweep over the sunlit landscape outside his window. It saddened him to know he'd be leaving Angels Crest soon, that they'd all be leaving. But what lay ahead was better.

He looked down at Sister Desirée. "Thank you," he said. "Now, let me send for someone to help move your things into her room."

"I'll be moving out of the dormitory?"

He cocked his brow.

She looked sorry she had displeased him and quickly said, "It will be moving?"

"Yes, temporarily. For the sake of bringing another into the fold. The most elegant suite in the chateau, gourmet room service from the dining room—"

"The stringed ensemble playing Mozart from the garden beneath the terrace?" she finished.

"Yes," he said.

"Just as you provided for my welcome."

"That's why I thought of you, shall we say, as her guardian angel?"

Sister Desirée looked thoughtful, obviously remembering her first days at the chateau. "Yes," she finally said. "I was a tough case to convince—*it* was a tough case," she corrected automatically. He fought the urge to pat the top of her head.

Instead, he nodded. "And so shall be Sister Theodora. You will understand her thoughts; you will answer her questions. Befriend her. Gain her trust. And when the time comes, you will be the one to travel with her to Atara."

Sister Desirée looked pleased. "It will be a privilege and a joy."

THREE

In her office the following morning, K.C. tucked an errant strand of hair behind one ear, mentally detailing all that was needed to meet her deadline for the *Pelican Journal*. The last thing she needed, today of all days, was to be out of the office. Because of her fierce, protective love for Aunt Theo—and of course her love for Father Max—she could not put off the trip to Sugarloaf Ridge. She'd walk to the ends of the earth for Aunt Theo and Father Max.

She decided, glancing at the stacks of work, there was no reason she couldn't continue to work on the deadline along the way. She gathered some files and stuffed them into a briefcase, dropping her laptop computer into the side pocket. Maybe she'd find a human-interest story along the way to fill her column.

And she had already asked Georgie to put in some extra hours selling ad space and to cover that evening's city council meeting. With Georgie's coming wedding—the most elaborate, the young woman loved to mention, in Pelican Cove's colorful history—she was more than delighted with the extra income.

"You ready?" Father Max asked, grinning at her as he opened the door.

K.C. nodded and gave him a wide grin. "We'll both feel better when we see Aunt Theo and know she's merely being held hostage by her latest group of conjured-up characters."

He nodded. "Then let's not wait another minute." He turned to open the door for her.

"There's a catch, though, Max," she said as she stepped through the doorway into the outer office.

He stopped. "What's that?"

"You'll need to drive so I can work." She nodded at the beat-up leather briefcase hanging from her shoulder.

His eyes brightened, and he grinned mischievously. "You don't mean the Morgan?"

"None other!" she confirmed, knowing how he loved her dear restored English sportster. Deep green, the color of a forest at twilight, it was the one pride of K.C.'s life. Well, almost. Her Abyssinian cat, Satinka, was the other.

She grabbed her sunglasses, perching them atop her head to double as a hair band, and had a brief word with Georgie; then the two headed out the front door of the *Pelican Journal* office. The sleek little Morgan was parked in the small lot behind the newspaper building. K.C. grinned as she matched Father Max's hurried stride.

"Top down, I assume," Father Max said as they rounded the corner and spotted the vehicle. His eyes were wide with boyish anticipation. He didn't bother to open the door, just stepped over the top and into the driver's seat, on the right side, in true British fashion.

K.C. quickly tied her hair back with a scarf, popped on her sunglasses, then settled in beside him. "A perfect day for it, dear sir," she said with a laugh. "Drive away!"

Moments later, Father Max, after donning a golf hat to keep his bald head from sunburn, had set the engine to a low roar, then accelerated as they moved out of the parking lot and onto the street. It was a short distance from the seaside village of Pelican Cove to the interstate, and Father Max easily maneuvered the sports car through what little traffic there was and headed into the gently rolling coastal hills dotted with live oak, elm, and fragrant eucalyptus trees. Soon they had left the brisk sea air behind them, and the sun beat on their shoulders as they sped inland.

After the road had straightened, K.C. pulled out the laptop, turned it on, then pulled out her notes for the upcoming column.

Father Max glanced across at her. "I'd put up my old Royal typewriter against that highfalutin electronic thing you've got any day," he said with a grin. "And mine doesn't even have to have its batteries recharged."

K.C. flashed him a smile. It was known all over Pelican Cove that he held the electronic age in disdain. He wouldn't touch a computer. He only shook his head at them and never missed a chance to put down their technology. Even research on the internet was of no interest to Father Max. "Give me the feel of a hardbound book in my hands any day," he'd said more than once.

K.C. went back to her notes for "Pelican Chat." Everything she had jotted down earlier now seemed irrelevant, at least compared to the feel of the wind in her hair, the sun on her shoulders, the fragrance of the air. And, of course, the nagging worry that something indeed might be wrong with Theo. She tried to push the thought from her mind and whispered a quick prayer for her aunt. Finally, she slid the laptop back into its case and zipped it snugly into place.

She glanced over at Father Max, noticing that he was knitting his brows again.

"You said this time you feel differently about not hearing from Aunt Theo. Why, Father Max? Did she say anything about her new book?"

"Only that it reached far beyond anything she'd come across before." He paused, swinging the car around a heavy pine cone that had fallen into the road, then downshifting as they began climbing the small mountains between the Sonoma and Napa Valleys.

"This may not have anything to do with what she's working

on, but lately she's been talking a lot about people disappearing, not because they're in trouble or in any immediate danger, necessarily, but for other strange reasons." He shook his head solemnly as they rounded a steep curve. "She never said what, who, or how many. Said she'd explain it all to me once we got together for the ballet and supper."

"It's the sort of thing a mystery writer might become obsessed with," K.C. agreed. "She may be following some lead. Got caught up in the chase and forgot to call about the ballet."

"You're right," Father Max said. "But I'll feel better once I hear it from her."

K.C. reached across and patted his hand, now resting on the gearshift knob. "So will I."

An hour later, Father Max guided the Morgan through the town of Sugarloaf Ridge, then a mile and a half beyond, into the cabin's driveway. Pine needles and squirrel-gnawed cones crunched under the tires as he slowly eased the car closer to the house. The small Lincoln-log cabin looked empty, though Theo's old Buick was parked near the front door.

K.C. and Father Max exchanged worried glances as they approached the front door. Moments later, K.C. knocked once, then again, louder. There was no sound from the other side of the door.

"Do you have a key?" Father Max asked.

"No, but I know where Theo keeps her spare." She led Father Max through a stand of scrub pines to the back of the house. At the edge of an herb garden, near a large clump of rosemary, was a smooth oval stone with the words *Water Me* etched on it. K.C. grinned at Father Max as she stooped to pick it up. With a quick twist the stone opened, revealing a house key inside. She tossed it to him, then brushed off her hands as she stood. They headed back around the house to the front door.

A moment later they were inside. The light was dim, and K.C. quickly stepped to a window and folded back the shutters. Father Max did the same on the opposite side of the room.

K.C. noticed there was no musty odor indicating the cabin had been closed for days. "Theo hasn't been gone long," she said. "Maybe she walked into town to visit a friend, decided to spend the night." The excuse sounded lame, but she wanted to believe it, wanted to believe something ordinary was happening.

"Wouldn't she have taken the car?"

K.C. shrugged as they walked to the kitchen. "I've been worried about her lack of exercise when she sits in front of a computer all day. She promised me she would try to walk more." She glanced around the kitchen and peered into the sink. "Look, her cereal bowl's still here, complete with a few soggy bran flakes."

"Well, now we at least know she left sometime after breakfast."

"We just don't know which day."

Father Max opened the refrigerator door. "Look, here's a leftover salmon steak and some mashed potatoes—all ready to slide into the microwave. No one would leave fresh fish unless they planned to return quite soon."

K.C. laughed lightly. "See, I think we've been worried for no reason. Let's sit down and wait. Maybe Theo's on her way home as we speak."

Father Max grinned sheepishly. "She won't like it that we've been snooping in her refrigerator."

"And that we discovered she didn't bother to wash her breakfast dishes."

Laughing, they moved into the living room and settled into two comfortable and worn overstuffed chairs. K.C. put her feet up on a three-legged footstool. The time passed pleasantly as

Father Max told K.C. about his recollections of Pelican Cove through the years, the families—especially those K.C. was related to—that had come and gone but had left a lasting imprint on the small community.

"But it's your mother and father I miss," he said, after a time. "Your father has a heart for serving God like few I've come across. He always felt God had called him into ministry, and for a long time didn't understand that ministry didn't mean he had to stand behind a pulpit telling people about God."

"I remember him saying you were the one who helped him understand that giving a child a cup of water in Jesus' name is the same as giving it to Jesus himself."

Father Max nodded slowly. "Ministry can be as simple, yet profound, as that." He sighed. "Most people don't understand."

K.C. sighed heavily and looked away from his concerned gaze. "I think it's always hard to understand God's plan— whether we're looking for ways to serve him or simply trying to figure out his direction for the rest of our lives."

Father Max leaned forward. "Maybe it's the same thing, K.C."

The conversation was getting too close to a heartache she was trying to forget. The sorrow with a big, bold name on it: Elliott Gavin, ex-fiancé. She drew a deep breath. Father Max had counseled her after the breakup and knew very well all she'd been through. He also knew how painful it was to talk about even now.

Figuring out the rest of her life? Once she thought it had been planned out meticulously. Gav and K.C. together forever. Serving God together. But now? Figuring out what stories to print in her little newspaper once a week was difficult enough. She pushed up her eyeglasses and gave Father Max a quick smile and changed the subject. "How about some tea?"

"Sounds good." He squinted toward the window as she stood to go to the kitchen. "You know, K.C., the shadows are getting long. I've been wondering if maybe Theo did go out for a walk, yesterday or the day before, planning to return within just a few hours. But what if she fell, or for some other reason couldn't make it back? She comes up here to be without telephone or fax or nearby neighbors. I can't really believe she might have gone someplace for an overnight visit."

"E-mail is her only concession to communication," K.C. agreed as she glanced toward the corner of the room behind Father Max. Theodora's big, scarred oak desk dominated the area. Her aunt's computer stood in the center of the desk, her papers, notepads, and books scattered around it. "I keep coming back to her research, thinking it may have led her off on some tangent," she mused, almost to herself. "The puzzle is why she wouldn't have taken her car."

Father Max followed her gaze and stood. "Maybe she left a note, a scrap of something?" They headed to the desk and rifled through some of the strewn papers. Father Max glanced up at K.C. "I can't help thinking we're invading Theo's privacy." He frowned, and K.C. patted his shoulder.

"I wonder if we can get into her e-mail messages," K.C. said, sitting down. "But let's take a look here first." She flipped through some of the papers. "These are mostly manuscript notations and pages from her last book. As far as her privacy is concerned, if Theo is in trouble, somehow I don't think she'd mind."

Father Max gave a worried shrug, and they began examining some of the papers again. K.C. read through her aunt's handwritten notes, one by one. She found nothing but a list of character names and place descriptions: a vineyard in autumn colors at sunset, a seaside cliff near Pelican Cove at sunrise, a raging winter storm coming off the Pacific Ocean. Theo's agent's phone number was noted with a reminder to call her in New York when the writer returned to Pelican Cove.

Father Max shook his head slowly after finishing the stack he was going through. "Nothing," he said quietly. "Not even a hint."

K.C.'s gaze landed on the computer. "If we could get into her e-mail, some of her messages might give us a clue."

Father Max shook his head. "That's going too far, K.C. I can't help thinking that's truly an invasion of her privacy. Maybe we are letting our imaginations get carried away." He smiled sadly. "You said that Theo's been talking about getting more exercise. Perhaps she did go on a walk...." He frowned as a new thought occurred. "This is rocky terrain. A twisted ankle could have her sitting on a boulder someplace, awaiting help."

She linked her arm through Father Max's. "Instead of that cup of tea," she said, "how about going for a walk? Let's see if we can catch up with Theo before dark. There can't be that many hiking trails around here."

He nodded, though his deep worry about Theodora was still evident. "Let's go," he agreed. "But I've got another plan if this isn't successful."

K.C. knew before he spoke what that plan was.

"The next step we should take, in my opinion," Father Max said as they walked through the door and out onto the porch, "if we don't find Theo, is to head into town to see the sheriff."

K.C. let out a pent-up sigh. She'd already decided the same thing. But the only local law enforcement in the tiny town of Sugarloaf Ridge was none other than Sheriff Elliott Gavin.

"Yes, I know," she managed to whisper. "Any other law enforcement agency would say it's too early for a search."

She swallowed hard. Of all people, it would have to be Gav.

FOUR

A few hours later, K.C. met Father Max's worried gaze as they sat together in Theodora's living room.

"Maybe you should ask someone from the Napa office to come up," Father Max said, frowning.

"I was just thinking the same thing," K.C. agreed. She had tried twice before to reach Gav, only to be connected to the Napa station after being told by the dispatcher, "Sheriff Elliott Gavin is currently unavailable. I'm sorry."

K.C. figured the Napa authorities might make them wait the required hours to file a missing person's report. Gav, on the other hand, wouldn't hesitate to act. He cared about Aunt Theo as much as she and Father Max did. It had been Theodora's idea for him to set up his residence in Sugarloaf Ridge and run for sheriff when he graduated from the police academy two years before. With the backing of the famous author, he'd easily won the election.

"I'll try to get Gav once more," she said. "Otherwise, we may have to settle on working to convince the Napa authorities." She picked up her cell phone from the nearby lamp table and punched in the number, expecting the same response as the two previous tries. This time, however, the phone rang several times without being picked up by the dispatcher.

K.C. moistened her dry lips. Not only was she becoming more distraught by the hour over Theo's disappearance, she was nervous about talking to Gav. It would be the first time they'd spoken since their broken engagement three years earlier.

The ring sounded once more before she heard the click of the telephone being lifted from the receiver.

"Sheriff's office," said Gav's deep, unmistakable voice. "Elliott Gavin here."

"Gav?"

There was a heartbeat of silence. They'd known each other since childhood, were sweethearts through most of high school and betrothed during their last few years at U. C. Berkeley. He would know her voice, even though all she'd uttered was his name.

"K.C.?"

"Yes, Gav, it's me," she said. He was silent, as if not knowing what to say. She decided to plunge right in. "Gav, I'm up here at Sugarloaf. At Aunt Theo's cabin. Father Max is with me."

"Is something wrong?"

"We're not sure. We can't find Theo."

"I just saw her last week," Gavin said. "She's been hard at work on her next book."

"I know. That's why we weren't worried. But Father Max and Theo had tickets for the San Francisco Ballet two nights ago. She didn't come home to Pelican Cove. Didn't call. No word at all. You know how she feels about the ballet."

"And about seeing Father Max." K.C. could hear the smile in Gav's voice.

"Anyway, we drove up this afternoon to check. Everything in the cabin points to her having left one or two days ago. We waited, thinking she'd gone on a walk, or maybe into town for groceries."

"You've looked around outside? Maybe she fell...."

"Yes, we just got back a bit ago. We checked some of the trails and roads around here. Nothing."

"I'll be right up," Gav said, and now K.C. could hear concern in his voice. "And I'll call Search and Rescue. We've got a great volunteer team up here."

"I've heard of them," K.C. said, feeling relieved that Gav was taking this seriously, no matter how angry, hurt, and filled with sorrow her heart was at the thought of seeing him again. "Thank you, Gav. I'm glad you can come." Her eyes met Father Max's. He gave her a slight nod, his expression filled with understanding of her still raw emotions.

"I know it's going to be hard for you," Father Max said when she'd hung up the phone. "But Gav's the best man for the job."

"I know," K.C. said, letting out a deep breath. "I had just hoped I'd never have to see him again. Ever."

He nodded slowly. "God's ways aren't always ours, child."

Father Max understood, more than anyone else, what their meeting would mean. He had counseled them both, together during their engagement, separately afterward. During the painful year that followed that worst week of K.C.'s young life—the week that Elliott Gavin both dropped out of seminary and broke off their engagement—Father Max never revealed anything that Gav told him about his decision.

She respected Father Max's strict rules of confidentiality, but she had long ago come to terms with the only obvious conclusion that made sense: Gav had been unfaithful to her. What else would send him out of her life and out of seminary at the same time?

She'd managed to push the pain of his betrayal into the farthest recesses of her heart, pick up the pieces of her life, and start over. The little newspaper she'd purchased was now her life, her identity. She had tried to forget that she ever felt the call to serve God in ministry—side by side with a husband who'd planned to become a pastor in a small town just like Pelican Cove. All that was past. She and Gav obviously had misunderstood their calling, their love, their future plans together.

Three years later she was the extremely independent K.C.

Keegan, editor of the *Pelican Journal,* driver of the enviable restored Morgan, and mom to sweet, adoring Satinka the cat. That comprised her life. That was all she needed.

She felt the heat of tears behind her eyes, and swallowed hard.

Father Max smiled, noticing her reverie. "God's ways aren't always our ways, child," he repeated.

While they awaited Gav's arrival, K.C. put in a call to Georgie O'Reilly at home, and Father Max headed to the kitchen to wash Theo's breakfast dishes and those they'd used when they had her leftovers for lunch.

"Hey, there!" Georgie said after K.C. said hello. "Did you find Aunt Theo?"

"No. She's left without a trace, Georgie. She may just be off doing research."

"You're going to stay over, then?"

"Yes." She hesitated a moment before continuing. "I called Gav to help in the search."

There was a soft gasp in the receiver. "Gav?" a pause, then, "Oh, K.C., are you okay? I mean, I know how you feel about that scoundrel—"

K.C. interrupted. "Look, he's the only game in town. Literally. And he loves Aunt Theo. As Father Max said, he's the best man for the job. Actually, he's on his way up here now with the local search-and-rescue team in tow. We're hoping they'll find Aunt Theo stuck, unharmed, on some cliff, taking copious notes about her experience for her next manuscript."

"I'll be praying for her—for you too, K.C. Don't worry about the paper. I scoured the town for ads this afternoon. Picked up a couple more. Also attended the city council meeting tonight. Nothing new there." Then she laughed. "Of course, Marigold Green was there ranting and raving about some neighbors who she says are building a six-floor guest house on their R1-zoned property."

"And are they?"

"According to her, yes. She spent two days sitting in a vacant lot next door to them, writing down the numbers of cement bags delivered, pilings, footings, or whatever they're called, siding, and heaven knows what else. She contacted an engineer and gave him the list of building materials. According to him, she said, it was enough to build a six-floor building—one room stacked on top of the other."

"I wonder if she ever considered he might be pulling her leg," K.C. laughed, picturing the big, indignant, spike-haired gadfly. Then she sobered. "Why don't you follow it up? Contact the homeowners. Find out what they're really planning. Someone needs to stop the damage this woman does to her neighbors' reputations. Not to mention the wasted hours she causes city officials when she calls in her complaints."

"I'll do it," Georgie said. "You want photos?"

"Yep. The building site with Marigold standing in front with her clipboard would be nice. The caption can detail the hours she spent there and her list of building materials. Last I heard from the city planner, Marigold's been photographing live oaks around town so she'll have a record if anyone does any illegal pruning. He might have a quote for you."

Georgie giggled. "Got it." K.C. could hear the scribble of her pencil as she took notes. "Anything else? How about your column? Want me to take a stab at it?"

K.C. started to agree, then hesitated as Aunt Theo's sweet face came to her mind. "No," she said finally. "I've just now had a brainstorm. Let me work on it. I'll fax it from town tomorrow."

"That'll give us plenty of time. As long as I've got it by five so I can get it to the print shop by six."

They said their good-byes, then Georgie added, "You're in

my heart and prayers—all of you. Even Gav."

"Thanks, Georgie. Especially remember Aunt Theo."

"I will, sweets. Take care!"

"You, too." K.C. hung up the phone.

Father Max strode around the corner, tea towel in hand, just as a knock sounded at the front door. His eyes met K.C.'s. "Want me to answer it?"

K.C. stood. "It's all right, Max," she said quietly. "I'll get it."

A moment later, she pulled open the door, trying to ignore the thudding of her heart. Elliott Gavin stood in front of her. He'd removed his hat, showing his dark hair, shorter now than when she'd seen him last. He looked handsome in his uniform, vigorous and healthy…and happy, she noticed with a pang. Even in that first glance, his expression held a sense of being at peace with himself. Breaking up with her must have been good for him, she thought bitterly. Briefly she wondered if he was still seeing the other woman.

"K.C." For an instant his eyes searched her face.

"Hi, Gav," K.C. said, feeling her cheeks redden. "Please, come in."

Almost reluctantly, it seemed, his gaze moved from K.C. to Father Max, still standing in the kitchen doorway, towel in hand. Gav strode toward his friend and greeted him with a bear hug. "Max," he said, stepping back to shake the priest's hand. "It's good to see you." His voice was subdued, K.C. noticed, the worry about Theo still very evident.

"I'm sorry about the circumstances," Father Max said, looking to K.C.

She moved closer to the two. "The search-and-rescue team's on its way?"

He nodded. "Some may have been in bed." He glanced at his watch. "It's after eleven." His eyes met K.C.'s again. "I'm sorry you couldn't get me earlier. The dispatcher said someone tried to call several times. She described a voice that sounded like yours."

"You don't need to explain—" K.C. said, then instantly regretted it. Of course he didn't need to explain.

"I was in class," he said, ignoring her comment. "It doesn't get out until ten." Then Gav glanced around the room, seeming to take in everything from the stacks of paper near Theo's computer to the books she had been reading on the coffee table. "Did you check her closet to see if any clothes are missing?"

K.C. felt foolish. She hadn't even thought of it.

"Or suitcases?"

"Wherever Aunt Theo went, she walked," K.C. said, tucking a strand of hair behind one ear, a nervous habit she thought she had gotten past years ago. "We can look, but I don't even know what clothes she normally wears up here. We can check for suitcases, but I doubt that with her small frame, she'd have gone far with anything to carry."

"I agree," he said. "But it's a place to start while we wait for the team."

K.C. led the way into Theo's small bedroom, flicking the wall switch by the door, illuminating the room from a single light bulb over the bed. The walls and floor were knotty cedar, and there were a couple of dark green scatter rugs flanking the antique brass-framed bed that was covered with a colorful handmade quilt. A spool-legged table stood near the bed; a reading lamp, a notepad, a small stack of paperback mysteries, and an open Bible were on its polished maple top.

K.C. went immediately to the note pad. She leafed through the penciled notations. "Ideas Aunt Theo thought of in the middle of the night. Character names mostly. Plot twists and turns." She scanned the contents, then closed the cover and checked for other scraps of paper on the table. After a minute she went to the clothes closet, a small walk-in.

Father Max peered over her shoulder as K.C. scooted hangers back and forth, checking the contents. Behind him, Gav was looking in a small linen closet. "Her suitcases are here," he said after a minute. "A garment bag and an overnight case. Was that usually all she brought with her?"

K.C. turned and nodded. "Yes." She went back to her search through the hangers filled with jogging suits and sweats. "I don't recognize most of these, do you, Max?"

He shook his head. "Theo said she only wears sweat outfits when working. Sometimes jeans. More comfortable when sitting at a computer all day."

"I do remember that she bought some better walking shoes last time we were together in Pelican Cove," K.C. mused as she knelt to go through the canvas shoes and sandals. "They're black with thick trapped-air soles." She grinned at the memory, looking back and catching Gav's eye. "Aunt Theo worried that they looked like old lady shoes. I told her she was safe. Shoes with air pockets in the heel are only purchased by yuppies and baby boomers."

"Are the shoes there?" Gav asked, coming closer.

"No, I don't see them yet." She lifted the lids of a couple of old shoe boxes. "Of course, she may have left them in Pelican Cove."

"Not if she promised you she'd start walking more," Father Max reminded her.

She crawled further back into the closet, checking shoe boxes and some old tote bags. "No, they're not here," she confirmed a moment later when she emerged. "But I found her empty hatbox. Theo never goes walking without her wide-brimmed straw hat."

Gav squinted in thought. "All that's missing, then, at least as far as we know, are her walking shoes and her straw hat."

"And her purse. We noticed it was gone when we first got here."

"It doesn't appear Theo left on a planned trip." He hesitated. "But something doesn't ring true about that, either. How many women do you know who take their purses when going on a walk?"

Father Max solemnly nodded in agreement as K.C. stood and brushed off her jeans. "You're right," she said. "None. But as you said, we've got to start somewhere."

The three glanced around Theodora's bedroom once more to make sure they hadn't missed anything, then Father Max and Gav stepped into the living room, and K.C. reached for the light switch. But she hesitated when the notebook caught her attention. She flicked through the pages, her focus again on the character names. One sounded familiar, but before she could figure out where she had heard it before, the sound of cars pulling into the driveway caught her attention.

She set the notepad beside the Bible and turned out the light. She headed toward the living room as Gav opened the door to welcome the search-and-rescue team members. Ten or twelve men entered the small living room. They were all ages, looking fit and ready to go to work. The easy banter between them and Gav spoke volumes about their respect for the sheriff.

She watched Gav explain the circumstances to the men. His stance was that of someone who knew exactly what he was doing...and enjoyed his job immensely. Some of the men asked questions, and she, Father Max, and Gav answered them as best they could. Finally, the briefing was over, and the team headed to the vehicles for high-powered flashlights, ropes, and climbing equipment. Father Max asked if he could come along, and the men agreed after a nod from Gav.

"I'm going to call Napa station for a helicopter," Gav said

once they'd left. "It'll take some time to get here, but the aerial spotlight may make the difference."

K.C. sank to the sofa, her head bowed into her hands. The reality of Aunt Theo's disappearance was setting in. Now she looked up gratefully. "Thanks, Gav, for all you're doing. The reason I didn't talk to the dispatcher at Napa was because of the forty-eight hour wait."

A flicker of disappointment crossed his face, then just as quickly disappeared. He walked over to where she was sitting and gently squeezed her shoulder. "It's going to be all right, K.C.," he said softly.

Their eyes met for the briefest heartbeat before K.C. looked away. She didn't want him to see the moisture in her eyes. Seconds later she heard the front door close and the crunch of gravel as Gav headed to his car to radio for the helicopter. Angry at her vulnerability, she quickly brushed the tears off her cheeks, then headed to the bedroom to get the bright yellow emergency flashlight-strobe-beacon-radio combo she'd noticed by Aunt Theo's bed.

Then she headed out the door, around the house, and up the path toward the voices and beams of light cast by the search-and-rescue team. She tried to ignore the fall of Gav's footsteps on the leafy ground behind her...and the sound of his voice calling her name.

FIVE

K.C. didn't even glance back when Gav called her name. Biting her lip and pretending she didn't hear his voice, she hurried toward the search party's lights and voices higher on the mountain. Soon he was lost to her as he mingled with crew members, and K.C. had pushed him from her mind, concentrating instead on Aunt Theo and her safety.

When the first pearl gray light of dawn arrived the following morning, it was apparent that, at least in the immediate vicinity, there was no trace of Theodora Whimple. An exhausted Father Max returned to the cabin to keep hot coffee brewing for the crew, but K.C. stayed, tramping up and down the cliffs until the sun was high in the eastern sky.

Wearily, she finally turned back to Aunt Theo's cabin. Before she did anything else, she needed to get her column written and faxed to Georgie. She planned to have a comforting mug of steaming coffee and get right on it. What she had to say in her column was almost as important as the search by Gav and his crew.

She let herself into the cabin. Father Max wasn't around, but when she glimpsed through the barely open bedroom door, she saw why. The weary rector was sprawled out on Aunt Theo's bed, sound asleep. She closed the door quietly and tip-toed into the kitchen to grind some beans in Aunt Theo's old-fashioned hand-grinder and brew another pot of coffee.

A few minutes later she was seated at the desk. She reached for the leather case to pull out her laptop, then hesitated, glancing at Aunt Theo's computer. Yesterday, they'd worried about invading her aunt's privacy. Now that seemed trivial next to their concern for the woman's safety.

Within minutes, she had the computer up and was scrolling through the folders: *Works in Progress, Bright Ideas, Character Names, Place Descriptions.* First she chose *Works in Progress,* opened the folder and again scanned the file titles. There were a few synopses, which she quickly read through. They contained sketchy information about a series set in Scotland, another in Ireland, and still another, more abstract than the others, about South African vineyards. Nothing relevant to anywhere Aunt Theo might go locally, so K.C. went on to the next folder, the one titled *Bright Ideas.* Still nothing.

Sighing, she stopped to head to the kitchen for coffee now that the brewing cycle was complete. Steaming mug in hand, she returned to the computer. Seated again, she took a sip of coffee, then opened the folder containing *Character Names.* She clicked the mouse on the file called *Names for Current Work.*

After the word-processing program opened, she read down the list, noticing that some of the same names appeared that she'd noticed the night before in the pad beside Aunt Theo's bed. This list was long, and in some cases, character descriptions were noted beside the names. Toward the bottom of the list, she noted three names with asterisks before them, though there was no indication why.

One name stood out: Keb-Kaseko Rodolphe, which she'd also seen in the notebook. Where else had she heard that name before? She took another sip of coffee and frowned in concentration. She couldn't remember.

She went on to scroll through the other files. To no avail. There were no clues as to where Theodora Whimple might have gone to do research.

Disappointed, K.C. decided to get on with her own writing project. Since she already had Aunt Theo's computer up and running, she decided she might as well use it instead of the laptop and create a new folder and file of her own.

For nearly an hour she wrote with speed and passion and had almost finished the column when a knock sounded at the door. She got up to answer it, but Gav opened the door and stepped across the threshold. She stopped in her tracks, not wanting to be alone with him, something she'd tried to avoid throughout the night before.

But she hadn't needed to worry. He got straight to business. "K.C., we're about ready to call off the air search," he said. "I'm sorry, but the men feel they've exhausted the options around this area."

K.C. sighed. "It was a long shot," she agreed quietly. "I couldn't help but hope they'd find some clues."

He nodded in agreement. "That doesn't mean we're going to stop looking."

"You've got some other ideas?"

"What if she walked down the hill to Oakville?"

"That's quite a distance. At her age? I don't know," K.C. said.

"She could have taken a bus, a taxi—maybe the train—someplace else from there."

"But why? She's got the car. If she were going any distance, it doesn't make sense that she wouldn't drive."

Gav looked embarrassed and cleared his throat. "I don't want to bring this up, but some of the men were asking about it, so I thought I'd mention it."

"What, Gav?"

"Some of them are avid mystery readers, and they mentioned the mysterious disappearance of—"

K.C. interrupted, knowing where he was headed with this. "Dame Agatha Christie?"

"Yes. Do you remember hearing about how she disappeared for months. She never did tell people where she'd been."

"Are you suggesting, Gav, that Aunt Theo's pulling some kind of stunt?" She was indignant, and her voice reflected it. "You know her nearly as well as I do. I can't believe you would even entertain the thought—no matter who asked about such a scenario. You should have set them straight right off." She paused, looking him straight in the eyes. "I thought I knew you better than that!"

"K.C., you don't know me at all," he replied, without missing a beat. His words now became clipped, and he sounded very much the law-enforcement officer. "People don't always behave the way you want them to—or expect them to. Life isn't often that way. The truth is, maybe Theo doesn't want to be found. Did you ever consider that?"

"You're wrong about her, Gav. She would never simply disappear. That's why I know she must be in danger."

"You have no proof."

"No, I don't. But I know my aunt."

He stared at her. "The way you knew me, K.C.?" Before she could answer, he turned and strode through the door, leaving K.C. standing in the middle of the room.

"K.C.—?" Father Max came up behind her and wrapped his arm around her shoulders. She took comfort in his gentle but strong presence. "People sometimes say things in anger when they're frightened."

"Father Max," she cried softly, when she turned to face him. "Why now? Of all times, why now? I wanted to put Gav in the past where he belongs. And now—when I'm feeling the most vulnerable—I can't avoid him."

"If it helps any, I think it's as hard on him as it is on you, dear."

She looked at him, searching his kind eyes. "How can it be?" she finally whispered hoarsely. "He's the one who left me."

Father Max smiled sadly. "Things aren't always the way they seem, are they, K.C.?"

She didn't want to think about his meaning, so instead, she gave him a shaky smile and asked if he'd like some coffee. He accepted, and K.C. went back to the computer to finish the last lines in her column.

A half hour later, glad that she and Theodora wore the same size, K.C. had pulled on a fresh pair of jeans and a cable-knit top, washed her face, and brushed through her hair. She traded her tortoiseshell glasses for sunglasses, and she and Father Max headed out to the Morgan.

She took the steering wheel this time, backed from the driveway, and headed down the tree-lined road to Sugarloaf Ridge. She didn't even glance at the sheriff's station as they passed. A ways down the block, she dropped Father Max at the drugstore to buy himself a razor and some toiletries, then she headed to the local stationers and the only fax machine in town. She would cross back over and pick up her own toiletries after she sent the fax to Georgie.

She pulled the Morgan into a parking space in the shade of a large elm and hopped out. Grabbing the sheet of paper with her column for the *Pelican Journal*, she hurried across the street to the stationery shop. A bell tingled, announcing her presence, and after conversing with the shop owner for a minute, she paid her money, then headed toward the fax machine in the back room.

Her first two tries didn't go through—the line was busy. She waited for a few minutes before trying again. She paid little attention to the bell ringing in the front of the shop, announcing the entrance of another customer.

But a moment later, a voice spoke from behind her. She didn't turn. She'd know the voice anywhere. Just as he'd known hers.

"I'm sorry for what I said earlier, K.C." he said. "It was uncalled-for."

She punched in the fax number again and hit "send" before finally turning toward him. Still she didn't speak.

"I had no right to say what I did back at Theo's," he said, watching her intently.

"You have every right to your opinions, Gav," she finally said softly. "What I wonder is why you never voiced them three years ago when you left me." She paused. "You never said why. That's the one opinion I've always wondered about."

"I didn't come here to talk about that now, K.C. This isn't the time or the place." His face had flushed beneath his tan. "I came to say I'm sorry for what I implied about Theo—that she might have wanted to disappear. I know that isn't true, and I pledge to you that I will stop at nothing to find her."

For a moment all that could be heard was the chitchat of customers who had just stepped into the shop, the ticking of a large wall clock above the fax machine, and the irritating song of a mockingbird outside the window.

Suddenly, K.C. couldn't bear one more minute of Gav's scrutiny. She gave him a quick, impersonal smile. "Well, thank you," she said finally. "It was thoughtful of you to let me know about your commitment." Then she swept past him and hurried through the door.

Gav stood watching K.C. leave, feeling his heart go with her. Then he noticed she had left her fax on top of the machine. He checked the printout to make sure it had gone through, then grabbed the fax and hurried to catch her. He had just stepped out the door when the dark green Morgan sped by, K.C.'s red hair gleaming in the sun, Father Max sitting beside her, holding onto his hat.

He stepped from the stationers and headed back down the block to his office. He was planning to ask K.C. and Max to accompany him to Oakville to ask people near the taxi stands, bus depots, and train stations if they remembered seeing someone matching Theodora Whimple's description. He had a snapshot of his own of Theodora, taken just a year ago. He'd already asked Andy, his part-time deputy, to make up flyers with copies of the photo and Theo's description, especially listing what she might have been wearing yesterday: heavy black walking shoes and a wide-brimmed straw hat.

But as he pictured K.C.'s hurt and angry face, he decided maybe he should pursue this angle alone. He doubted now that K.C. would want to accompany him anywhere.

As he headed back to his office, he glanced down at the fax K.C. had just sent to her newspaper office. He smiled. Ah yes. Her column for the *Pelican Journal*. She didn't know it, but he read her paper weekly, cover to cover, just after Theo finished her own perusal. He was proud of what K.C. had accomplished with the paper; he also enjoyed her take on Pelican Cove's events and people. K.C.'s voice came through in her articles, loud and clear. He cherished reading her work almost as much as he once cherished being with her.

He began to read as he walked.

Dear Readers, K.C. began. *Today, I write with hope that you, dear people of Pelican Cove, can help in the search for one of our own citizens. Though she spends her writing days at her cabin at Sugarloaf Ridge, Pelican Cove is still her real home.*

I'm writing about Theodora Whimple, three-time winner of the prestigious Edgar award, mystery-writer extraordinaire, and favorite author of millions, and—most important—lovable friend to all of us.

Theodora was last seen exactly one week ago, though we have reason to believe that more recently than that, she decided to take a journey whose destination was known only to her.

Someone mentioned that Theodora might have disappeared in much the same manner as Agatha Christie, that she might have wanted to get away without telling anyone of her whereabouts.

I wish to dispute the idea, the rumor, before it gets started in our little town. And I will tell you why:

Theodora Whimple is honorable, honest, and forthright. She loves her Lord and God with all her heart, and in that heart there is no guile. Instead, her heart is filled with love and compassion and an inability to hurt others.

There have been those in our town who compare our Theodora to the fictional writer played by Angela Lansbury in Murder, She Wrote. *There might be some resemblance. However, where television characters have scripts to follow, Theodora has none. She plays out her actions on the stage of her heart, a heart that is held in safekeeping by a loving God.*

Please, help us find Theodora Whimple. If you know anything about where she's gone, or if you remember something she mentioned in passing that she's investigating, please call the Pelican Journal *office. We will have someone taking calls twenty-four hours a day. Thank you, my friends, for myself and for all those who care about our beloved Theodora. Thank you.*

And it was signed with K.C.'s scrawling signature.

Gav folded the paper and stuck it in his uniform pocket. He hurried along the sidewalk now, wanting to be on his way. Once in the office, he picked up the flyers and sprinted to his black-and-white sheriff's vehicle, a four-wheel drive Jeep Cherokee, at the rear of the building.

He pulled out of the driveway, but instead of heading down the hill as he had planned, he headed straight up the hillside to Theo's cabin. He only hoped he would arrive before K.C. and

Max took off to search for Theo on their own.

As he wound along the road, the phrase K.C. had written about Theo played over and over in his mind: *She plays out her actions on the stage of her heart, a heart that is held in safekeeping by a loving God.*

He thought about those years when he and K.C. had been in love. He wondered if she had guessed that he had been unable to play out his actions on the stage of his heart. And why.

Had she known? And his next thought stabbed through him like a knife. Had K.C. guessed that he blamed her for his own inability to be honest before God?

SIX

K.C. met Gav at Theo's front door. For a moment she regarded him without speaking, then invited him to come in.

"I'm heading down to Oakville," he said, hesitating as he glanced toward Theo's computer. He recognized the on-line graphics for an Internet-access program. "I thought you two might want to come along." He briefly explained that he'd had the flyers made up and thought they might want to help distribute them. They readily agreed but asked him to first take a look at something they had discovered on the Internet.

"You've got to see this, Gav," K.C. said, a flicker of hope in her expression. He followed her across the room to Theo's desk. "Father Max—who claims to be a Net newbie—figured out a way to get us on the Internet. Still can't get into her e-mail, but we found some web sites she's visited recently. I'm curious to see what you think."

Father Max was sitting to the left of Theo's computer. K.C. quickly seated herself again in front of the keyboard. Gav pulled up another chair on her right.

"Okay," she murmured as she pulled down a "Favorite Places" menu from the top of the screen. Absently, she read through the list. There were at least twenty-five sites. "Here it is," she said, highlighting one of the titles toward the end. "Look at this one." And double-clicked the mouse.

Moments later the web site appeared. Gav leaned forward, now closer to K.C., acutely aware of her fresh-scrubbed fragrance of soap mixed with a touch of her cologne, a woodsy scent that had always reminded him of wildflowers and clover.

"Here!" she said excitedly. "I noticed in one of Aunt Theo's files this morning that she's planning a story set in South Africa. Maybe using a vineyard as a backdrop. On a whim, Father Max and I decided to see if we could find any indication of her on-line research. Random web site 'hits' would be nearly impossible to trace, but Theo's made a list of favorite places, indicating she's visited the sites more than once."

"'The growing wine industry in South Africa,'" Gav read aloud, then scanned through the lead article. Then he looked up at K.C. and Max. "I don't understand. There's really nothing here—"

K.C. interrupted him. "At first glance, no. But read on," she said. "One of the articles is written by someone who claims to be a famous vintner from Napa Valley." She highlighted another title and double-clicked the mouse. Seconds later, the article by the French vintner Keb-Kaseko Rodolphe appeared.

Gav frowned as he began scanning the article in which Rodolphe listed point-by-point the differences between soils in the Napa and Sonoma Valleys and in the new vineyard regions in South Africa. Gav looked up again. "I'm sorry, I still don't see the connection," he said.

"I found Keb-Kaseko Rodolphe's name listed in two different places—in the notebook beside Theo's bed. Also in a computer file of possible character names."

"Perhaps Theo liked the sound of the name."

"Aunt Theo never uses real names in her books," K.C. pointed out. "As she's said more than once, 'Not in this litigious society.'"

"Okay, so there's a connection," Gav said. "Have you taken it beyond the web site?"

"We were just about to try again," Father Max said. "Let me show him, K.C.," he said proudly, leaning toward the keyboard and grabbing the mouse.

He clicked on Theo's e-mail icon, a little mailbox with a flag. A message appeared in the center of the screen, asking for the password. Father Max let out a deep sigh.

"Corresponding with someone of Rodolphe's stature would be something Aunt Theo would do," K.C. said. She suggested a few ideas for Theo's password. Father Max keyed them in. Nothing. He tried another. Still nothing. He scratched his head and frowned.

"Okay, think, guys," she said. "What password would you use if you were Aunt Theo? I've just tried her birthday, different combinations. That's obviously not it."

Father Max and Gav made suggestions. "How about character names?" Gav asked. "Does she have a favorite? Place of birth, maybe? Mother's maiden name?"

K.C. punched in a few more letter combinations, again to no avail. Finally, she turned in her seat and glanced at him. "We're wasting precious time." She looked disappointed. "I really thought we might have something here."

Gav touched her hand, and her eyes met his. "Hey, you *do* have something here, Kace." Her eyes widened in surprise when he used her nickname. It was as if it had been yesterday, not three years ago, since he'd called her by the name only he used.

He went on. "If Theo's doing research on wineries, maybe she's gone to visit one around here. Some even have B&B's on the premises. Let's try to find out where this vintner, Keb-Kaseko Rodolphe, is employed and go from there." K.C. gave him a grateful smile, and his heart skipped a beat or two. He swallowed hard. It was getting more difficult by the moment to be near her. "Why don't we head into Oakville," he said, "hand out the flyers, and ask around? Maybe we can think of some passwords to try on the way."

Father Max and K.C. agreed. A few minutes later, Father

Max pulled the front passenger seat forward and settled into the backseat of Gav's two-door Cherokee. K.C. took her seat in front, though reluctantly, he noticed. He was sure she would have rather had Max take the front seat.

Before they started out, Gav used his radio to call the dispatcher in Napa to run a check on Keb-Kaseko Rodolphe. Then he backed out of the driveway and headed down the hillside toward Oakville. He glanced over at K.C.'s profile, one he knew so well. Years before, he'd watched her grow from a long-limbed, gangly child into a self-possessed, creative, intelligent, and graceful woman. The best part about K.C., though, was that she was totally unaware of her beauty. If she thought about her looks at all, it was only to bemoan the fact that her red hair was stick straight, her white skin sunburned too readily, and her eyeglasses too often slipped down her small nose.

K.C. turned toward him as if she knew he was studying her. In the instant before he returned his focus to the road, their eyes met. Her eyes had always reminded him of the waters of Pelican Cove at twilight, a color more gray than green or navy, yet a color that seemed to speak of the ocean's depth. Once they'd beheld him with unabashed love, as deep as that ocean, he thought. As deep as his for her. But now? He pushed the thought from his mind. All that was in the past, and he was determined not to let nostalgia rule. He and K.C. had practically grown up together. They'd been childhood friends before they'd fallen in love. Perhaps they could be friends again.

Gav swung the car around the final wide hairpin turn leading into Oakville, deciding that was the way it had to be. Friends.

Just before reaching town, Gav pulled the car into a California Highway Patrol substation. "Wait here," he said to K.C. and Max as he set the brake. "I'll be right back."

Father Max spoke first. "You're hoping they might have something on Rodolphe?"

Gav nodded. "The dispatcher I called from the cabin sent the request to all law enforcement agencies in California. Requests like this get instant results—if there is any information. I can pick up the printout anywhere."

But when he got inside, there was nothing to report. No such person seemed to exist. Of course, that could mean he'd simply never been fingerprinted or received a social security number. Two distinct possibilities if the man was not a U.S. citizen.

Gav headed back to the Cherokee and told K.C. and Father Max the bad news: They were back where they had started. For the next hour, the three handed out the flyers Gav had brought along. And they asked questions of people they met at the bus station, the dispatcher's office for Oakville's single taxicab service, and the train station.

They were just turning to leave the train station when K.C. pointed out a downcast woman sitting alone at the corner of the building. A supermarket basket filled with dirty clothes and blankets stood next to her.

K.C. headed toward the woman, leaflet in hand.

"Let her handle this one alone, son," Father Max said when Gav started to follow. "This woman might not want to talk to the law."

Gav nodded and watched as K.C. knelt down and began to speak earnestly to the woman. The woman nodded tentatively at first, then looked at the flyer and nodded again. She pointed north along the tracks, then said a few more words. Several minutes passed, then K.C., a wide smile lighting her face, hurried back to where Gav and Max waited.

"She spotted her!" she announced. "Yesterday morning! It was the hat and shoes that caught her attention. Especially the shoes. She said she'd give the world to have some like them." She smiled into both their faces. "I told her we'd see to it she

71

gets a pair." She looked back to the woman and waved. The woman blew her a kiss, and K.C. turned back, a wide grin on her face. "Size nine."

Father Max hugged K.C.'s shoulders. "Tell us what else she said. I saw the woman point north. I take it Theo boarded the train and headed that direction."

K.C.'s face was alight with hope as the three started back to the sheriff's car. "Yes! She took the wine-tasting train to Calistoga."

"She could have gotten off anywhere along the line," Gav pointed out, opening the passenger-side door for K.C. and Max.

"I know. But at least we've got a starting place." K.C. slid into the front seat.

Gav didn't point out that there were sixty or seventy wineries between Oakville and Calistoga. The hillsides were dotted with them. "It's a starting place," he agreed. If indeed she was visiting a vineyard.

When they were buckled in and ready to go, he started the engine and let it idle for a moment.

"Is something wrong?" K.C. asked when he didn't back out.

He nodded slowly. "Yeah, two things. First, why would some world-famous vintner, writing articles on the Internet, supposedly from Napa Valley, be unknown here? And second..."

"If Theo boarded the tourist train of her own accord, why are we looking for her?" Father Max finished. "She's off doing research and perhaps doesn't want to be bothered."

"Exactly," Gav said. "It's good news to know she wasn't whisked away into danger. Wherever she's gone, she obviously chose to go there. That means she's safe."

K.C. was looking out the window, back toward the train station. She shook her head slowly. "I know all that makes logical sense. But there's still the ballet—"

"She may have forgotten we had tickets," Father Max said. He looked sad.

K.C. let out a sigh. "I suppose you're right. We should wait to hear from her...give her time to contact us."

Gav backed out and headed into the street. He glanced over at K.C., who was still knitting her brow. "You're still not convinced, are you?"

She turned toward him. "I'm worried. You hear about people going off to meet people they've met on the Internet. Maybe Keb-Kaseko Rodolphe is one of those sleazy—"

Gav interrupted. "It's children and the very naive who are taken in by that sort of thing. Not Theo. She's too bright." He concentrated on the road a minute. "And we don't know that this Rodolphe has anything to do with her trip on the tourist train. I still say, let's give her some time to contact us, then if we don't hear from her in a few days, we'll pull out all the stops. I promise."

"All right," K.C. sighed. She said nothing more the rest of the way to Sugarloaf Ridge and Theo's cabin.

The following day at noon, Gav was going over some reports in the office when the phone rang. He picked it up.

"Gav—?"

"Hello, K.C." He hadn't expected to hear from her so soon. "Do you have news about Theo?"

"Yes, something came to my attention this morning. It may not have anything to do with Aunt Theo, but I wanted to see what you think."

"What is it, Kace?"

She hesitated, and he wondered if hearing the endearment affected her as much as it did him when he said it. "I wrote

73

about Aunt Theo's disappearance in my column. It was in today's paper."

"I know." He explained that he'd read the fax.

"Well, this morning we had a call from Marigold Green. Do you remember her?"

He chuckled. "How could anyone forget?" The woman had lived just down the street from his family when he was growing up.

"She called in a rumor the day we left for Theo's. Something about Theo's friend Ariel Tilman having joined a cult that believes people can be reincarnated as angels."

"What does that have to do with Theo's disappearance?"

"Marigold called this morning after reading my column. She said she found something on an Internet bulletin board that's been discussing Heaven's Gate."

"Heaven's Gate?" He sat forward, leaning on his elbows. K.C. was right. There was reason to worry.

"Yes, Gav."

"Who else is posting messages on the same board?" he asked.

"Theo...and Keb-Kaseko Rodolphe."

He let the information sink in. "I'll be right over, Kace," he said quietly.

"Thank you, Gav," K.C. whispered. "There's something else."

"What is it?"

"Marigold Green says there have been other disappearances."

"Besides Ariel Tilman?"

"Yes. Marigold knows someone in Marin County who also left friends and family to join a cult in Napa Valley. The woman, Desirée Scott, was married to one of *the* Scotts, as

Marigold refers to them. She and her husband cofounded a computer software business."

"Marigold's always been good with details," Gav said dryly. "I've heard of the company. Did she say the Scott woman is widowed?"

"Yes. Marigold said they'd met months before Mr. Scott died. She was quite proud of the fact she was Mrs. Scott's drama coach in a small theater production. Desirée Scott was to play the lead but had to drop out just before the first performance. Her husband died of a sudden heart attack. She was devastated."

"A wealthy widow is a prime target for a cult leader," he said.

"She's heard of other disappearances, and she thinks there might be a connection." K.C. swallowed hard as if to keep the shaking from her voice.

"Go on," Gav said.

"She doesn't think Aunt Theo knew about Mrs. Scott, maybe none of the others, either, but she did post a message about the cult that Ariel joined, a group called Angels of Fellowship. She asked if anyone had heard of it."

"And had they?"

"The person who came forward saying he had information was Rodolphe. The final message was from Keb-Kaseko Rodolphe telling Aunt Theo he would e-mail her with private information."

"We've got to find that password."

"Father Max and I have already started."

"I'm on my way." Gav didn't wait to hear K.C. hang up her cell phone.

~ ~ ~ ~ ~

After hours of trying different combinations, the three finally gave up, exhausted and discouraged. K.C. phoned an order for a pizza, which was delivered just before nine o'clock. She was rummaging around in the kitchen for paper plates and forks when the idea struck.

She headed back to the living room. "We don't need the password to correspond with Rodolphe," K.C. announced as she pulled out a slice, slid it onto a plate, then handed it to Father Max.

"There's another way?" Father Max pensively took a bite of pizza.

"On my laptop," K.C. said with a grin. "I don't know why I didn't think of it before. We can go to the same bulletin board. Leave some sort of enticing message—leaving my e-mail address for his answer." She shrugged and took another bite of pizza. "I'll call Marigold Green to learn exactly how to find the place where she saw the messages posted from Aunt Theo."

"And using your e-mail address, he won't be able to trace our posts back to Theo," Gav added. "We may also hear from every crackpot who comes across the message."

K.C. agreed. "It is a fishing expedition. But I can't think of anything else to do right now."

"It's a good plan, Kace," Gav said softly. "He'll take the bait. We'll make sure it's a message he can't ignore."

"And then we'll wait to hear from him," Father Max said sadly. "I wonder how long it will take."

Unspoken was the conclusion they'd all reached: Keb-Kaseko Rodolphe was somehow involved with Aunt Theo's disappearance. Dangerously involved.

SEVEN

On her third morning at Angels Crest Vineyards, Theodora woke to the soft chimes of bells, pealing from a sound system in one of the chateau's turrets. Her suite was luxurious, almost too much so, she thought as she threw back the down comforter and stepped onto the plush rug beside her bed.

Her clothes, freshly cleaned and pressed, had been laid out for her, just as they had been each morning since her arrival. Though she'd also been given one of the Angels of Fellowship robes, she had promptly placed it in the rear of the large walk-in closet, giving it not even a cursory second glance.

Theodora was increasingly worried that the comfortable surroundings were masking her earlier concerns about Angels Crest. Outwardly, the place seemed genteel, sophisticated, and benign. Even Randolph's attempt to drug her that first night no longer seemed the threat it once had.

No, the real seduction came from the spalike vacation atmosphere. Gourmet foods at her disposal, superb classical music played throughout the gardens and chateau, intellectual discussions of the arts and politics in small groups scattered around as well. Though she woke that first morning expecting jail garb and armed guards, instead she'd been served breakfast in bed, then treated to a facial, a seaweed wrap, and a swim in the chateau's indoor pool.

But today, she decided, she'd seen enough, and it was time to get out. She planned to tell Randolph right after the morning meeting that she had completed her research and would appreciate a ride to the train station.

After dressing and running a brush through her hair, Theodora crossed the living room area to the east-facing French doors, pulled them open, and drew in a deep breath as she stepped outside on the veranda. The sun was just rising, splashing patches of golden light across the smooth stone surface. All around her, flowers cascaded from pots and urns, and in the corner a fountain bubbled from where it was almost hidden by a surrounding tangle of pink, white, and crimson impatiens interlaced with ferns. A sparrow twittered from the branch of a small ficus tree, then hopped to the fountain for a drink.

Across the lawn beyond the balcony, two women and a man strolled in their robes, walking slowly, deep in discussion. The Angels of Fellowship members had been another surprise. Instead of mindless zombies in barracks, she had met friendly, outgoing, and seemingly happy people.

"Sister Theodora?"

Theodora turned to see the woman who shared her suite approaching through the French doors. "Desirée, good morning!"

Desirée, a pretty woman in her fifties, returned the friendly smile. "Are you ready for morning meditations?" she asked.

Today she would at last view the entire population of Angels of Fellowship in one place.

She nodded to Desirée. "Of course, dear," she said. "I am." She didn't add that it was mostly because she wanted to find Ariel Tilman and figured her friend would be among those attending the morning meeting.

Desirée frowned, and Theodora remembered. In one of yesterday's discussions with some of the Fellowship members, she'd been told about their pronoun *I* rule. She grinned. "Oh, that's right. I'm not supposed to say *I*, am I?"

Sister Desirée almost laughed, then caught herself.

"Look," Theodora said softly, trying to read Desirée's heart beneath the beatific smile so often on her face. "You might as well know that the more you tell me about your Fellowship, the more certain I am that I'm not interested."

"It can be a wonderful life for you," said Desirée, ignoring Theodora's words, "if you'll only allow it. There are higher powers—the Ataran Angels—who will guide us into a life of higher consciousness. We can be brought to a place where all awareness is more acute than what ordinary beings experience."

Theodora shook her head. "I might as well tell you now that my heart belongs to Another—"

Desirée frowned. "What do you mean?"

"Jesus Christ."

A swift darkness crossed Sister Desirée's face. It was the first time she'd shown any hostility toward Theodora in their hours spent together. "Brother Randolph knows things about other worlds that will change your life. How can you—without understanding the universe and its glorious creatures—judge something you don't understand? Something that will only serve to enhance what you already believe?"

Another robed devotee entered the room, looked around, then joined Theodora and Desirée on the veranda. "Your discussion is carrying into the hall, ladies. Can anything be clarified?" She carefully avoided using the outlawed pronoun.

Theodora knew that they could not be overheard from that distance. Of course, the suite was bugged. Forewarned is forearmed, she thought. The crack in the polished facade of the compound was widening.

"Sister Theodora is being challenged by our doctrine, Sister Vesta," Desirée said sweetly, putting a positive spin on their conversation. That was something Theodora had also noticed. Rance Randolph discouraged negativity of any kind.

The two women watched Theodora carefully, awaiting her

response. She gave them a quick smile. "Actually, your doctrine is not a challenge at all. I understand it completely. I'm simply not interested."

The two devotees exchanged worried glances.

Theodora went on. "I'm sure you've been encouraged by Randolph to show me all the wonders of becoming an Angel of Fellowship member, but ladies, you might as well save your energy." She looked at them intently. "My heart isn't up for grabs. It belongs to the only God of the universe. He says, 'I have loved you with an everlasting love. You are mine.'" She paused, then added quietly, "He also tells me to love only him, my Lord and God, with all my heart. You see, besides there being no room for any other so-called god with so-called rules—your leader and his angels are masquerading as God."

"The Bible is filled with stories of angels. Brother Randolph believes in God—" Sister Vesta countered.

"And so does Satan," Theodora countered. "The second epistle to the Corinthians says that Satan masquerades as a beautiful angel. Think about his work in the Garden. He offered Eve a godlike understanding of the universe—just as you've been offered by Rance Randolph."

"So you are comparing Brother Randolph to Satan?" Desirée breathed, her eyes wide. "And the Ataran angels also?"

Theodora saw through her dismay and understood from the slope of her shoulders that Desirée knew she had failed in her mission. Mixed with the anger in her eyes was fear.

Just then the bell-like chimes sounded again from the chateau turret. "It's time for meditations," Sister Vesta said.

Theodora nodded. "Let's go, then."

The three women filed down the stairs to the ground floor, then crossed the compound to a large auditorium. Outside its tall wooden entrance doors, dozens of devotees waited silently in line. Theodora, flanked by Desirée and Vesta, took her place at the end of the line. She bowed her head, folded her hands, and prayed that the Lord would be with her through this day, that he would strengthen her and give her wisdom.

She looked up to see Sister Desirée watching her intently, as if knowing Theodora had been praying. But she said nothing and turned away when the line ahead of them began filing through the doors to enter the auditorium.

There was an unearthly hush as the devotees filed into the meditation hall. Theodora was astounded as she looked around. There were more followers than she could have imagined. Hundreds of people stood in rows spread across the massive room. Their eyes were closed, and their fingertips were steepled in an attitude of contemplation. She stood silently with them.

She glanced around, looking for Ariel, but also taking in the beauty of the room. Light spilled through the tall stained-glass windows, causing a rainbow splash of color to light the plain ivory robes of the devotees. Dark walnut beams, carved in a Spanish motif, spanned the high ceiling, rising to a point in the center. The effect was one of stepping back in time to a monastery or medieval castle.

Theodora bowed her head, conscious of the staged setting and the atmosphere it was supposed to evoke. Words and phrases from a psalm filled her heart, bringing her comfort and strength.

"The LORD is my light and my salvation—whom shall I fear? The LORD is the stronghold of my life—of whom shall I be afraid?

"One thing I ask of the LORD...that I may dwell in the house of the LORD all the days of my life, to gaze upon the beauty of the LORD and to seek him in his temple.

"For in the day of trouble he will keep me safe in his dwelling; he will hide me in the shelter of his tabernacle and set me high upon a rock.

"Wait for the LORD; be strong and take heart and wait for the LORD."

A sudden hush fell over the group, and Theodora looked up to see Rance Randolph, robed in shimmering pale gold, entering the room from a side door. As if one body, the devotees stood, heads bowed reverently. He held up his hands, and his followers lifted theirs.

From the back of the room a drum began to beat, slowly, seductively, then gradually building in speed and complexity. The followers swayed to the pulsating rhythm, arms lifted, eyes closed.

Randolph began the chant. "Atara-Atara-Atara," he said, and his followers answered, the word reverent on their lips. "Atara-our-home-in-the-heavens. Angels of Atara, come for us. Save us. Atara-Atara-Atara."

Theodora slipped to the rear of the room, gradually moving out of the view of Randolph, Desirée, and Vesta. But she needn't have worried; eyes closed, and they were sinking into a trance.

She hid behind a pillar in the rear of the auditorium, watching. Her heart beat faster, and she felt as though she might suffocate from her nervous, shallow breathing.

Even before Randolph silenced the drums and began to speak, she knew that for the last three days, she'd indeed been lulled into thinking this group was harmless. She'd been seduced. And suddenly she wondered how many of the others—those dancing to the pulsating drums—had been brought in the same way.

"Brothers and sisters," Randolph said when his followers were seated on the floor, "as the world races toward a disaster worse than anything we mortals can imagine, we gather here in our compound, where no harm can befall us."

There were murmurs of agreement.

"I told you some time ago that I had details of this event, details I was encouraged to keep from you until I received permission from the Ataran angels to take you into our confidence."

Theodora moved around the pillar just enough to see his face.

"I can now disclose more information." He paused dramatically before continuing. "As you know, scientists have recently expressed belief that it was the impact of a meteorite with Earth that caused the end of the age of dinosaurs."

There were nods of agreement. He smiled broadly. "And lately, as many of you are also aware, cryptologists have found encoded messages in the Old Testament texts." His voice dropped dramatically. "These messages—had we known about the encoding—foretold the assassination of JFK, its date and exact location. That's just one example. These codes have also predicted astounding events, momentous events, in this world's history! Wars. Earthquakes. Devastating hurricanes. Volcanoes." His voice dropped. "Meteorites."

He shook his head slowly, appreciatively. "Now, dear brothers and sisters. This is a book that is more than merely the collection of myths of a simple people. It is—I daresay—a book left as a map by the Atarans for us to use, when the time is right.

"And that time is now!"

A low murmur of speculation rose from several places among the audience.

Randolph held up a hand, and even as his followers continued to chatter like children, he spoke. "What I have to tell you is something no one else on Earth yet knows." He repeated the words to be sure all had heard. Now a hush prevailed. "Even as we sit here today, a meteorite is hurtling toward Earth. Impact *will* occur. Soon. Very soon."

There were a few moans, and Theodora looked around to see some of the older women hide their faces in their hands.

"Dear friends," Randolph said softly. "We don't need to concern ourselves with what is or isn't going to happen to this old world. It's a spaceship. That's all it is." He laughed lightly. "A spaceship that is soon going to be destroyed. Now, listen, and I will tell you how."

There was not a sound in the room except the charismatic tones of Randolph's voice.

"The first meteorite will slam into Earth causing a spray of dust that will obliterate the sun.

"It will then break apart, sending millions of smaller particles into the atmosphere. These will be pulled back to Earth by gravity. They will rain down upon this poor planet, causing raging global firestorms."

Again, Theodora heard sounds of weeping from someone near the front of the room.

Randolph ignored it. "All mankind will soon be annihilated by this meteorite shower." He was almost shouting now and gesturing wildly. "Make no mistake about it. Every living creature on Earth will be destroyed."

Theodora drew in a deep breath, almost unaware that she'd been afraid to breathe. If she didn't know any better, she, too, would be taken in by his earnest delivery.

"But there is hope, my friends," he continued. "This will not be the end for us." He smiled broadly and held up his hands. "Have no fear. We are about to embark on a journey that will whisk us away from this world…," he paused dramatically and dropped his voice, "…before the first meteorite hits."

His piercing gaze moved from face to face across his audience. For a moment he didn't speak.

Journey? Theodora frowned, considering the word. Where would Randolph take his followers? She briefly thought of Brigham Young taking his followers to the Great Salt Lake and the new frontier to escape persecution.

But what new frontier could Randolph be considering? Mars? She almost chuckled at the thought. After the JPL triumph with the *Pathfinder* probe, she'd heard someone had started a list for volunteers who wanted to colonize the red planet. Maybe Randolph was jumping the gun to give his followers something to look forward to. Or perhaps a carrot to dangle before their noses.

"Our journey won't be like that of any other mortal before us."

She frowned again. Mortal? That ruled out the Mars colonization.

"No," he said. "We will be freed from our bodies." He leaned forward, his piercing gaze flicking across the room, touching here and there, lovingly, on the faces of the devotees. "Freed," he repeated. "Because we will be traveling through the universe with a speed these mortal frames could not bear." He laughed lightly. "And believe me, I'm ready to leave this ol' tired and used-up frame behind. I'm ready to exchange it for the angelic frame we're promised."

Applause broke out as waves of nausea washed over Theodora. Long-ago television images of Jim Jones and the nearly one thousand bodies of his followers found in the Guyana jungle filled her mind. The more recent news of the Heaven's Gate tragedy crawled in beside it. She was suddenly filled with anger, horror, and despair.

He's talking about mass suicide!

85

Did they know what he had planned? All around her people were talking about it as if he'd just announced a trip to Disney World.

Oh, Lord, she breathed. *Show me what you would have me do. He said soon. The journey will be soon. And they don't know the horror of what's ahead. They don't know!*

She looked up to see that Desirée had followed her to the rear of the auditorium. The woman's eyes had filled with tears, and she was shaking her head slightly.

"Are you all right?" Theodora whispered.

"It's my family," she said. "I must get them to join me here so they can be saved. You see, that's what this is all about. Those who enter our gates will be spared Earth's destruction. From now on, as Brother Randolph has said, none of us will be allowed to leave."

Theodora's heart stopped. "No one?"

Desirée shook her head. "Those who enter our gates may lose their physical lives, but ultimately they will be saved."

"To go to this other planet?"

"Yes," Desirée said earnestly.

"I must ask you, dear," Theodora said, taking the younger woman's hand. "Does Randolph include me in this scenario?"

Desirée's response was halted when Rance Randolph raised his hands for the members to again silence themselves. "You are among the privileged, my friends. For we will all leave this earth to join the Ataran angels.

"And the harvest will be soon, dear friends. Very soon!" He smiled, his face almost glowing. "Take this thought with you as you go about your mission preparing to greet our visitors: Life's greatest journey lies ahead! And the time is short. We need to gather as many as we can into our vineyard before our journey begins."

"Desirée?" Theodora urged as Randolph finished, doing her best to keep the creeping panic from her voice. "Does Randolph expect me to stay here?"

Desirée smiled softly. "Well, yes. I thought you knew that."

As soon as the meeting was over, Theodora wove her way through the throngs of followers and hurried across the compound to the front gate. Her only thought was to get away from the estate as quickly as possible. Even her rapid fall of footsteps seemed to echo the words: *Escape! Escape! Escape!*

Devotees milled about after the worship service, and no one seemed to notice as she slipped away from them, winding through the eucalyptus trees and around the estate's buildings.

She forced herself to breathe normally, though her heart was racing as she hurried along. Several minutes later, she reached the guardhouse at the side of the ornate front gates. The rotund guard was just taking his place at the guardhouse when she approached.

"Good morning, Sister Theodora," he called out with a beatific smile. "What brings you this way on such a fine morning?"

Theodora gave him a dazzling smile. "Well, good morning to you, Brother! I have an assignment that perhaps you can help me with."

"And what might that be, Sister?" He was still smiling.

"Ah, me," she said, fishing in the robe's pockets. "It appears I've lost my map." She shook her head as if at her own absent-mindedness. "I've been sent to collect some clippings from certain grapes in the south vineyard. Sister Vesta told me it would be wise to travel through this gate to the place. Can you tell me where the carneros vines are grown? It would be those ready for immediate harvest." She'd heard just enough talk about the harvest, the location of the carneros vineyards, to sound somewhat knowledgeable.

"I would be happy to help you," he said, and Theodora breathed easier. She waited impatiently for him to open the gate. But the gate didn't open. Instead of triggering the electronic opener, he picked up a telephone and spoke into it without taking his gaze from her.

After a moment, he stepped from the guardhouse and walked toward her, still smiling. "You'll need to come with me."

She looked up at his round face, hesitating.

"Please," he said pleasantly. "I'll show you the way."

Her heart sank as he took her firmly by the arm and led her back up the cobbled road toward the chateau.

The large glass doors were locked, but he deftly unlocked them and escorted her inside, across the foyer and up the wide spiral staircase to the third floor.

Moments later she pushed open Randolph's office door. He looked up without surprise from his desk. His discarded robe hung haphazardly over the back of his leather chair; he'd shed it like a snake sheds its skin.

"What a pleasure to see you, Sister Theodora," he said, standing. "And thank you, Brother Dakota, for a job well done."

Brother Dakota obviously knew he was being dismissed. He gave Randolph a curt nod and exited the room.

"Don't you 'Sister Theodora' me," Theodora muttered when he'd left, barely able to contain her anger.

"Please, please," he continued as if she hadn't spoken. "Come in, and sit down. I've been meaning to send for you. You merely saved me the trouble."

She didn't move from where she stood opposite his desk. "I

know where you're about to lead your followers," she said.

He gave her a wide smile as if delighted with her news, but his eyes remained cold. "Do you, now?"

"And it's not to another planet," she said. "You can't do this to them."

He laughed.

"I'll do everything in my power to block what you have planned. I'll contact the authorities, relatives of your members. Someone will listen. Together we'll stop you—"

"Really," he said nonchalantly, seating himself again.

She took a few steps closer to him. "My visit is over. I will be leaving immediately."

"I am greatly disappointed that you don't seem to appreciate our fine hospitality. I thought that a woman of your refinement and intelligence would see that we have so much to offer."

"Offer?" She practically choked on the words. "It seems all you plan to offer your followers is the same kind of journey the followers of Jones, Koresh, and Applewhite were given." Her words were followed by a cold, almost palpable silence.

After a moment, Randolph spoke again, his voice flat. "You have no idea what you're talking about." He paused. "Now, you've wasted enough of my time with your idle speculation." He dismissed her with a flutter of his fingertips.

"I will need transportation to the train station in Calistoga." She hesitated. "Second thought, I'd just as soon walk."

"You might want to reconsider," he said as she turned to go. "As I remember, you'd hoped to spend time with our esteemed French vintner."

"Keb-Kaseko Rodolphe?" A flash of hope brightened the darkness inside her. Perhaps he could help. He was obviously held in great esteem: Perhaps he could convince Randolph that his plan was that of a madman. "Has he returned?"

"Actually, he was never gone."

"What do you mean?"

"You see," Randolph continued, "I know the real reason you came to us. That you've suspected there's been 'some sort of bizarre, dangerous, mind-devouring cult behind the facade of Angels Crest Vineyard.' That you came here, not to do research for your next book, but because you were curious about our activities, especially the disappearance of your childhood friend, our dear Sister Ariel Tilman."

He had quoted her exact words from the e-mail posts she'd exchanged with the vintner, the man who had seemed so sympathetic to her search, the man who had actually suggested she visit Angels Crest in person.

"Keb-Kaseko Rodolphe?" she whispered again, suddenly aware of the trap she'd led herself into, aware of all she had divulged about herself, her work, her family.

She took a step backward, feeling unable to breathe. It was as if the air had been sucked right out of the room.

"Yes," he laughed. "The one and only Keb-Kaseko Rodolphe." And standing again, he bowed with a flourish. In a split-second flash of recognition, she realized the statue was indeed his likeness.

He added, his lip curling, as he straightened, "But see that you never speak the revered name aloud again."

EIGHT

Back in Pelican Cove, K.C. rose early. The dawn was unusually bright for summer on the northern California coastline. In that first instant before becoming fully awake, she almost forgot the heartache of her aunt's disappearance. It seemed Theodora had been missing more than a few days. K.C. had left several messages on the Internet bulletin board, but Keb-Kaseko Rodolphe hadn't yet taken the bait.

The day before, after hearing a note of frustration in Georgie O'Reilly's voice, she'd finally headed back to the *Journal* to spend the day in her office, setting things in order for the next week's issue. Now that K.C. had her computer set up for communication at Aunt Theo's, she and Georgie had worked out a system so they could stay in contact, handling all decisions and workload together via e-mail and modem.

She'd also tried to trace Ariel Tilman's family, remembering everything Theodora had told her about her friend. But so far she'd been blocked at every turn when she tried to follow leads. It seemed the elderly woman had been alone in the world after her husband died, leaving her a small fortune, but no surviving children or relatives. She'd grown up in Pelican Cove and had a multitude of friends, but those K.C. called said Ariel had cut off all contact with them weeks ago. They also confirmed that she'd indeed been quite taken with the beliefs of a cult called Angels of Fellowship and had been in contact with its leader. Unfortunately, no one knew the leader's name or where the cult was located.

K.C. hurried around her apartment, watered a few plants, and started to put out more food and water for Satinka, whom a neighbor had been caring for, when she stooped to pet the lanky feline. "Sweet, sweet baby. I hate to leave you again." She lifted her and kissed the top of Satinka's striped head.

The cat responded with a rumbling purr and curled into her lap. "Tink," K.C. murmured. "How would you like a little vacation?" She grinned, making the quick decision. Satinka would be happier at Aunt Theo's while K.C. was there. Why not take her along? She headed for the carport storage area and the cat carrier, scooped up the necessary pet paraphernalia, and placed it all in the Morgan.

The sun was just rising when she backed out of the apartment driveway and headed through town. On the seat beside her, Satinka let her know with a series of yowls that riding in a car wasn't her favorite way to travel.

But the top was down, and enjoying the breeze on her face, K.C. headed east on the interstate. The traffic was light this early in the morning, and she pressed harder on the accelerator, now eager to get back to Sugarloaf Ridge.

She had just rounded the first curve in the coastal foothills, when her cell phone rang.

She half expected the call to be from Georgie, so she was surprised when Gav's deep voice said, "Kace—?"

"Yes—Hi, Gav," she said, trying to ignore the way her heart seemed to drop to her toes every time he said her name.

"We got a message. Rodolphe finally responded." Gav sounded excited.

K.C. slowed as she rounded a curve. "What did he say?"

"He didn't give out any information about himself but seems willing to correspond with 'Satinka.'"

K.C. grinned as she glanced over at the now sleeping cat. They'd created a new screen name on K.C.'s Internet access account: Satinka.

"Have you answered him?"

"Father Max did. Baited the hook again…" He laughed. "Our skeptic has really taken to this Internet business. He's accessing the net like a pro."

"What's the bait this time?"

"Satinka said she's looking to correspond with a like-minded soul interested in fine wines, classical music, and art. She also said she's young, a mystic, and interested in the supernatural."

"Sounds good," K.C. said, braking for a ground squirrel that darted across the road in front of her. "Anything else?"

"Father Max has a theory about people who are pulled into cults, so he also added that Satinka is alone in the world, lonely, looking for companionship and love, if she can find the right person."

"Nice touch."

"We just sent the reply a few minutes ago."

"If he's still on-line, we may hear back right away."

"We're hoping so." Gav hesitated, and his voice softened. "How long until you can be here, Kace?"

"About a half hour, I think."

There was a heartbeat of silence, then Gav cleared his throat. "We—ah. I've missed you," he finally said.

"Don't start, Gav…" she warned. "Please." She didn't have to say what she was talking about.

"I'm sorry," he said after a moment's hesitation.

"We'll talk later, Gav. But not about us," she said. "I'll be there soon."

"All right, then," he said formally. "Good-bye."

"Bye, Gav." And she replaced the phone in its holder.

∾ ∾ ∾ ∾ ∾

After her encounter with Randolph, Theodora hurried to her suite. Her heart pounded, and every fiber in her body continued telling her to flee. She needed to think of another plan. And fast. There had to be a way!

As she moved across the opulent and charming living room area, she felt a familiar sense of oppression. A feeling she had been ignoring for the past three days.

"Sister Theodora—?"

Theodora looked up to see Desirée approaching from her bedroom. The woman's eyes were red and puffy from crying. Theodora forgot her own fears and immediately went to Desirée, taking the woman's hands in hers.

"Dear, what's the matter?" She led her to one of the couches, and they settled into it.

Taking a shaky breath, Desirée fished in her pocket for a tissue. "The news today…" she began, then her voice faltered. "It's just so terrible I don't know if I can bear it. Just the thought of what's about to happen to our world…"

"It's a lie," Theodora said evenly. She didn't know if Desirée was using her distress as a ploy to keep her from leaving, or if the woman was truly upset. But either way, she had to tell the truth and convince her that Rance Randolph was a phony. "Randolph is deceiving you—and frightening you—with his wild ravings about the end of the world."

Desirée shook her head. "No," she whispered. "He's not like that. He wouldn't do that to us."

"How do you know?"

"If you knew him better you wouldn't need to ask that question. I've spent hours with him. He is an intelligent, compassionate man."

"Has he offered any proof about his predictions?"

Desirée shook her head. "He doesn't need to. I believe him."

This was going nowhere. "You are an intelligent woman, Desirée." She nodded, her eyes still tearful. "Consider just for a minute that Rance Randolph is a con artist. That this is all some strange game to feed his very large ego."

"But it isn't—"

"Please," Theodora interrupted. "Just think about it. What if everything he's told you is a lie?"

She sniffled again. "He wouldn't lie about such a thing. Why would he? Say it's *not* true for the sake of argument. He would be giving up everything of importance. For what? To simply die? All of this—" She gestured toward the grounds and vineyards outside the veranda. "All would be lost. All this would then have no meaning. There would be no journey. It makes no sense that he's trying to con us."

"He's trying to convince *you*—not himself—that the end of the world is coming." She took Desirée's hand in hers. "He's trying to convince *you* that the only way out is suicide. If he does, and that mass suicide occurs, he'll not lose anything. You will die. But the end of the world will not occur."

Indignant, Desirée yanked back her hand. "It isn't death he's talking about!"

"Do you really think he's got a spaceship waiting out in one of the vineyards for this journey?"

Desirée didn't answer, but there was a flicker of fear in her eyes.

"Come with me, Desirée," she said suddenly. "Leave this place with all its secrets and dangers. Leave with me, now!"

Desirée looked at her with mournful eyes. "I can't leave."

"Why not?"

"I have nowhere to go."

Theodora felt a stab of pity as the realization sunk in. "You've given everything to him?"

"To the Angels of Fellowship," she corrected, and again Theodora could see her fear.

"You can stay with me," Theodora said, though she knew it wouldn't make any difference.

Desirée shook her head. "I can't leave this place," she said. "What if he's right? What if this is the only place of safety?" She looked thoughtful. "The world is full of mystery. There've been too many UFO sightings to ignore. What about the alien ship that crash-landed in Roswell, New Mexico?"

She didn't give Theodora time to answer, but rushed on, almost breathless as her words spilled out. "Even the Bible says that we entertain angels unawares. Perhaps the angels that Brother Randolph speaks with are those very angels."

Theodora held up her hand. "You can be sure the angels referred to in God's Word are not from UFOs." She frowned, leaning closer. "Desirée, cults often mix just enough Scripture in with the lies of an egotist to convince people they're somehow close to Christianity. Randolph is no different than any of the others. He's attempting to manipulate you with fear."

This time Desirée reached for Theodora's hand, an imploring look on her face. "Please, don't go. Stay, and help me…and maybe some of the others figure a way out of this." She hesitated. "Stay, even if it is only to convince us he is lying."

It was a challenge, and Theodora wondered if it had come from the lips of Rance Randolph himself to keep her from leaving. It really didn't matter; she couldn't ignore Desirée's plea for help.

"I can probably do more for you on the outside," she said. "I'll stay and talk with you today. But I definitely must leave in the morning."

Desirée squeezed Theodora's hands. "Thank you, Sister," she said. "What you've said has given me something to ponder. I gave up everything to come here. Everything. I can't consider leaving until I can think things through. Decide exactly what my reasons are for staying—and if those reasons are valid."

"I understand."

"No, I don't think you do."

"Is there something more, Desirée?" Theodora had been trying to identify something she'd noticed in the woman's face every time Rance Randolph's name was mentioned. Now she held her breath, somehow guessing what Desirée might tell her next.

Desirée nodded slowly, and her cheeks reddened sweetly as she began to speak. "It's about Brother Randolph..." Her voice faltered. "The reason I trust him."

"You think you're in love with him?"

"Is it that apparent?"

"I don't know if it is to everyone. But I noticed."

"You see, when I met him I'd been newly widowed. My Clarence was the only man I'd ever loved. We'd been married thirty-five years when he died, and I thought I couldn't go on. Life was empty...so very empty...until I met Brother Randolph. It was as if the sun came up after a very long night."

Desirée's face lit up. "Oh, we attended plays and concerts, and he took me to some of the finest restaurants in San Francisco. We danced and talked till dawn." She giggled like a schoolgirl. "One night, we even walked in the rain, just because it was a romantic thing to do." She sighed. "He filled my empty days with laughter...with ideas about life. Ideas I'd never before considered."

"Ideas about Angels of Fellowship?"

"Yes, and other things."

"And you fell in love."

"Yes. That's why I came here. I didn't really care about some other universe with another world filled with angels, Ataran angels. I only believe it because he does."

97

"Because he wants you to," Theodora corrected. "Do you miss that close relationship with him? I mean, you're not seeing him in the same way, are you?"

Desirée laughed. "Oh, no. It wouldn't be right. I understand that. But, there's still something between us. Something beyond the relationship he has with the others. I watch him when he's speaking to the group, and he seeks me out. Our eyes meet, and I know he remembers our times together with as much fondness as I do."

"That's why you can't leave. It's not because you're afraid to, or because you believe in the coming destruction."

Desirée drew in a deep breath. For a moment the room was silent. Finally she nodded. "It's Rance Randolph I can't leave."

The sun was bright against a sapphire sky when K.C. turned the Morgan into Aunt Theo's driveway at Sugarloaf Ridge. She rolled to a stop just behind Gav's Cherokee with the sheriff's insignia on the side.

Grabbing Satinka's carrier, she headed to the porch and pushed open the door.

Gav, in jeans and a pullover sweater, and Father Max, also sporting jeans, with a flannel shirt, were seated in front of her computer. Gav turned as she entered the room. "You were right. Our vintner had indeed stayed on-line."

She placed the carrier on the couch and flipped it open. Satinka hopped out to sniff her new surroundings. "What did he say?"

Father Max looked up from where he'd been composing an e-mail post. "He said that he knows of others besides Satinka who're trying to find meaning in this confusing world."

K.C. pulled another chair to the desk and settled into it. "I knew it! He's the key." She scanned Father Max's message. "Ask him where Satinka might meet him," she said, smiling.

"You took the words right out of Satinka's mouth." Father Max began to type. A moment later, he clicked the mouse on 'send,' and the three settled back to await the reply. "If he's still on-line," Father Max said.

And he was. It took only a few minutes for Satinka's mail-box icon to blink. Father Max clicked it twice, and the three began to read through the post.

"Bingo!" K.C. breathed after a minute. "Angels Crest. He wants to meet her at Angels Crest's five-star dining room."

"He swallowed the bait," Gav said.

"Hook, line, and sinker," Father Max added, then sat back in his chair and nodded slowly.

"He didn't say he's affiliated with Angels Crest," K.C. pointed out. "Only that he wants to meet Satinka there."

"Why else would he pick the place?" Gav said. "It doesn't make sense unless he's somehow connected to it." He looked thoughtful. "Besides, people like this are usually more comfortable on their home turf."

"Why don't we ask if he's connected to Angels Crest?" K.C. said, frowning. "I want to find out everything I can before I agree to meet him."

"Meet him?" Father Max raised a brow. "Don't tell me you're actually thinking of playing the role of Satinka?"

K.C. nodded. "I might, but I want to see what we're getting into first."

"I can't let you do that, Kace," Gav said earnestly. "It may be dangerous."

"What Aunt Theo's gotten into may be far more dangerous, Gav. I'll do whatever it takes to find her. Including meeting this elusive vintner as the equally elusive Satinka." She gave them both a reassuring smile, then took over the keyboard and typed,

My dear Keb-Kaseko,

Though it is tempting to meet you, I am a bit of a recluse and leave my home only when necessary. I must admit, five-star dining would be a delight, however, and I am seriously considering your dinner offer.

Could you tell me more about Angels Crest? I am able to overcome my tendencies toward agoraphobia by finding out every detail I can about those locations to which I venture forth. I need to know that I will feel safe.

Satinka

K.C. grinned. "That will give him something to mull over for a while." She clicked the mouse to send the message. The real Satinka had nosed around Aunt Theo's living room, and now hopped on K.C.'s lap, then onto the top of the computer. She stretched out, obviously enjoying the warmth of the monitor.

Gav stroked Satinka's sleek back and turned to K.C. "I won't try to talk you out of your plan, Kace. But how about if you and I drive up to Angels Crest Vineyards this evening? Nose around. See what we can find out."

She nodded. "The three of us can go—" she began, but Father Max, looking wise, interrupted.

"I'll stay here and continue sending messages on behalf of the agoraphobic Satinka," he said with a grin. "You two can do this leg of the sleuthing without me."

A few minutes later, the two were in the Morgan, K.C. driving. She pulled out of the drive, swung onto the road leading through Sugarloaf Ridge, and down the hillside to Oakville.

"It's all fitting together," she mused as she drove. "Aunt Theo searches for Ariel via the Internet. She's answered by the world-renowned French vintner. Though we don't know what their e-mail exchanges contained, mystery writer that Theo is, she may have done the same thing we did—"

"Played the role of someone she's not?"

K.C. frowned as she came to a stop sign, watched for traffic, then revved the engine again and sped away. They had nearly reached Highway 29, leading through Napa Valley, and she slowed the Morgan as traffic increased. "She had no reason, at that point, to suspect Keb-Kaseko Rodolphe. She may have simply used her own name, but perhaps made up some reason for connecting with him."

Gav nodded slowly. "If he was so quick to ask our Satinka to meet him, he may have done the same thing with Theo."

"That's the only thing that makes sense."

"So Aunt Theo met him—perhaps at the same restaurant—then didn't leave. Why?" It was a rhetorical question.

"The names, Gav. Think about it. Angels Crest Vineyard. Angels of Fellowship, the cult that Ariel joined." She glanced at him then back to the road. "That's got to be the connection. They've got to be one and the same."

"But cults are sprinkled throughout the state...the nation. People join. They leave. They go on to something else that catches their fancy. Very few are like the dark, secretive, dangerous cults we hear about on the news."

K.C. found herself concentrating on the familiar resonance of his voice as much as the thoughtful, detailed facts he was giving her.

"Those few are more dangerous than we know, Kace," he continued. "Many of the leaders are paranoid. They've got to have absolute control. When that's threatened, there's usually trouble. Once people join, they're not allowed to leave. Mainly because of the flow of information the leaders don't want outside their gates."

"Do you think that's why Aunt Theo might be considered a threat—if our scenario is correct?" K.C. asked, frowning. She braked for another intersection, then swung the Morgan north

101

on Highway 29. "It still doesn't make sense."

"It's the only lead we've got," Gav said.

They rode along in silence for several minutes. K.C. tried to ignore the memories that Gav's presence evoked. "Law enforcement suits you, Gav," she said finally.

He glanced over at her, meeting her gaze. She quickly turned her attention back to the highway.

"I'm enjoying it," he said blandly.

"Is that what you've decided to settle into, as a career, I mean?" She was getting dangerously close to memories too sorrowful to face, memories of the life of ministry they had once planned together. She immediately wished she hadn't asked.

"I probably won't stay in law enforcement. Entirely, I mean," he said, keeping his eyes forward. "I'm not sure."

I should have known, she thought bitterly. Once fickle, always fickle. She couldn't help wondering about the woman in his life, the one she was sure had stolen his heart three years before. She wondered if the woman followed him to Sugarloaf Ridge or perhaps lived somewhere in the Napa or Sonoma Valleys. She pushed the thought from her mind, unable to stand the stab of pain.

Gav turned to look at her, almost as if reading her mind. A veil seemed to close over his eyes, shielding his soul from her scrutiny. She didn't expect him to continue, but he did. "I'm going back to school, Kace."

She almost laughed. "You are?" She wanted to ask if he thought he might stick with it through graduation, but she kept her lips tightly shut.

"I'm getting double graduate degrees in psychology and social work."

She was surprised, and felt more than a little chagrined for her bitter thoughts. "That's...that's wonderful, Gav. Is that why you're unsure about leaving law enforcement?"

He nodded. "I will use both in the future—with or without staying in law enforcement."

For a moment K.C. didn't know what to say. "It sounds like you're still called to help people, Gav," she finally said quietly. He didn't answer but just kept his eyes on the road.

"We're coming into Calistoga," he said after a moment, almost as if relieved to talk about something else. "The vineyard's up in the hills to our left." He pointed west.

K.C. inched the Morgan through the bumper-to-bumper traffic, and they made their way along the main street of the charming town. The shops were filled with tourists, and she stopped several times to let pedestrians pass in front of them.

Finally, Gav nodded to an upcoming intersection. "Here's where we turn," he said.

"Let's do it." K.C. swung into the left-hand lane and dodged the cars in the oncoming traffic as she turned. A few minutes later, she shifted to a lower gear, and they headed up the hillside.

Soon the road wound through acres of vineyards on rolling hills that stretched out of sight. "It's beautiful," K.C. whispered. "Just look at this setting!"

They rounded another curve, then K.C. suddenly pulled over and stopped. "Look, Gav. Up ahead."

There was Angels Crest Vineyard at the top of the hill, the rock walls of the chateau gleaming in the sun, its canopy of live oak trees providing the perfect frame.

She was so busy staring at the stunning chateau, that she was startled when Gav touched her shoulder. "Over there," he said and nodded toward a distant field.

She followed his gaze. There, along the hillside, were a dozen or more robed figures, stooped over the grapevines. "They look like monks," she said. "Those robes…" she squinted. "They've even got hoods."

"Take a look at this fence," Gav said. He got out of the car and moved toward the nearest segment. K.C. guessed it had to be at least ten feet tall, barbed and spiked at the top. Gav studied it for a few minutes, then turned back to her. "There's heavy-duty surveillance here, Kace." He frowned. "I'd bet this whole thing is electrically charged. And take a look at the strobe lights on top—motion sensors."

"I wonder if it's to keep people in—or out."

"Probably both," he said solemnly, and K.C. knew that his thoughts also were on Aunt Theo.

A few minutes later, K.C. rounded the corner and they spotted the guardhouse. "Odd that there aren't more people around," she muttered to Gav as they awaited the approaching robed guard.

"Welcome to Angels Crest Vineyard." The guard had a round, cheerful face. He looked genuinely sorry as he shook his head. "If you've come for a tour and wine tasting, you'll have to come back at another time. You see, we only give tours by appointment."

K.C., trying to hide her disappointment, looked over at Gav. They exchanged glances, and he suddenly gave the man a big smile and got out of the car. He strode over to where the guard stood by K.C..

"We're so disappointed," Gav said, still smiling. "You see, my wife and I are here on our honeymoon. We can't be here long, and we'd so hoped to see Angels Crest Vineyards. Take the tour, see the gift shop…the whole shebang." His tone was light. "Any chance of making an exception?"

The guard seemed to hesitate. He narrowed his eyes in thought. "Let me check," he said, and disappeared into the guardhouse.

"Honeymoon, Gav?" K.C. whispered angrily when the guard was out of earshot. "I really don't care what cover you make up for us. But from now on, don't you dare call me your bride or your wife!"

The guard stepped out of the small building before Gav could answer. K.C. quickly exchanged her scowl for a smile.

"I'm sorry," the guard said. "We really can't make an exception. You can return tomorrow, however. Our CEO has offered you a private tour for your trouble."

Again, K.C. and Gav exchanged glances. "And who heads up Angels Crest?" K.C. ventured.

The guard smiled. "Rance Randolph, CEO and vintner."

"Vintner?" Gav repeated. "We understood that your vintner is the world-renowned Keb-Kaseko Rodolphe."

The guard seemed to study their faces as if memorizing their features. His cold look chilled K.C. "It's odd that you'd be aware of our dear Keb-Kaseko," he said finally. "That's not information known to the general public." He paused, almost dramatically. "Rodolphe is known only in certain quite elite circles."

K.C. and Gav shrugged, laughing together as if at their newlywed poverty. "Well, my goodness, I had no idea we traveled in any kind of a circle," said Gav.

"Nor did I," laughed K.C., playing the lighthearted bride. "Imagine such a thing! Next we'll be jet-setting around the world."

But as the Morgan turned away from the estate and headed back down the hill, neither was laughing.

"I think we've found the place," K.C. said, gazing out at the robed and hooded figures in the vineyard. Again, a shudder skittered up her spine.

NINE

That night after curfew, Randolph sent for Sister Desirée, and a short time later she was ushered into his office.

"Please, dear, come in and sit down," he said. He smiled into her eyes and noted her expression of adoration. She settled into the chair across from his desk.

"I want to commend you on the excellent way you handled our dear sister this morning."

She frowned. "Sister Theodora?"

"Yes, of course," he said. "I couldn't have orchestrated the conversation better myself. You played the role of a teary, vulnerable apostate so beautifully that even I was convinced…that is, until the end when you pleaded with her to stay."

"You overheard our conversation?" Her cheeks flamed.

He turned to a console on a credenza beside his desk, flicked a switch, and she heard the voices of two novices discussing the morning announcement about the meteor. After a moment, he turned the volume down, and as their conversation continued, the murmur of voices could be heard in the background.

"You overhear everything?"

"When I choose to." He paused before going on. "Visionaries are often belittled by those with small minds," he said after a moment. "They are afraid to consider worlds outside their own limited beliefs and value system." Her eyes cleared; he was getting through to her. He smiled. "Those who believe in a personal God are particularly narrow-minded," he said solemnly. "Theodora Whimple is one of these, I'm afraid. I really thought that she'd come seeking something more in her life, the intellectual, the beautiful, the fellowship of like-minded superior beings. But I read her wrong, and I'm sorry that she's so afraid to expand her mind."

"She says she will leave tomorrow," Sister Desirée said. "Perhaps it's for the best."

"I have not released you from your duty—that which I spoke of the first night she was here."

Sister Desirée swallowed hard and nodded. "Why not just let Sister Theodora go her way?"

"The Ataran angels are convinced she belongs with us," he said, his tone quiet but filled with absolute control. If there was one doubter among his followers, there would soon be others. And that he would not allow, especially this close to the culmination of the plan he had spent a decade to develop.

Even before the declaration of love he'd overheard, Randolph had guessed how he could keep Sister Desirée from doubting, from voicing her doubts to others.

"You, dear Sister Desirée," he said, his tone now soothing, "are among the chosen. Though I haven't said, I've known it from the first time I met you." He stood and walked around the desk to stand next to her. Reaching down, he lifted her chin with his fingertips and caressed her cheek with his thumb. "There will be royalty on our new planet," he said softly. "And you, my dear, are to rule with me."

There was clear love in her eyes, and he reached for her hand, pulling her to stand in front of him. "Do you understand what I'm saying?"

She shook her head, and he laughed lightly, seductively. "I'm asking you to marry me, my sweet Sister Desirée, to become my bride on this earth as well as on the next."

When she tried to speak, he touched her lips to silence her. "It was ordained from time's beginning that you and I should become one—to travel together through the universe. To populate a brand-new world. Our bodies will be young again when we arrive there, Desirée. Our children will rule for the generations that follow."

He was delighted to see the transformation in her face, and he became caught up in the world he was creating even as he spoke. "You may wonder about those we are taking with us on this journey—those who are here at Angels Crest. They will be our subjects, but it is our line that will continue on as royalty." He chuckled. "Our own House of Atara."

"Royalty?" she finally managed to whisper, her eyes wide. "Us?" The wonder on her face told him she was convinced.

"My Ataran queen," he breathed, drawing her close. He kissed her gently on the lips. "May we rule forever."

She reached her arms around his neck. "I'll treasure this moment always," she said, kissing him back.

The next morning in her suite, Theodora awoke to the ringing bell in the chateau's turret. But when she looked for her freshly laundered clothes in their usual place, they were missing.

Frowning, she threw back her comforter and slipped out of bed. She strode through the dressing room doorway and across the marble tiles and flicked on the ornate gold-and-crystal lamp. She pulled open the door to the large walk-in closet and turned on the inside light.

Her skirt and blouse, her lovely Australian straw hat, her walking shoes and stick, all were missing. Instead, she found a hooded robe and set of undergarments, as well as a pair of the thin canvas slippers.

The message was clear: She would not be leaving.

A few minutes later, Sister Vesta escorted her to the morning worship service. Immediately after, she was given her assignment for today and each day that would follow: She would help with the harvest of the carneros grapes.

It was backbreaking labor, and from the first hour, she didn't know how she could last. She stopped often to rub her back and stretch her bent spine.

"Sister Theodora," Sister Vesta said sternly from the end of the row each time she attempted to rest. "There's no time for daydreaming on this job."

Theodora lifted her tray, supporting it on one hip, and bent over the staked grapevines once again. Her fingers, already stained purple, gently twisted the clumps of fruit from the vines. She rubbed her back and reached for another clump of grapes.

She looked around for a means of escape. She'd already surveyed the electronic fences and knew exactly where the guards were posted. But it seemed impenetrable, and she was concluding that this was where God wanted her to be. She looked up into the heavens, seeking comfort from her Lord's presence.

I am the true vine, my beloved, and my Father is the gardener.
Remain in me, and I will remain in you.
As the Father has loved me, so have I loved you.
Do not be afraid, my child. Remain in my love.

Theodora drew in a deep breath and gazed for a moment across the vine-covered hillsides. She thought of the verse that had come to her many times during her hours laboring at Angels Crest: "My command is this: Love each other as I have loved you. Greater love has no one than this, that he lay down his life for his friends."

Again, she looked heavenward. "Oh, Lord," she breathed, "is this the sacrifice of love you require from me? Is it my life?"

Do not be afraid! I am with you, my beloved child. Remain in my love.

TEN

KC. and Gav drove back to Angels Crest the following morning for their ten o'clock appointment. Again, the guard met them at the gate. This time he was dressed in street clothes and smiled broadly as he saw them approach.

"Ah, here are our newlyweds again!" he called out as he walked toward them. "Welcome to Angels Crest. This time I can be a bit more hospitable." Clipboard in hand, he leaned into the car on K.C.'s side. "We were just closing yesterday when you arrived. And because of our preparations for the coming harvest, our hours are limited. I'm sorry."

She gave him a tentative smile. "We understand."

"Now," he said, leaning closer, "I need to ask you a few questions before you go in. Do you mind?"

"What kind of information do you need?" K.C. glanced over at Gav. He shrugged, leaving it to her.

"The usual—name, address, reason for visit."

"Don't most people come for wine tasting and the tour?" K.C. asked, keeping her voice light.

The guard smiled again, but his eyes held a brittle look. "Not always," he said, then he glanced over at Gav. "You are Mr. and Mrs.—?"

"Elliott Gavin," K.C. said, turning away from the guard to send Gav a daggered look. Gav smiled into her eyes, then leaned forward so that he could see the guard. "We're Elliott and Katherine Gavin." K.C. shot him another warning look, and while the guard was writing their names, Gav shrugged again, still smiling.

"Address?" the guard asked. "It's for our mailing list." He

paused, seeming to study their faces. "We have a wonderful home-tasting program we'll tell you about later," he added.

"We don't yet have a permanent address," she said smoothly.

The guard looked up in surprise. "I see."

Gav leaned forward again. "We'll be happy to send it to you once we're settled." To emphasize his point he gave K.C. a loving smile. Her back to the guard, she glared at him.

Finally, the guard gave them parking instructions, then stepped into the small guardhouse, opened the electronic gate, and waved them through. Gav gave him a friendly smile and a mock salute as K.C. put the Morgan in gear and drove slowly into the estate.

K.C. headed the car along a small road leading to the rear of the chateau and the parking lot on an upper level. To one side of the drive was a sculptured English garden, to the other a sweeping lawn dotted with live oaks, eucalyptus, elms, and weeping willows. The hillside behind was heavily forested with more eucalyptus, so large they appeared to be centuries old.

Gav shook his head in awe. "This place *is* impressive," he said. "But there's something about it…"

"I know," K.C. agreed. "It's beautiful, the setting, the grounds, the architecture. But…" she hesitated also, frowning. "I'm not sure why, but it just seems, well, too perfect."

"I was thinking secretive. But maybe it's just our imaginations, Kace."

"Katherine," she corrected. Her voice softened. "It's been forever since anyone's called me that."

"Ah yes, Miss Katherine Cassandra Keegan," he said. "It was definitely too long a handle for such a skinny tike." He met her gaze. "I still remember when you changed it to K.C.—fifth grade, wasn't it? You'd had it with teachers calling you Katherine Cassandra every time you got in trouble. You figured with K.C. they wouldn't be able to draw out those two short syllables with quite the same dramatic effect."

She flashed him a grin as she pointed the Morgan into a parking space and turned off the engine. "You've got quite a memory," she said, irritated with the way her heart seemed to take an elevator ride every time their eyes met.

For a moment neither one moved to exit the car but sat looking at each other.

"The show begins," he finally said as he stepped out. Coming around to her side of the car, he opened the door for K.C.

Yes, a show. That's all it is, she thought grimly. Gav took her arm, and they headed to the reception area where the guard had said their tour would begin.

A slim, pretty, middle-aged woman met them at the door. She was dressed exquisitely in a navy skirt and cream knit top, a jaunty cranberry scarf tied at her neck. It set off her blond hair and ivory complexion.

"Hello," she said. "My name is Desirée Scott. I'm so glad you could join us today." She smiled and reached to shake their hands. "I understand you two are newlyweds!"

K.C. and Gav exchanged glances, and Desirée laughed merrily. "Good news like this travels fast," she said. "Actually, Dakota called ahead to announce your arrival."

"Dakota?"

"Our lovable guard. Isn't he a character? You'd think he owns this vineyard—as protective of the place as he is."

K.C. couldn't help liking the woman. What Desirée Scott didn't know was that the exchanged glances had more to do with her name than with calling them newlyweds. Desirée Scott, Marigold Green's widowed friend from Marin County, cofounder of the computer software empire. K.C. watched her now with renewed interest.

"My name is Katherine, er, Katherine…Gavin," K.C. finally managed.

"And my name is Elliott," Gav said, putting his arm around K.C.'s shoulders. "Elliott Gavin."

Desirée seemed ready to clap her hands together in delight. "We are so glad you stopped by today. Please, follow me, and I'll take you on a short tour as we head for the chateau. Mr. Randolph is awaiting your arrival."

They followed Desirée Scott outside, and as they walked along the path leading to the front of the chateau, she explained some of the estate's history.

"Historically, our roots go back to 1853," she said. "The land on which the estate is located today was originally rich farm land. It was owned by Maude and Bernard Hudson. The hard-working couple soon discovered that their land was perfect for growing grapes.

"Maude Hudson's brother, who lived in France at the time, visited the family in 1857, bringing with him cuttings from some of the finest vineyards in the Loire and Rhône Valleys. Of the more than three dozen cuttings he attempted to bring by ship, only seven survived."

K.C. and Gav looked appropriately impressed.

Desirée Scott stopped and looked out to the vineyards. "Many of the vines you see here today are descendants of those original cuttings and their resulting vines."

She started walking again, speaking as they followed. "To our right and up the hillside is a wine cellar that was built in 1876. At first it had a flat roof which was used to unload the grapes, then in 1884, second and third stories were added by Chinese workmen.

"Mr. Randolph will lead you on the tour through the limestone tunnels in the mountain directly behind the wine cellar. These were chiseled by the same Chinese laborers. It took them years to complete the labyrinth of caves and tunnels. Some of them reach hundreds of feet into the mountain.

"They keep a year-round temperature of fifty-eight degrees. You will notice when you descend into the tunnels that a black moss still grows on their walls. That moss was quite a blessing because it kept the air dry and pure."

"Are the tunnels where the wine was aged?" K.C. asked.

"Oh no, my dear," Desirée laughed. "That is where the barrels were aged."

"So empty barrels were stored there?" Gav asked.

"Yes, barrels made of both American oak and French oak. As you may know, some wine connoisseurs can tell the difference quite readily between wines that are identical in every way, except for the wood of the aging barrels."

"Are the caves used for anything now?" K.C. asked.

A strange look crossed Desirée's face, then she shook her head, almost too quickly. "Oh, no!" she laughed. "They haven't been used for years. I've heard there are some empty barrels still stacked in some of the back caves, but that's all."

They had arrived at the front of the chateau, and Desirée led them up the stairs to the portico, through the double pillars, and into the entry hall. Overhead hung a crystal chandelier, casting rainbows of light around the room. Dark beams and white walls added to the castlelike atmosphere. The floors and their borders were made of gleaming oak inlaid with other woods, perhaps mahogany, maple, and walnut. Elegant curtains looped around gleaming brass rods fell dramatically on either side of the wide hall's floor-to-ceiling windows.

"Please, follow me." Desirée led them to a side room and opened the door to the library.

"The estate fell into disrepair in the 1920s largely due to Prohibition," she said. "It was purchased in the 1930s by a Hollywood producer who turned the original farmhouse into a country manor. He hired the famous Albert Schroepfer of San Francisco to make the changes you see here today."

K.C. glanced around at the library. The cozy room was lined with bookcases and ornamented with statues and paintings, the perfect setting to relax and read.

After a moment, Desirée led them through some broad double doors to the dining room, which she explained was now used as a meeting room for the winery's board of directors. Again she touched on the history of the architecture and furnishings. They stepped through the outside doors to the veranda, which afforded an excellent view of the gardens and sloping lawns shaded by massive oaks and brightened by flowers of every hue.

"It's beautiful," K.C. murmured, and beside her, Gav agreed.

"The country manor house was designed almost in the same way that country inns are today," Desirée said. "On the fourth floor we have suites of rooms that we reserve for guests from time to time. The two middle levels are used for office and storage space, and the ground floor is exclusively used for our guests. Tours, seminars, and such."

They headed back into the entry hall and crossed to the other side.

"And this," Desirée announced dramatically, "is our lovely Angels Repose." She opened the French beveled-glass doors and invited them to step inside.

Angels Repose was filled with a golden, rosy warmth from sunlight spilling through jeweled windows depicting angels of every description, from classic Victorian depictions to contemporary, almost alien-looking creatures. Cozy chairs and sofas were gathered in nooks and corners, and vases of fresh flowers were placed tastefully on small window and tea tables, along with elegant silver coffee and tea services. A Bach piano concerto played softly through a flawless sound system.

The wine-tasting table was set up in one corner with gourmet snacks. K.C. stepped closer to read the small jar labels touting the ingredients of smoked artichokes and fire-roasted chili dips. Plates of dainty crackers were nearby.

Bottles of wine were arranged in baskets lined with straw, almost as if suggesting their use for picnics. Shirts and barbecuing aprons sporting the Angels Crest Vineyard logo were tucked into baskets. Wine glasses, with a gold embossed ACV, were arranged under spotlights, giving them the appearance of fine crystal.

K.C. glanced at Gav to see if she could read his expression. He gave her a slight nod as if agreeing with her silent assessment. This was no ordinary gift shop, or even tasting room. Angels Repose invited people to come in and sit down, look through the reading materials while sipping glasses of wine or—surprisingly—cups of gourmet tea or coffee.

"You'll later finish your tour here in Angels Repose," Desirée said with another of her friendly smiles, "and have a chance to look through some of our fine reading materials. We also have a video for you to view. But first, I would like to take you up to Mr. Randolph's office and introduce you. He will personally escort you during the remainder of your tour.

"Please, follow me," she said again, and stepped back into the entryway. They headed toward the wide spiral staircase at the rear of the entry hall, climbed to the third floor, and moved soundlessly down a long carpeted hallway.

A pleasant young woman, whom Desirée introduced as Ms. Bastancherry, looked up from her computer as they approached Rance Randolph's outer office.

"This is Mr. and Mrs. Gavin," Desirée said. "Mr. Randolph is expecting them."

Ms. Bastancherry stood and shook their hands. "Welcome," she beamed.

A moment later, Desirée held open the door and stood back to let them enter Randolph's office.

A tall man with graying hair, a thin face accentuated by a dark goatee, and an oily manner of moving, stood and strode across the room to greet them. "It's good to have you here with us today," he said. "I'm so sorry that we had to turn you away last evening. But perhaps we can make up for it with a personalized tour. After all, we're always happy to have newlyweds join us. A commitment such as yours is all too rare in today's world."

"I'd have thought you were much too busy to give us a personal tour," Gav said. "We thank you."

Randolph's smile seemed to freeze in place for an instant. "Well," he laughed lightly, "yes, of course, normally I am otherwise occupied. But as I said, I believe this is a special occasion. It certainly warrants a bit of a celebration, don't you think?" He reached for K.C.'s hand. "May I offer you my best wishes," he said, squeezing it gently. She fought the urge to withdraw her hand.

Then he shook Gav's hand. "My congratulations to you, Elliott. May every happiness be yours."

Gav met K.C.'s gaze over Randolph's shoulder. She could have sworn that he was ready to roll his eyes. Instead, he merely gave the smooth-talking CEO a curt nod.

Randolph led them from the room, down the staircase, and through a back door leading out to the grounds once again. The man provided a running commentary about the history of Angels Crest, filling in details that Desirée Scott hadn't covered.

They came first to a long concrete slab outside a plain rectangular building. On it, large metal equipment stood silent and empty. Randolph explained that the equipment first separated the grapes from the vines and leaves, then crushed the grapes. These were used only at harvest, which had just begun by picking the champagne grapes, he added excitedly, always first to ripen. And it was an early harvest because of the heavy rains the previous winter, followed by an abnormally sunny spring. "A good year for winemakers!" he concluded.

Next he led them into the building which housed the stainless fermentation tanks, explained the process, then moved into the first of several state-of-the-art barrel-aging rooms.

"This series of aging rooms give us the capacity to produce premium wines in a controlled environment," he said, almost as if by rote. "The fifty-five-gallon French oak barrel cooperage is, of course, the ultimate for finishing our chardonnays, cabernet sauvignon, fumé blancs." He gave them a saccharine smile. "We'll see to it that our happy newlyweds go home with a choice bottle of our finest private reserve chardonnay. There's none to compare with it in the world. And it can only be purchased on our premises."

He turned to lead them out of the building. "Next, we'll tour one of the buildings I'm proudest of here at Angels Crest. Many people, even from the local areas, have no idea that we also run a culinary arts school. Each year we bring some of the finest young people from all over the world to train with five-star chefs."

"So you have a restaurant here as well?" Gav asked as they followed him along the path to an outer building. They were now walking beneath a canopy of oaks draped with Spanish moss. The day seemed darker somehow to K.C., though the sky was still a brilliant blue.

"It's small, but very exclusive," Randolph said. "Very exclusive."

A moment later, he opened the door to the school, and they stepped inside. Again, K.C. was impressed by the decor. It was open, airy, and light, and when they stepped into the dining room itself, she let out a small sigh of delight. Everything was white, the marble floor, the long tablecloths, the plush, canvas-padded chairs. Even the ceiling had billows of gauze stretched its entire length. The only color was that of delicate tropical palms and bright Caribbean paintings gracing the walls.

"It is nice, isn't it?" Randolph said, the pride evident in his voice. "It's five-star."

"So we've heard," K.C. murmured without thinking.

"You've heard of our dining room?" Rather than seeming pleased, Randolph was watching her carefully.

Gav came to her rescue. "We're constantly reading travel magazines, dreaming about places we'll probably never be able to afford. I'm sure it was in one of them, do you think, dear?" He looked at K.C.

"I'm sure it was, Elliott," she agreed sweetly.

"We don't advertise our culinary arts school—or its dining room," Randolph said. "There's no need. It's provided for guests of the chateau. And, of course, for friends of our staff."

"I see," said Gav. "Could we have a look at the kitchen?" It was diversionary. Gav was no more interested in examining a state-of-the-art sauté pan than he was in designing counted cross-stitch.

"Of course, of course," Randolph said, and K.C. let out her breath, hoping the man wasn't giving much thought to her comment.

After the kitchen tour, Randolph headed back through the forest of Spanish-moss-draped oaks to the old cellar. "Did Desirée tell you the history of our catacombs?"

"Catacombs?" K.C. frowned.

Randolph laughed. "Well, that's what we call them—in jest, of course. In reality, they're tunnels dug by Chinese laborers in the mid-nineteenth century."

"Oh yes, the tunnels," Gav said. "She did tell us about them. They sound intriguing."

"And mysterious," K.C. added. Randolph was walking faster now and she hurried to catch up. Gav was right behind her, and his presence was comforting, considering where they were headed.

"Ah yes. Mysterious indeed," Randolph said. "There have been stories passed down through the decades about the tunnels—everything from secret hiding places created during Prohibition to skeletal remains being found from people buried years ago." He laughed lightly. "Some say, people buried alive." He seemed to pause to let his words sink in before continuing. "Of course, we know that's nonsense."

"But you did—or someone did—find remains?" K.C. asked.

"The first was when the house was being refurbished in the 1930s—the skeleton of a young woman was found in one of the hiding places created by Prohibition."

"Did anyone ever find out her identity?" K.C. asked.

"No—though some of us have our suspicions," he said, but didn't go on.

"You said 'the first,'" Gav said. "There've been others?"

But Randolph didn't answer. The three-story stone cellar rose before them, its crumbling stone walls covered with ivy and surrounded by wild, overgrown foliage. "This is it," said Randolph. "This is the heart and soul of the first wine-making efforts on this property nearly a century and a half ago." He paused dramatically. "After all that time, you can still almost hear the voices of those who labored here."

"It's in use today?" Gav asked.

"Oh, no. But the only way to reach the tunnels is through this building." He pointed toward the steep hillside behind the building. "The limestone caves are located deep inside."

K.C. hesitated, looking up at the hillside, its dark canopy of oaks, its tangle of unkempt brush. There was something about it that disturbed her. A feeling of suffocation. If it weren't for Aunt Theo, she'd run as fast as she could from this place.

At once, she was aware of Randolph's cold assessing gaze. "Is anything wrong, Mrs. Gavin?"

Gav stepped up and circled his arm around her shoulders. "I believe my wife is tired," he said. "Perhaps we could return another day to finish the tour."

"No, Elliott," she said. "I'm quite all right. Let's go have a look."

Randolph nodded slowly, still watching K.C. carefully. "Afterward, we'll head back to the chateau. Mrs. Gavin can refresh herself at the lovely Angels Repose. We have some wonderful wines for you to sample," Randolph said, now striding toward the imposing old building.

He unlocked and then opened the door of the decaying cellar. He stood aside while K.C. stepped into the dimly lit, musty room. Gav followed behind her, and she was glad when he reached for her hand.

Randolph stepped inside and motioned for them to follow.

ELEVEN

Gav walked very close to K.C. as they entered the first tunnel. The walls were indeed lined with moss, just as Desirée had told them, and the air was surprisingly fresh, especially after the dank outer room. Randolph flipped a switch. A crude system of wires and dim lightbulbs were now evident running the length of the tunnel's ceiling.

From the set of K.C.'s shoulders, Gav knew each step was increasingly difficult for her. When they were children, she'd once chased a kitten into a pitch black crawl space under her house. She became stuck fast, but no one was home to hear her calls for help. The kitten soon scampered to safety, but hours later, the hysterical little girl had to be rescued by the fire department. Gav remembered how her mother told him that K.C. couldn't sleep without the light on for almost two years. She'd never admit to being claustrophobic, but Gav was one of the few people who understood her terror of underground places.

They rounded a corner, then stopped before a thick wooden door. Randolph unlocked it and led them into a cavelike room where dusty barrels were stacked to the ceiling. Randolph's narrow face twisted into a smile. "This is quite atmospheric, don't you agree?" He glanced proudly at the old barrels. "These are French oak, some nearly one hundred years old. They're now too porous to use, but I find them too fascinating to give up." He laughed lightly. "Actually, this room is fascinating in its own right, even without the barrels.

"This was where, it is said, a Frenchman was murdered by the original owner."

"Not Maude Hudson's brother?" K.C. asked.

"Yes, actually, it was." Randolph looked pleased that K.C. had paid attention to the earlier part of the tour. "Hudson's entire acreage was almost destroyed by phylloxera—a destructive little plant louse—that made its way from France into the eastern part of the U.S. in the 1860s. During the next twenty years it destroyed nearly all the vineyards of Bordeaux, Burgundy, and Champagne as well as most other vineyards of Europe and California.

"As the plants here began to die, the distraught Hudson blamed his brother-in-law for bringing the cuttings from France in the first place."

Gav frowned, wondering why Randolph seemed to take such delight in the tragic story. "So he killed the man?"

"Actually it was quite ironic. He poisoned his wife's brother, not knowing that he held the secret to the fight against phylloxera. Had he waited only one day, the young man could have explained that he'd discovered a way to make the plants resistant to the little louse."

The cave was silent as Gav and K.C. waited for Randolph to continue. Somewhere in the distance water dripped, echoing through the tunnels. Gav squeezed K.C.'s hand when he felt her shiver.

Randolph chuckled again. "All Hudson needed to do was graft North American cuttings—from vines brought to California years earlier by Father Serra—to the French vines. The so-called native vines were highly resistant to phylloxera. Problem solved." He snapped his fingers, "Just like that."

"But it was too late for the poor Frenchman," K.C. said.

"Ah yes. You're right about that. Poor fellow. He was found years later in one of these barrels. You see, as far as everyone else knew, he'd returned to France. No one ever knew for sure what happened. But the remains of the Frenchman were found decades later—"

"In this room?" K.C. finished for him.

Randolph's lip curled, as if he enjoyed the story immensely. "Yes, in one of these very barrels. I mean that in a generic sense, of course. That particular barrel was given to the local gendarmes for their investigation."

"Did they find out the cause of death?" K.C. asked. "Did he suffocate?"

"Forensics showed a trace of poison still in the man's system. Probably administered with wine."

"Wine?" Gav was now uncomfortably aware of Randolph's scrutiny. "How would they know that?"

"It's quite easy to doctor wine before the bottle is even corked or labeled," he said with an easy smile. "Quite easy, considering many poisons are tasteless and odorless. Undetectable."

"How about the murderer? Did they find out who did it?" Gav asked.

"They couldn't prove it, but all signs pointed to Hudson, who was an old man by this time. No charges were ever brought against him, but it's said his wife never spoke to him from that day until the day he died years later.

"Now, shall we continue on? This is perhaps the most colorful room in the catacombs, but we have some others that are equally fascinating. We won't have time for the entire labyrinth, but I'll show you a few more. Please, follow me." He switched out the light, leaving them temporarily in absolute darkness.

"And, here we are." And Randolph flipped on another light, leading them into another tunnel.

K.C. clung to Gav's hand as they wound deeper into the earth.

~ ~ ~ ~ ~

K.C. settled into the plush sofa in a quiet corner of the Angels Repose room and leaned back, closing her eyes. Gav watched her tenderly. He knew the toll the catacomb tour had taken on her. Her fear had been almost palpable.

"You okay?" he asked when she opened her eyes and saw him watching her.

She nodded, and sat forward with a sigh. "How soon can we get out of here?" She kept her voice low so she wouldn't be overheard. "This place is giving me the creeps."

"I agree, but we should at least have a sip of wine, play the role a bit. Maybe take them up on looking through their reading materials. Watch their video."

"I don't even like wine," she said. "But I think I'd rather sample wines and cheeses than watch a dry video on the history of Angels Crest Vineyard."

He nodded. "It may not be as dry as we think. We came here for information, Kace. We need to glean every little bit that we can."

"I've got everything I need to play *my* role," she whispered.

"You're surely not still thinking about meeting Rodolphe?" he whispered back incredulously.

Just then, Desirée Scott approached with a tea cart as if serving high tea at the Ritz Carlton. The silver cart held an elegant display of finger sandwiches, crackers, cheeses, fruits, and wines.

Smiling, she settled across from them and proceeded to explain about the different wines, beginning with the whites, the most mild, then moving toward the more robust reds.

After they'd tasted several, she opened a bottle of the Angels Crest private reserve chardonnay and poured them each a glass. She also poured just a splash into her own glass. "This is a special occasion," she said, "deserving of a toast. Then I will leave you two to enjoy this complimentary bottle on your own."

Gav and K.C. looked at each other and held up their glasses to clink them together.

"To love," Desirée said with a wide smile as if she knew the wonder of it herself. "May it last forever!"

The three clinked the glasses together, then she gave them some reading materials and mentioned again that the video would be at their disposal.

"I'm sorry, Gav," K.C. said when Desirée was out of earshot. "A sip or two this time of day is one thing—but an entire bottle?" She frowned at him. "What shall we do?"

He grinned, taking a sip. "It's really pretty good wine. Maybe we could have her cork it and we'll take it with us."

"Is that considered tacky?"

"Probably."

"Maybe we could pour some into the vases," she suggested facetiously.

"Talk about tacky," he said, taking another sip. "Really, Kace. Try it. This is one of the best chardonnays I've ever tried."

"As if you're some sort of wine connoisseur," she teased. "How many chardonnays have you actually tried in your lifetime, Mr. Gavin?"

She tucked a strand of hair behind one ear and pushed up her glasses. The familiar gestures tugged at his heart. He wanted to reach over and take her hand, but that would be assuming too much.

She sipped her wine, watching him over the top of her glass. Her eyes still teased him, and he couldn't help smiling back. "Hey," he said. "I didn't think you liked this wine."

K.C. suddenly sobered and put her glass down.

"What's wrong?"

"I was just thinking about the story of the Frenchman's death in the aging barrel. What an awful story to tell your guests."

He nodded and set his glass down as well. "I wondered about the same thing. Yet Randolph seemed more animated telling us about that than about anything else on the tour."

"With the exception of the five-star dining room."

"Which reminds me, Kace. Please don't think about coming here alone to meet Rodolphe."

She obviously didn't want to talk about it and looked away. Noticing the brochures and booklets that Desirée had placed on the tea cart, she reached for one.

"Look at this," she said. "I had a feeling this would come up sooner or later." A grim look crossed her face as she examined it. "Here's the heart of what this is all about," she said still scanning the paper. "Angels of Fellowship. It's all about it," she whispered. "Especially its history and its leader."

"Who's at its head?"

"Three guesses—"

Gav nodded, knowing the answer. "The CEO, Rance Randolph."

He settled close to K.C. on the sofa to have a look. She thumbed through the booklet. There were slick photographs of Randolph, the vineyard, and smiling Angels of Fellowship members in their monklike robes performing various activities around the grounds. Captions described the peaceful beauty of the compound, the camaraderie of the community, the joyful hope the members had for their future in an uncertain world.

"It says nothing about their beliefs," K.C. said.

"From what we've heard, they're pretty basic. They worship the finer things in life: good wine, good food, good music."

"I wouldn't call them harmless," K.C. said, "in light of Aunt Theo's disappearance."

"We don't know for sure she's here."

"That's what we've got to find out." She looked up from the booklet. "That's why I've got to meet Rodolphe here. He's the key."

The smiling and pleasant Desirée Scott approached them again. "Can I get you anything, dears?"

"No, we're fine," Gav said with an equally saccharine smile. "But we would like to see that video you mentioned." He glanced at the booklet in K.C.'s hands. "We're very interested in the Angels of Fellowship. It just sounds so…" He searched for the word.

"Peaceful," K.C. filled in. "Yes, so peaceful in such a disturbing world."

Desirée beamed. "Why, certainly. That's at the core of our beliefs, and we'd love for you to learn more about it. Please, follow me. The viewing room is just around the corner."

Gav sat close to K.C. on a narrow, padded bench. The lights went out and the performance began. Music swelled and images danced across the screen, and Gav grew increasingly dismayed.

Randolph's appeal targeted the intellectual, the egotistical, and the lonely. He promised a world of hope to them all. Working toward reaching your highest intellectual and creative potential was a theme, as was joining a community of other intellectuals, those who enjoy the finer things in life, so a person would never be lonely again.

But that which made Gav believe Rance Randolph was a raving lunatic was the mention of a planet called Atara populated by forty-four angels. Angels of Fellowship followers here on earth were assured of passage to Atara where they would rule the universe, simply by obeying the Ataran angels' edicts.

The rest of the video paled in contrast to that core bit of information. At the top of the list of thing cults had in common was a leader who ruled as if he were a god. Topping the list of the usual characteristics of cults was a leader who promised his followers would progress to deity if they obeyed the rules. There was also the insidious belief that knowledge beyond human attainability could be reached.

The serpent hasn't changed his tactics, Gav thought grimly. In this beautiful Garden of Eden known as Angels Crest Vineyard, the serpent was alive and well.

He thought of Theo and breathed a prayer for her safely. If she was indeed here, she was in greater danger than he had first believed. They needed to find her quickly.

"Sister Desirée, my dear, come in." Randolph stood to greet the lovely woman who would soon become his bride. "Tell me, how did you think the newlyweds enjoyed their tour?"

"I think they'll be back," she said, sitting in a chair across from him. "They told Brother Dakota they haven't yet settled where they plan to live. That probably means their plans are rather up in the air, as newlyweds' sometimes are. I wouldn't be surprised if they might want to know more about our little community."

He nodded. "There are two reasons I disagree with you. The first is the woman's mention of Keb-Kaseko Rodolphe to Brother Dakota yesterday. Why would she think dear Keb-Kaseko is our vintner? His, ah, relationship is given out to a privileged few. I'm very careful about that." He smiled. "I use the information as a tool for exactly this reason."

She looked at him sharply. "And the second?"

"Their deportment today. They were nervous about something, though I couldn't put my finger on it." He frowned. "Nervous and quite curious at the same time."

"Is that so unusual, Brother Randolph?" She frowned. "This

can be an overwhelming experience."

"Yes, yes, of course it can, dear." He turned to look out the window, letting his gaze move out to the vineyards. "How is our Sister Theodora doing?"

A dark look crossed Sister Desirée's face, and her voice dropped as she spoke. "I think you're making a mistake with her, Broth—"

"Who thinks what?" he thundered suddenly, and she jumped, startled. Her cheeks flamed in embarrassment.

"I—it thinks you're making a mistake," she said, her eyes downcast.

He got up from his chair and went around his desk. He lifted her chin and kissed her cheek. "That's better," he said softly. "Now, what were you about to say about my mistake?"

"She's too old to be laboring in the vineyards," Sister Desirée said softly. "I—it sees her rubbing her back. She's in pain."

"Sometimes people are reached through adversity when prosperity can't touch their spirits," he said. He took Sister Desirée's hand and helped her stand.

"It hopes you're not talking about breaking her spirit." Sister Desirée looked sad.

He gave his intended a hard look, and she hesitated as if trying to decide whether to speak further on Theodora Whimple's behalf.

"If breaking her spirit is what it takes," he said finally, "then so be it. After all, the end justifies the means, doesn't it, dear?"

She didn't answer, and he tilted her face toward his. "Doesn't it, dear?" he repeated. She gazed into his eyes, and finally nodded wordlessly. He wondered if it was his imagination, or if the adoration he was used to seeing in her gaze had dimmed.

TWELVE

K C. pressed her foot on the Morgan's gas pedal, anxious to be away from Angels Crest. They followed the winding road down the hillside. "I don't care if I ever see another grape," she murmured, ignoring the beautiful spread of vineyards on both sides of the road. The sun was high, now beating down on their shoulders. A nagging headache caused her to squint and rub her temple absently.

"Are you okay?" Gav asked, looking across at her.

"Yeah, just tired, I think," she said, her gaze back on the road. "Maybe we should stop and put the top up."

"Good idea. How about letting me drive? It'll give you a rest," he offered.

K.C. gave him a grateful smile. "Good idea, Sheriff Gavin." She headed for the next turnout and shut down the engine. She'd just opened the door and stepped out when she noticed a group of robed figures working in the vineyards.

"Harvesttime is just beginning," Gav said as he helped her fasten the roadster's canvas top. He opened the door on the passenger side, and she stepped in.

"I wonder why they pick the grapes by hand," K.C. said, after he slid into the driver's seat. "You'd think a machine would be more efficient."

"It's because certain grapes are too delicate, I think," Gav said, but his attention was on the dash of the little roadster. He started to turn the ignition key, but K.C. stopped him.

"Gav—?" She squinted toward the robed laborers sprinkled across a distant vine-covered hillside. He looked up. "That's backbreaking labor. Do you think they're working as volunteers, or are they forced?"

He followed her gaze, squinting against the bright sunlight. "One of the brainwashing tactics of people like Randolph is to physically wear out his victims...deliberately subject people to physical and psychological hardship. It's often the first step in altering thoughts, attitudes, even actions."

K.C. shook her head. "It's hard to believe that thinking people can be pulled into something like this."

"The ironic thing is that Randolph appeals to those who consider themselves intellectuals. They go a step beyond pride of intellect and sophistication...the promise of godhood for themselves. They decide at some point that to become a deity, they'll follow any order, obey any rule, no matter how humiliating." Gav still watched the laborers, stooped over the vines, the harsh noon sun beating down on them. "This brainwashing process is meant to totally cleanse the mind of one set of ideas and replace them with another.

"Followers can be forced to publicly confess past crimes or errors—usually having to do with rules made up by the cult leader. This breaks the spirit, and opens the way to re-education to the new ideas and beliefs."

"How could someone be forced to confess?" K.C. asked. "Please don't say it has to do with physical violence." Aunt Theo's sweet face flashed before her mind's eye, and K.C. felt the sting of a sob in the back of her throat.

"Cult tactics are more sophisticated than that, Kace." He turned to look at her, his eyes gentle as if he knew her thoughts about Aunt Theo. "Lack of sleep and food are usually successful. Isolation from families and familiar surroundings."

"Isolation," K.C. murmured. "Do you think that's what's happening to Aunt Theo?" She looked out at the field again with new curiosity, reviewing the possibilities. "She came here to investigate. For some reason, Rodolphe—or Randolph himself—decided to cleanse her mind, bring her into the Angels of Fellowship. Could that be?"

Gav nodded, his gaze sweeping along the hillside, across the robed laborers. "It's occurred to me, Kace. Especially after watching that video a few minutes ago. Some of the points Randolph made were right out of the textbook on cult leaders, especially the part about godhood and the planet Atara."

She looked up at him, surprised. "How did you learn all this, Gav? Seminary?"

"No. I did a paper on it for one of my psychology classes last year. It's a fascinating study. Something I plan to explore further."

"No matter how sophisticated this guy Randolph is," K.C. said, "one thing I know for certain—Aunt Theo is unbrainwashable!"

For a moment Gav didn't answer, then he said, "It's not just the cult leader the victim must watch out for. The most diabolical leaders have extensive understanding of psychology and neurophysiology, and they use their followers to create a false family for the victim. Peer pressure plays into the psychology. There are usually self-criticism and mutual criticism sessions creating a feeling of guilt that everyone else has accepted these new ideas as absolute truth.

"Group pressure can be a powerful tool, Kace. Even someone as strong as Theo might bend."

"Her belief in God is too strong," K.C. said. "Besides, she's as stubborn as they come."

"She needs our prayers, K.C."

"There hasn't been a moment that Aunt Theo is not in my prayers."

Gav nodded. "Mine, too, Kace. Mine, too." He looked out at the fields again, thoughtfully. "I know how people like

Randolph operate." He turned back to K.C. "We need to get in there—beyond where we were shown today."

"I agree. That's why I'm planning to meet Rodolphe as planned."

"We both need to go in, K.C."

"As seekers?"

He nodded. "Not quite. I'm thinking that we need to slip in and nose around without officially being brought in as seekers."

She considered his words. "This place is highly fortified—armed guards, electric fences. We don't even know where the followers are housed. He showed us nothing of the back acreage."

"I still would rather figure out a way to break into the compound undetected so that we can explore—look for Theo—without someone watching us every minute."

"I don't know how we can get in," she said, "unless I go through with my plans to meet Keb-Kaseko Rodolphe as Satinka. Maybe I can find a way to slip you in that same evening."

"The trunk of the car?"

She grinned. "Lucky for you it won't have to be this tiny trunk. They would remember the Morgan, so we'll have to take Aunt Theo's old Buick."

He started the little car, pulled onto the road, and headed down the hillside. "You'll need a disguise, too, Kace. If you come across Randolph while dining with Rodolphe, he'll remember you."

"I know," she agreed. "I've already thought of that. Let's stop at the thrift shop in Napa on the way back to Theo's."

"Something slinky and feline for the mysterious Satinka?" he teased with a lifted brow.

"Leopard skin!" she said. "Just the thing."

They chuckled and talked companionably as they sped

around the curves leading into Napa Valley. They had almost reached Highway 29, and Gav braked the car for a stop sign. It seemed so natural when he reached over and took her hand.

Reality settled in, and K.C. withdrew her hand. "You don't have to pretend now, Gav," she said, thinking about their cover at the chateau.

"K.C., we need to talk," he sighed. "About us."

"There is no 'us,' Gav." She looked across the car at him. He was concentrating on the road as he turned the Morgan onto the highway leading south. "It's taken me three years to get my life back on track since you left—left with no explanation, I might add." Her tone was bitter.

"Kace, I couldn't talk then. I was drowning and taking you under with me. I simply had to leave."

She fought her tears, the familiar anger seeping into her heart.

"I know now that I shouldn't have left the way I did. But at the time, I thought I didn't have a choice. I just couldn't face you."

Of course he couldn't, she thought, not with the news he'd found someone else.

"I thought we could talk about anything...everything," she said, her voice little more than a whisper. "Remember the way we used to talk on the phone till dawn, even after we'd spent the day together?" Her voice broke, and she couldn't go on.

"Of course I remember, Kace," he said, his voice low. "Besides loving each other, we were best friends." He slowed the car for passing traffic, shifted, then sped up again. "K.C., we talked about everything—except what was haunting me the most. That one thing I couldn't tell you. I wanted to; I just couldn't find the words."

K.C. felt she couldn't breathe. She had considered all the reasons a million times back then. Even so, she had hoped she might someday find out she had been wrong, but his words just now told her she hadn't been. The thought of Gav in someone else's arms invaded her mind once again. He'd been unfaithful. He couldn't enter the ministry because of it. He couldn't marry her for the same reason. That same woman might still be in his life, and her heart nearly broke with the thought.

She looked at him, trying to steady her voice. "If you couldn't tell me then, I don't want to hear it now, Gav. Bringing up the past after all this time is only making it harder for us both."

He let out a deep sigh and reached for her hand. "K.C., won't you let me explain? I'm finally ready to talk about it. I've had so many things to sort out."

"Why, now, Gav?" She fought the urge to lift his hand and kiss his slender fingers that were wrapped around hers.

"I've never forgotten you," he said. "You're part of me—a very important part, even after the years we've been apart. Just being with you the last few days has stirred all those feelings I thought I'd put behind me."

"Nostalgia, Gav," she attempted to keep her voice light, other-wise all this was too painful. "That's all. We were friends before we fell in love, and we can be friends again. We tried the love part, and it didn't work, that's all." She withdrew her hand from his and gave him a playful punch on the arm. "Do you remember teaching me how to throw a spiral football pass?"

He laughed, and their sad mood was indeed broken, just as she had hoped. "How could I forget?" he said. "You brought every little girl in the neighborhood over for lessons. But you told me not to dare show them the exact way to place their fingers on the laces. You wanted some buddies to play football with, but you still wanted the upper hand."

"Still do," she said with a chuckle. "I still do."

"Kace," he said as he guided the car along the winding road.

"Yeah, Gav?"

"I still care, you know." His voice was low, and his eyes stayed on the road. "I always will."

K.C. didn't answer but just kept looking out the car window as they sped along, wondering if the dull ache in her heart would ever lessen. It was too late. Gav knew it, and so did she.

They didn't speak the rest of the way to Napa. When Gav pulled into the parking lot of the thrift shop, though, K.C. grinned at him as he took her hand to help her from the car.

"Wait'll you see what I've got in mind," she teased, to keep their conversation light.

"Not the leopard skin, please!" he groaned.

"Nothing but!" she said, and twenty minutes later they exited, laughing as they carried their bundles to the car: a 1960s long, dark "fall" wig; a 1970s faux leopardskin jacket and matching hat; a 1980s pair of lace-up, square-toed boots; and a 1990s black, billowy, ankle-length skirt.

Their tone turned serious again as Gav turned the car onto the road up the mountain to Sugarloaf Ridge, and they discussed the details of their undercover plan.

"I'll have to take a couple more days off from work," Gav said, "since this isn't an official investigation."

"Can you get backup, though, should we need it?"

He nodded. "Since we can't prove foul play, it might be hard. I've already let my deputy know what we suspect. I can call him on your cell phone, if we need help."

"Unless Randolph's security includes a cell-phone scanner," K.C. said solemnly.

"Or if electronic communication to the outside has been blocked," Gav added.

∼∼∼∼∼

Father Max greeted them at the door with a wave and a grin as they pulled into the driveway and parked behind the Cherokee. "How did it go?" he called as they gathered their packages from the back of the car.

"I think we're on the right trail," Gav said, and the three entered the house. "Angels of Fellowship is firmly in place there." He shook his head. "What an ingenious cover—the award-winning vineyards and beautiful grounds, the delightful tours of buildings with their colorful past and promising future."

"Do you think Theo's somewhere inside?"

"She's got to be, Father Max," K.C. said, and she went on to explain their plan. "Everything points to Angels of Fellowship. We're going to find a way to get both of us inside the estate."

"I'd like to go in with you," Father Max said. "Theodora means the world to me. I can't stand by helplessly."

Gav and K.C. exchanged glances in silent agreement. "It's not a good idea, Max," K.C. said. "We need someone on the outside we can communicate with. I'm going to take my cell phone. We'll pick up a phone to plug in here. We really need you to stay here, stick by the phone."

Father Max looked momentarily disappointed, then nodded. "Actually, I've got a plan rattling around in my head. I may pull it out if worse comes to worst." K.C. and Gav exchanged glances, but Father Max just looked wise. "You'll see." Satinka wound around his legs, and he said, "Oh, I almost forgot to tell you. I've been corresponding with Rodolphe quite regularly today."

K.C. was putting the packages on the sofa. She stopped and looked up.

"He's encouraging Satinka to meet him tomorrow night—at the Angels Crest dining room."

K.C. made her way across the room to the desk where she'd left her notebook computer next to Aunt Theo's. She punched a few keys, and her e-mail server appeared on the screen. She scrolled through the messages from Rodolphe with Father Max and Gav reading over her shoulder.

"There's the last one," Father pointed out, and she clicked on the title—Dinner with a Friend—and the message appeared.

My dear Satinka, it read. I do understand your reticence to venture forth and meet me. But I also understand your loneliness and heartache. Many of us feel alone in today's world, but don't lose hope, my friend.

I want to introduce you to a family of friends who understand exactly what you're going through. We've all been there at one time or another.

I sense you are seeking fulfillment in this life and peace in the next. We can offer you these as well.

Satinka, I feel I've grown close to you through our cyberspace exchanges, and I so look forward to meeting you in person.

Please agree to meet me at Angels Crest Culinary Arts School dining room. I'll understand if you decline. But my dear, my heart will soar if you accept! You do not need to decide this moment. Consider my words, and know that I'll be awaiting you at eight o'clock tomorrow night.

Yours faithfully,

Keb-Kaseko Rodolphe

K.C. rolled her eyes. "'My heart will soar'? Oh, please!"

"Sounds like an old movie script," Gav added.

"A bad movie script," Father Max said, shaking his head.

"Now, Father," K.C. said "You've got to fill me in on all you said to Monsieur Rodolphe on Satinka's behalf." The real Satinka had curled into K.C.'s lap and was purring loudly. "It must have been good to elicit a response like this."

Father Max grinned. "Read the messages yourself. I created Satinka's persona from one of the characters in Theodora's latest novel. You'll find facets of the lovely, lonely, and very Southern Anastasia Goodenough mentioned in each post—her idiosyncrasies, her strange habits, her talents."

"Genius," K.C. said, opening the first message. "I read the book not long ago and know the character well. It's a script I can follow."

"K.C., are you sure you want to go through with this?" Gav was now scrolling through the electronic messages and scanning each one. He looked away from the monitor screen and met her gaze.

"Of course," she said. "There's no other way."

"You may change your mind after you read this post." Gav moved his chair to one side so she could lean closer to the screen. It was not sent to "Satinka" personally but had been posted on the bulletin board—the same board where Satinka had left the first enticing message to Keb-Kaseko Rodolphe. It was from Marigold Green.

To Whom It May Concern:

I have taken it upon myself to police this and other message boards, reporting my research of fraudulent claims and other dangerous nonsense. In today's world, someone must take on this role because it seems no government is willing to take the risk to do it. You know, freedom of speech and all that. Ha!

"That sounds like Marigold," K.C. murmured as she scrolled down to the next paragraph.

"Read on," Gav said earnestly. "It gets better."

Alert! Alert! Alert!

People formerly affiliated with Angels of Fellowship claim that a

mass suicide is imminent among current group members. These vic-
tims—yes, victims!—think they will be traveling through space to
another planet called Atara. Ha! again! Keb-Kaseko Rodolphe, a
world-class impostor, is at the heart of this deceit.

This is a warning! Pass it along to all you know:

Stay away from anyone affiliated with Angels of Fellowship. I
am currently beginning more research on its connection to the disap-
pearances of many people who have gone into this cult, never to
return.

I will be repeating this message on every bulletin board I can find
on the Internet dealing with cults. If you have any additional infor-
mation, please post it here!

Join in the fight against con artists like Monsieur Rodolphe! Help
me spread the truth around the world.

Marigold Green
Pelican Cove, California

K.C. looked up at Gav, then across to Father Max. "Whether this is true or not, Marigold could be charged with libel." Suddenly she feared for the woman in all her brazen courage.

"The greater question is the one of truth, Kace," Gav said quietly.

"Do you suppose there's any truth to her accusations?"

"If there is, you're putting yourself in great danger." Gav was gazing at her with a look of tender concern.

"Can't we let the police handle it, Gav?" Father Max asked. "You certainly have connections. Let them search the grounds for Theo…for the others who are missing."

"I don't think we'd better consider it. The images of Waco and Jonestown are too vivid. Whoever this Angels of Fellowship leader is—Rodolphe or Randolph—if he's considering mass sui- cide, he's thought it out carefully. He knows exactly how he'll do it. Make no mistake, he's poised and ready to carry out the act."

"If the police rush in, you think it will push him over the edge?" K.C. asked, her heart sinking.

Gav nodded, standing. The other two stood across from him. "Not only that—I'm worried that if there's even a hint that he's being investigated—he may act."

"Oh, Lord," K.C. cried softly, covering her mouth. "If Theo's in there…"

Father Max circled her shoulders with his arm. "Greater is he who is in us than he who is in the world. Remember that, child."

K.C. looked up into his lined face, so wise and strong and filled with compassion. She swallowed hard. "I know," she said, frowning. "But I think it's hardest to remember when we slam into something so diabolical."

"Maybe circumstances like these let us catch a glimpse of God's greatness, K.C.," Father Max said. "Without them, we might not ever know his power."

She nodded, thinking of Aunt Theo. "Why don't you pray for her, Father? For us all?"

He grasped Gav's and K.C.'s hands in his, pulled them closer, and bowed his head. "Lord," he prayed, "your child Theodora needs you this very moment. We all do. We need to see evidence of your power in this situation.

"Though Theo's whereabouts are unknown to us, you are holding her near your heart—just as you do each of us. You are in control of her life—of ours.

"Nothing takes you by surprise. You have led her to this place, and we know you never make mistakes. Show Theodora what you would have her to do. Strengthen her, Father, for the task. Protect her with your love."

K.C. breathed in the sweetness of this communion with God. Father Max spoke as if God was his most intimate friend. There was no need for pretense with his Lord and Savior, for his Creator knew him better than Father Max knew himself.

"And for each of us…" Father Max continued. "Lord, give us strength for what lies ahead. Prepare us with the armor of faith to fight this battle against the forces of darkness. We stand ready, Father, for love is our banner, and we lift it high. Your love is our standard!

"In the glorious name of Jesus Christ we bring our petition to you, our Lord and Savior. Amen."

K.C. had begun to weep quietly as they prayed. After he said amen, she looked up and gave Father Max a watery smile.

"Thank you," she said softly. Suddenly, the emotion of the day, the worry over Theo, the nearness of Gav all seemed to wash over her. K.C. leaned back against the desk to catch her balance.

"Kace, are you all right?" Gav asked, frowning.

Through her blur of tears, she nodded. "I'm fine," she whispered.

But Gav paid no attention. He gathered her into his arms, and K.C. wept against his shoulder.

THIRTEEN

As soon as Gav and Father Max had left in the Cherokee for Gav's place in town, K.C. went to the computer and sent a message to Keb-Kaseko Rodolphe, confirming that she would meet him for dinner the following evening.

Her next electronic communication was to Georgie O'Reilly in Pelican Cove to remind her about the ad space they still needed for this week's *Pelican Journal*. She also attached the article she had been working on for her column and a couple of shorter pieces for fillers.

When she finished, she picked up her cell phone and dialed Marigold Green's number. There was no answer, and she was surprised when Marigold's answering machine didn't click on. She'd only heard it a few times, but it was unforgettable. While sounds of drums and tropical birds played in the background, the music to "George of the Jungle" swelled, then Marigold's voice came on, almost shouting, "It's a jungle out there! I'm doing my part to make this a better world. What are you doing? If your answer's 'nothing,' don't bother leaving a message."

K.C. waited a half hour, then tried the number again. Still no message machine. She tried once more, trying to push from her mind the nagging sense that something might be wrong.

She fed Satinka, pulled on her pajamas, and slipped under the covers of Aunt Theo's small bed. Earlier she'd found a copy of Aunt Theo's latest release, *Southern Comfort,* and placed it on the lamp table. Now she picked it up and reread some of the passages describing Anatasia Goodenough. Finally fatigue settled in, and she turned out the light.

Outside, crickets sawed noisily, and from a brook at the rear of the cabin, frogs lifted their voices in a din. A mockingbird sang from a nearby elm, its haunting song disturbing in the dark night.

K.C. was just falling asleep when Satinka leaped on the bed, startling her. Now she was wide awake again, worrying about Marigold Green. She flipped on the light and padded into the living room for her phone. She checked the number, punched it in, and hit the send button. Again the phone rang several times. Still no answer. No voice message.

She sighed and dialed the phone again, this time calling Georgie O'Reilly. A sleepy voice said, "Hello—?"

"Georgie? It's me. K.C."

"K.C., what's up? I got your e-mail earlier. I was planning to write you back tomorrow."

"Don't worry about it. That's not why I called."

"What's wrong, K.C.? Is it Aunt Theo?"

"Aunt Theo's trail has definitely led us to Angels Crest—make that Angels of Fellowship. They're one and the same." Georgie was wide awake now, and K.C. explained about their visit to the vineyard that morning.

"But there's something else that's worrying me, Georgie. I need you to check it out for me."

"Sure, babes. Shoot."

K.C. told her about the message Marigold Green posted on the Internet bulletin board. "If Rodolphe sees that, Georgie…and if he's as dangerous as she says…she may be in real trouble."

"You've said that Marigold Green makes things up just to get authorities to investigate," Georgie pointed out.

"I know that, and you know that—but Keb-Kaseko Rodolphe doesn't. Besides, maybe she didn't make this up."

"You tried calling her?"

"I've tried several times. No answer. No 'George of the Jungle' message."

"You want me to drive over right now?"

"I know it's late, but I think it might be a good idea. Do you mind?"

"Nope," Georgie said good-naturedly. "But I'll make sure you repay the favor someday. Just watch out!"

"Hey, Georgie—?"

"Yeah?" she said through a yawn.

"Thanks."

"No prob, boss."

"Take someone with you, okay?"

"Yes, ma'am. As long as I'm up, I may as well wake the neighborhood." Then her voice turned serious. "Actually, I'll call Casper. Get him to come along."

"Good idea." Casper was a big, burly journalism student at the local community college. He filled in when needed, sometimes ghostwriting. He was the one who came up with his nickname, and it had stuck, even though he'd advanced far beyond ghosting.

"I'll call you as soon as we check out her house." There was a pause, then Georgie added, "If she turns me in to the city for disturbing the peace, or rather, *her* peace, because she's got an out-of-order phone, K.C., you've got to go to court with me."

K.C. laughed. "I'll be there with bells on. I just hope she's okay."

"Me, too."

They said good-bye, and K.C. pressed the button to break the connection. She went back to the bed, placed the phone on the lamp table, and gently pulled the sleeping Satinka close.

Now the only sounds outside were those of an owl in the distance and the low murmur of the wind in the pines. K.C. shivered and tried not to think of what lay ahead, her dinner with Keb-Kaseko Rodolphe the next day, or smuggling Gav into the compound in Theo's trunk.

She finally drifted into a light sleep. When the phone rang she flipped on the light and squinted at her watch. It was after midnight.

"Georgie—?" she said sleepily.

"Yeah, K.C. It's me. Casper's here with me."

"Where are you?"

"At Marigold Green's."

K.C. was instantly awake. "What's happened? Is she okay?"

"There's no one here. It's eerie. The front door wasn't locked, so after we'd raised quite a ruckus knocking and ringing the doorbell, we pushed it open and went in."

"And?"

"The place is a mess."

"I think it usually is."

"No, K.C., this is different. Someone was looking for something. Stuff everywhere. Furniture tipped over. But no Marigold."

K.C. sighed. "Did you call the police?"

"Yes, they should be here any minute."

"Georgie, go home and get some rest. Call me in the morning if the police find out anything."

Georgie yawned. "Okay, babes. I'm on my way. Of course, I've got to drop off Casper."

"Thanks, again, Georgie. Thank Casper for me, too."

"Hey, wait. K.C.—?"

"Yeah?"

"Take care of yourself. This whole thing is giving me the creeps. People disappearing and all."

"I know."

"I'll be praying for you."

"Thanks, Georgie. Gav and Father Max, too."

After she and Georgie said good night, K.C. dialed Gav's apartment. After a few rings, he picked up the phone.

"Gav, something's come up."

"What is it, Kace?"

She told him about Marigold Green. His silence spoke volumes: he was more concerned than she. Finally, he sighed into the phone. "K.C., everything points back to Angels of Fellowship."

"I know, Gav. I didn't say so at the time, but when I saw that Marigold Green had not only left her name on the message, but also mentioned Pelican Cove, it was almost as if she was taunting Rodolphe to come after her."

"I thought of the same thing. Marigold Green is not exactly a common name," he said.

"And Pelican Cove, with its population of ten thousand, is an easy place to find someone. She had to know that."

"What we're getting into tomorrow's going to be dangerous, Kace."

"I know."

"If Rodolphe came after Marigold so quickly, the group—its leaders—may be more paranoid than I thought."

"There may be more people besides Aunt Theo who need our help. I wonder how many are being pulled into this organization against their will?"

"And the clock's ticking...."

"As Father Max prayed, God's in control," she said quietly.

"Kace—?" His voice was husky with sleep, and K.C. sighed, wishing she didn't love the sound of it so.

"Yeah, Gav?"

"What I said today...about loving you?"

She didn't answer, but felt her heart thudding beneath her ribs.

"Well," he continued. "I overstepped the line we'd put

between us. I'm sorry. It won't happen again. You're right about our being friends. We should have kept that boundary in place all along."

For a minute, K.C. didn't answer. Finally she swallowed hard. "That's what I was trying to tell you earlier, Gav. I've missed your friendship during the last three years. Let's not make the same mistake again. Let's keep it on that level."

He sighed, and she could hear him stretch. "Friends it is." Then he paused, and there was a smile in his voice when he spoke again. "But, Kace, keep in mind that friends do love each other."

She smiled. "I know," she said simply.

They said a few more words, then once again K.C. hung up the phone and turned out the light.

Sometime during the night, she dreamed that she heard Aunt Theo cry out for help. A chorus of crying voices, maybe those of Ariel Tilman and Marigold Green, joined her aunt's weeping.

K.C. stood by a mist-enshrouded lake. There was a light on the other side, and K.C. tried to move toward it, but her legs and feet wouldn't move. No matter how she struggled, she couldn't cross to help those who cried out.

Then she heard Father Max's voice. "Be not afraid, little one." Or was it Someone else's? "I am with you, K.C.!" said the loving voice. "When you pass through the waters, I will be with you. I will never leave you." The voice seemed filled with thunder and rushing waters yet seemed as soft as the fragrance after a summer rain. And she knew it wasn't Father Max's voice.

Suddenly Gav was beside her, watching her with caring eyes. He held out his hands to help her cross the lake, but she looked at him with bitterness, then turned away. The mist over the waters turned to snow, and her heart, which she held in her hands, turned to ice. It shattered, and she knelt to gather the pieces, frantically trying to put them back together. But there were too many, and they wouldn't fit.

On the other side of the now frozen lake, the weeping grew louder, and K.C.'s voice joined the chorus. When she woke, her cheeks were wet with tears, and for a long time she couldn't push the strange images from her mind. After that, she slept fitfully until dawn.

Father Max and Gav arrived at Theodora's cabin at noon, just as K.C. finished another article for the *Pelican Journal*.

"We're bringing Theo's cabin into the twentieth century!" Father Max said, holding up an old dial phone and a two-pronged telephone jack. "Now she'll have a phone and still be able to plug into the Internet."

"I doubt that she'll keep the phone after she comes back," K.C. pointed out with an answering grin. She refused to think that Aunt Theo might not come back. "That's why she comes here to write. No phones. No television. No distractions."

She looked up to meet Gav's eyes, and for a moment considered her strange dream from the night before. She thought about the bitterness that had shattered her heart, something she knew still lay deep inside. Oh yes, she could admire Gav in his worn blue jeans and V-neck cotton pullover; and she could wonder whether he looked more handsome in his sheriff's uniform or in the down-home, masculine style he was sporting today. She could resist the urge to reach up and brush back the few strands of dark hair that had fallen across his forehead.

But could she face the truth about her source of pain and sorrow? She didn't think so, at least not yet. It was better to keep him at a distance.

"We need to go over our plans," Gav said, pulling out some

notes he and Father Max had already made. She settled onto the sofa next to him, and they discussed the evening's activities, from her dinner conversation with Rodolphe to where to hide the car when Gav drove it back through the gates alone, disguised as K.C.

By four o'clock, they'd settled on a strategy that included Father Max's help in getting Gav back into the estate once the security system was deactivated.

"I brought something along, Kace," Gav said, "that I'd like for you to wear." He opened a small plastic case and pulled out a wireless microphone. "I'll wear an ear device, so your voice won't be overheard on my end. I suspect that compound has more electronic bugs than a stagnant pond has mosquitoes on a hot night."

She held the microphone in her palm, frowning. It was no larger than a matchstick. "If anything does go wrong at dinner," she said, "I don't know what you could do—with both of us on the compound, we're at their mercy."

"We have that covered as well. Gav will have the car phone and can call me," Father Max said. "I'll get word to the authorities."

"I'd feel better, K.C., if you'd agree to it," Gav said earnestly.

She nodded slowly. "All right—but you mentioned something about an electronic scanner picking up cellular phone transmissions. Wouldn't the same device also pick up a mike?"

Gav and Father Max exchanged glances. "This puts out a much weaker signal, Kace. It's unlikely it will be picked up, but even so…" He didn't finish.

"It's worth the risk?" She gave them both a brave smile.

Gav nodded solemnly. "And if you are in trouble, I can reach you in seconds."

"Ah, my knight in shining armor!" she said with a grin. "But then who will rescue the two of us?"

They looked at Father Max, who raised both hands in the air. "Fear not, my children. I'll be there," he said. "Right after I call out the cavalry!"

All three laughed, but judging from Gav's and Father Max's grave expressions, K.C. knew humor was only a mask for their misgivings about tonight.

By seven o'clock K.C. had dressed and stepped out into the living room. Gav and Father Max looked up in surprise. Satinka was stretched out on the couch between them.

"My, my!" Father Max said, his eyes wide. Even the cat sat up and eyed K.C. curiously, her ears cocked forward.

Gav raised a brow and let out a low whistle. "Wow, K.C., you've done it. It's perfect!"

K.C. grinned. "The new me, or maybe I should say, the new Satinka!" The outfit was indeed a wonderful disguise, from its loose-fitting fingertip-length jacket to the long black skirt and boots that made her petite feet look even smaller. The final touch had been slipping in her emerald contact lenses, those she saved for special occasions. Quite a contrast, she thought, to her new hair, the color of a raven's wing.

"You look great," Gav said, fingering the wig's long black strands. His expression was tender. "But I miss that redhead underneath it all."

"We'd better go, Gav," she said quickly. "Are you ready?"

He handed her the microphone, and she clipped it on the silk blouse beneath the jacket. He put the receiver in his ear, and they tested the transmission from various distances. "Great," he said. "It's working well."

"God be with you, dear friends," Father Max said when

they were finally ready. "I'll be praying for you."

"We're counting on it," Gav said, shaking the priest's hand.

K.C. gave Father Max a quick embrace, and a few minutes later, she was backing Aunt Theo's old Buick from the driveway, Gav beside her on the worn bench seat.

The big car ran smoothly, and K.C. maneuvered it down the hillside with ease. They passed Sugarloaf Ridge and headed toward Oakville and Highway 29. Dusk was settling across the Napa Valley, and by the time K.C. swung the car north toward Calistoga, the sky had turned an ashen gray.

They said very little, both lost in their own thoughts. K.C. had just turned off the highway onto the narrow road leading to Angels Crest when Gav said, "Better pull over here, Kace."

She nodded and swung the car off the road and into a thicket of elms and oaks. They both got out and went around to the back. K.C. unlocked the trunk and lifted the lid.

They were standing very close, and Gav touched her cheek lightly with the backs of his fingers. "I guess I should say, 'break a leg,' K.C."

She gave him a brave smile. "I'm more concerned about Aunt Theo and the others than I am about us. After all, what can Rodolphe do or say in full view of the other diners? I'll be safe. Just pray that I'll get the information we need to find Aunt Theo."

"You'll be in my thoughts every minute." His voice was husky.

"And you'll be in mine, Gav."

He stepped into the trunk and pulled an old pea green army blanket over him. Looking up at her, he grinned. "Hey, Kace—?"

She was ready to close the trunk and stopped. "Yeah?"

"Don't forget to unlock the trunk when we get there."

She grinned back. "Don't worry, Gav. Not too long ago I'd

gladly have kept it locked. But you're lucky, you've gotten back on my good side."

He chuckled. She tossed in her hat to give her an excuse to open it later, then pushed down the lid until it clicked snugly into place.

A few minutes later, K.C. pulled up to the guardhouse. The same guard who'd let them in on their earlier visit came to the car and stooped to look through the open window.

"Hello," she said, with a sweet Southern drawl. "I'm here to see a Monsieur Keb-Kaseko Rodolphe."

"And you are—?" He checked his clipboard.

"Satinka," she said with a smile. "Just Satinka."

"You don't have a last name?"

"I don't use one, honey," she said, smiling. "I find people usually remember me without it."

He gave her a friendly look, raising a brow. "Well, I'd certainly agree with you there, Miss."

"Make that Ms., sugar," K.C. said sweetly. "Ms. Satinka."

"Ah yes, here it is." He was looking at his roster again. "Mr., ah, Keb-Kaseko Rodolphe said you would be meeting him at eight o'clock."

K.C. nodded, looking at her watch. "And it's getting close to that now. Can you tell me the way? I'll also need to know where to park."

He pointed toward the upper parking lot where she and Gav had parked the day before. "Mr. Rodolphe said he would meet you on the front portico of the chateau, however, rather than the dining room."

K.C. felt a twinge of alarm. Rodolphe had changed the plan. Flipping back a strand of the long black hair, she smiled at the guard. "Well, I appreciate all your help. Thank you, honey. Now, you have a good evening."

He opened the gates and signaled her through.

She gave him a shy little wave and turned the car toward the upper parking lot. They were inside the compound! For better or worse, the first step of their plan was unfolding.

"Gav," she whispered into the matchstick microphone, knowing he was listening. "Here we go!" Suddenly, she wished she could hear the comfort of his voice in reply.

Moments later, she chose the most secluded parking place she could find, in the corner, under an elm. The large lot was surprisingly empty.

Though it was nearly dark, a full moon was just rising behind the silhouette of oaks. Its light already illumined the parking lot. As K.C. headed around the car to the trunk, she whispered a quick prayer, hoping no one was watching.

She lifted the lid to retrieve the leopardskin hat. The only evidence of Gav was a lump under the army blanket.

"Sugar?" he whispered with an exaggerated accent from underneath it. "Honey?"

"Watch out, or I'll lock this thing yet," she threatened, barely moving her lips for fear someone might be watching from one of the buildings.

She reached for the hat. "Did you get where I'm meeting him?"

"Yeah, I did." Gav's voice was serious. "If he takes you someplace besides the dining room, give me some clues so I can follow."

"I will, Gav," she whispered back. She hesitated, then added, "Blessings, dear friend."

"Kace," came the muffled reply from under the blanket, "I've decided I don't want to be friends."

"Shhhh," she said, pulling the hat down over the wig. She closed the trunk. This time she didn't let it click shut.

The moon had now cleared the hills and its eerie silver light blanketed the grounds and buildings. An ancient oak with a twisted trunk leaned into the towering chateau and, in the evening breeze, cast dancing shadows across its walls.

K.C. shivered as she stepped onto the path that wound through the formal English gardens leading to the front portico. The scents of honeysuckle and roses mixed together, filling her nostrils as she walked, but their overpowering sweetness reminded her more of a funeral parlor than a pleasant garden.

She turned the corner, and the portico was now dead ahead. Sensing she was being watched, K.C. looked up to see the dark silhouette of a man leaning against one of the twin pillars. Though he faced her, it was too dark to see his features.

She gazed up at him, aware that his tall, thin frame was somehow familiar. After a moment's hesitation, she climbed the stairs, and he turned toward her, his narrow face now illumined by the light behind a nearby stained-glass window.

K.C. caught her breath and halted, suddenly realizing where she'd seen him.

"Monsieur, ah, Rodolphe?" she stammered, almost forgetting her Southern accent.

"I'm sorry," Rance Randolph said. "But our esteemed vintner was unable to meet you tonight. He's asked me to take his place."

He stepped closer and peered into her face, studying her carefully. "And you must be the lovely Satinka I've heard so much about."

She blinked and swallowed hard, unable to speak.

"Welcome," he said smoothly. "Welcome to Angels Crest Vineyard."

FOURTEEN

Gav listened carefully for voices...for any signs of activity. When he was reasonably certain there was no one near the car, he raised the trunk lid a couple of inches and scanned the area. After a moment, he slipped out and sprinted toward the cover of some giant eucalyptus trees to the north of the parking lot. Again he examined the buildings and grounds, watching for security personnel. All was quiet, and taking a deep breath, he left his hiding place and sprinted toward the chateau.

He had almost reached the rear of the building when he heard K.C.'s voice followed by a burst of static. Halting, he made an adjustment to the receiver, then held his breath as he heard her stammering words. For a moment, he tried to understand what caused her nervousness. Then the realization sunk in. Not only did Rodolphe not meet her as planned, it sounded as though it was Randolph who'd taken the vintner's place. Randolph had spent enough time with K.C. to know the shape of her face, the sound of her voice.

Gav only hoped the entire persona K.C. had adopted would be enough to keep Randolph in the dark.

Gav reached the rear of chateau and flattened himself against the wall, inching closer to the portico. K.C.'s transmission was clear again, and he was glad to hear that her confidence had returned. Her voice was silky smooth and Southern to its core. If he wasn't so concerned about her safety, he'd be grinning ear to ear and cheering her on.

She was chatting away, her voice calm, about how disappointed she was not to be meeting Keb-Kaseko Rodolphe.

"I'd love to see the grounds in daylight," K.C. said, "though I must say, moonlight shows them off nicely."

Randolph's voice was harder to make out, but when he stepped close enough, Gav could get the gist of his end of the conversation. He was now saying something about K.C. returning during daytime hours, or perhaps spending the night in the chateau's guest quarters.

There was some garbling of the transmission, then K.C.'s voice came through again. "Why, dear sir," she said, smooth as glass, "I would be honored to take you up on your hospitality. But as dear Keb-Kaseko may have told you, I'm afflicted with a terrible malady that keeps me confined to home." Her voice dropped as if taking him into her confidence. "You see, it was only the promise of learning more about the Angels of Fellowship that enticed me out tonight."

"What a sweet darling you are!" Randolph had obviously moved closer to K.C. because his voice was now clearer. "Keb-Kaseko was right—just as he usually is about these matters. If it is solace, companionship, and a deeper meaning in life you're seeking, you've come to the right place. We are the ones who are honored and privileged to have you among us—even for a short visit."

K.C. gave him a demure little laugh. "Please, then, my dear Mr. Randolph, tell me more."

"Call me Rance," he said. Gav could practically hear him breathing into the microphone, he was so close to K.C. He clenched his fists, wanting to rush onto the portico and shove the man headlong into his manicured English garden.

"Well, of course, it would be an honor, Rance," K.C. said.

"We have a table waiting in the dining room. Shall we go?" Randolph said.

"That sounds wonderful," K.C. said. "Will others be joining us?"

"No. This is not a night we normally serve, so we'll have the entire place to ourselves," he answered.

"All alone. Now won't that be something!" K.C. repeated, a signal for him, Gav realized. "I call that personal service," she laughed.

Gav slipped back into the shadows just as Randolph took K.C.'s elbow to help her down the portico's steps and onto the walkway. They chatted as they walked to the culinary-arts building.

Gav followed at a distance, watching until they'd disappeared inside. He slipped closer and made his way to a side window, glad for the cover provided by some healthy Australian ferns. The dining room was aglow with lights from candles and chandeliers. It was indeed empty except for Rance Randolph and K.C., who entered from a side door. Randolph pulled out K.C.'s chair, and she gracefully settled into it, smiling up at him.

Across from the table, which was located in a small, partially curtained alcove, a quartet of musicians filed in and took their places on a carpeted platform. They seated themselves behind waiting music stands, holding violins, a viola, and a cello. Moments later the music of the ensemble drifted toward Gav.

A male server dressed in formal attire approached K.C.'s table with a wine list.

"I would recommend our 1984 cabernet sauvignon private reserve," Randolph said. He didn't wait for K.C. to reply but nodded to the server who exited the room, only to return a few minutes later with the bottle.

A white towel draped over his arm, the server then proceeded to uncork the wine and pour a small amount into K.C.'s glass.

She smiled at Randolph, then held the glass to the light—as if she did this every night of the year—to inspect its color. Gav couldn't help smiling. They'd learned the proper way to examine wine on their tour the day before. K.C. swirled the deep red liquid to the upper edges of her glass, and again held it to the light.

She nodded to Randolph with a smile. "Nice legs," she said like a pro, meaning the number of drips trailing down the inside of the glass. Gav watched as she lifted the glass to her lips and drew in a deep breath, again swirling the liquid slightly. "Fragrant," she said, taking a sip, "and very lovely."

The server was still standing by the table, awaiting her response. Finally, K.C. murmured, "This is wonderful," and the young man filled her glass, then did the same with Randolph's.

"A toast," he said, lifting his glass toward her. K.C. followed suit. "To knowledge, to inner peace, to fulfillment."

K.C. tucked a strand of her long black hair behind one ear and, smiling sweetly, clinked her glass against Randolph's.

Gav figured the meal would take some time, and as he and K.C. planned, he had work to do while she was dining. Reluctantly, he turned away from the scene and headed stealthily toward the front gate.

The stout security guard, again dressed in his hooded robe, was inside the guardhouse reading, it appeared, by the light of one small overhead lamp. While Gav inspected the electronic fence, searching for the place to later short out the system, he kept his eye on the motion detector lights, careful to dodge their reach. The guard looked out into the night as if sensing something was wrong, stood and walked to the doorway, scratched his head beneath the hood, then went back inside.

There was a burst of static from K.C.'s microphone, followed by the reassurance of her soft, calm voice. Another burst of static followed, and Gav turned down the volume on the slim chance that the security guard might overhear.

Gav slipped further into the shadows, waiting. After the

guard opened his book, Gav crept along the inside of the fence, assessing the exact distance from the guardhouse and estimating the time it would take to reenter the estate once the electronic gates were deactivated. He and Father Max had figured his best chance was also to take out the electricity, putting the compound, especially the guardhouse, completely in the dark for just those few seconds. And it would be only a few—seven to be precise—before the auxiliary power kicked in.

He also needed to make the incident appear to be caused by natural happenstance so the area would not be searched. It had been Father Max's idea for a child's Mylar birthday balloon, half-inflated, to "settle" into the wires as if it had been carried from a distance. Mylar balloons were the bane of all power companies; they'd recently been reported to have caused more power outages than any other source.

Satisfied with what he'd found, Gav smiled to himself and crept away from the fence, at the same time turning to slip back to the culinary-arts dining room.

The full moon was now high and the grounds were awash in its light. A breeze kicked up, whistling through the live oaks, elms, and eucalyptus trees on the hillside, ruffling the leaves of some nearby sycamores.

Except for the wind in the trees, the compound was eerily quiet, and Gav wondered where the devotees were housed and why he couldn't at least hear their voices or see some of them walking around the compound. It seemed odd to him that the place would be deserted. Why was there no evidence of life here, other than Rance Randolph and his security guard?

He suddenly realized he hadn't turned up the volume on his receiver. He adjusted the minute dial, only to hear nothing but the same static he'd heard before. No voices. No clatter of silverware on china. No background violins.

His next thought caused the hair on the back of his neck to

stiffen. What if Randolph had indeed gone over the edge? What if he'd already caused his group to commit mass suicide? Gav's heart began to pound as he thought of Marigold Green's message on the Internet. What if her words had triggered the event?

What if Randolph suspected K.C. was wearing a disguise and… His imagination took wing, and in his hurry to get to K.C., he began to move less cautiously. Through thick late summer foliage of lilacs and oleanders, small palms and tall ferns, he sprinted toward the dining room on the other side of the estate.

He stepped across a stone-covered footpath, then froze as he triggered a sensor floodlight. Not daring to breathe, he slipped behind a live oak trunk. The grounds around him—a small koi pond covered with water lilies, and some nearby eucalyptus trees—were flooded with an intense light. He half-expected sirens to wail and pit bulls to be set loose, but nothing happened.

Just then, two robed figures approached, speaking in subdued tones, obviously thinking they'd triggered the floodlight. When they'd passed, Gav let out a deep sigh and stepped from behind his hiding place.

Proceeding more carefully now, he crept along the shadows, keeping nearer the buildings than the walkways. Finally, up ahead, he spotted the culinary center. He moved closer to the dining-room window where he'd stood before, slipping behind the Australian fern. But when he stood and peered inside, K.C. and Randolph's table was empty. There was no server, no string ensemble.

It was as if they had never been there.

~ ~ ~ ~ ~

Rance Randolph escorted K.C. back to the chateau, up the stairs to his private office. She hoped that Gav was listening…and following. She'd ended the dinner early, feeling increasingly uncomfortable in Randolph's presence. But rather than allowing her to leave, he'd insisted that she come up to his office so he could give her more materials on Angels of Fellowship.

He'd spent the entire dinner speaking about his conversations with angels that he said resided on a planet called Atara. When he'd spoken the planet's name, chills had crept up K.C.'s spine. Marigold hadn't been exaggerating when she posted the warning about this group and their beliefs. Odd though, that her warning had been about Rodolphe, not Randolph.

She didn't know about Rodolphe, but Randolph was certifiably nuts, of this she was certain. She settled back, assessing him, as they talked in a cozy sitting area in his large, well-appointed office.

"My dear Satinka," he was saying, "I feel I've known you much longer than just one evening. I suppose when two like-minded people communicate as much as we have, it does eliminate those awkward first moments of their meeting." He gave her a beatific smile as if he could see into her soul.

K.C. shivered, hoping her nervousness didn't show. "Electronic communication is indeed a wonderful invention," she said sweetly. "Especially for a near-recluse like me." She paused a moment. "Now, sugar, you said you had more reading materials for me to see. And I've got some questions I'm just dyin' to ask you before I leave."

"Of course, Satinka—but first—how about a glass of sherry? I have some superb after-dinner drinks."

"No, thank you," she said firmly. Her one glass of cabernet

sauvignon at dinner, plus the tastes she'd sampled yesterday, added up to more alcohol than she normally consumed in a year's time. "Really, I would not care for anything more," she emphasized with a curt nod.

He gave her another wide smile. "Might I offer you some tea or coffee? I have a wonderful selection of gourmet-quality brews." He raised an eyebrow. "Also a crème brûlée that will knock your little old Southern socks off." He chuckled. "How about it?"

"I'll have a cup of tea—of your choice. But please, the dinner was perfect, Rance. I couldn't hold one thing more."

He beamed as if he'd just won some contest and stood to get the tea. When he'd returned and set the silver service on the table, it occurred to K.C. that it seemed too well planned, as if he knew she would want the tea.

"May I serve?" He started pouring the fragrant liquid into a cup. "And dear Satinka, do you take sugar or cream?"

"No, thank you," she said, sensing that something wasn't quite right. He was too eager. But she took the cup and saucer and placed it on the table beside her.

"Now, to my questions," she said. "Suppose for a moment that I might want to become one of your devotees. What would be my first step?" She settled back into her chair as he told her about leaving her family and friends and moving to the estate.

After a pause, she went on. "And say I decided to come here to live—after cutting off all ties with family and friends, as you suggested—where exactly would I live?" She twirled a lock of hair around her finger and smiled. She leaned closer. "And sugar, please don't tell me I'd have to give up my things—" She drew out the word. "—such as my unique way of dressin'? My little ol' hat?"

She shook her head sadly. "I noticed as I drove onto the

estate that your cute little guard was wearing a hooded robe. Please don't tell me that's what I can expect in my future here."

He laughed as if delighted with her Southern sweetness. "It's no different, really, than prep school children wearing a uniform. You'll become quite used to it."

"And about the place where I would live?" she persisted.

"Here with us on the compound."

"Exactly where on the compound, sugar?" She smiled.

"We have lovely facilities. In fact, for someone of your stature, I would have you stay here in the chateau as my guest. We have lovely suites upstairs."

K.C. leaned forward. "Do many of your devotees stay here—I mean in the chateau—long-term?" She wondered if Aunt Theo might be upstairs this very minute.

He laughed. "They usually soon find they'd rather be with the others in our family. Most move into the dormitories quite soon after their arrival."

"On the same grounds? I saw no one as I drove onto the estate this evening."

"My, my, aren't we curious?" he said good-naturedly. "All in good time, my dear."

"I am curious, Rance," she said, her voice now earnest. "Not just about where I'll be living, but also about your, er, religion. Your Fellowship…"

"Actually," he said, "we are not just another religion—"

"I didn't think the Fellowship was a religion at all," she challenged, unable to keep that opinion to herself.

He laughed pleasantly. "On the contrary. We are much more than a religion. We are a way of life—the only way of life—here on earth and through eternity. It is only through the plan of salvation set forth by Ataran angels that we can be rescued from the coming end of time as we know it."

"So you believe that the world will soon end?"

"I know it for certain. You see, the recent uncovering of messages in the Bible verifies what's been prophesied for centuries."

"Bible cryptology."

"You're familiar with the science, then."

"I'm not sure I would call it a science," she challenged again, then reminded herself why she was here: not to challenge, but to play a role. She smiled sweetly. "At least, that's what I've read."

But he barely noticed, so caught up was he in explaining the recent decoding methods of the Old Testament, and those of his own. He droned on about his discovery that these messages were left by the Ataran angels. "You see," he was saying, "though it's a myth, even the biblical version of the event—set forth in the Revelation—tells of the coming holocaust."

"It tells of Jesus Christ coming for his own," she murmured, almost unaware she'd said the words aloud.

"Ah, you've touched on a serious matter," he said. "The matter of how the great prophet fits into the tenets of our beliefs."

"The great prophet?"

"Yes, Jesus of Nazareth, as we prefer to call him. There have been few to compare with him through the annals of time. He is second only to Muhammad."

"Then how does Jesus Christ fit into your, ah, Fellowship?" she asked, hoping the reverence with which she said her Lord's name didn't give her away. She was unable to speak his name any other way. Even her Southern accent had faded. "Do you follow his precepts?" She wanted to ask how Jesus of Nazareth could be such a great prophet: either he was a madman or a liar for claiming to be God incarnate. Or he was telling the truth and was no prophet at all. He was the Son of God. There was nothing in between.

"He is one to be honored for his precepts," Randolph was saying. "Truly! I'm sure he's on his way to earning godhood in another life, perhaps on his own planet. He is our brother angel," he finished with a satisfied sigh.

K.C. held her lips together and breathed slowly to keep from blurting out the truth of her Lord's deity, his place in the Trinity. God became man, she wanted to shout, to die an excruciating death on the cross to save sinners like you! No matter what you've done...no matter how you've blasphemed against him...the God of the universe came to earth to save each of his lambs that you are leading astray! To save you!

Choking back the words, she felt her cheeks flush. It wasn't yet time to reveal whose child she was. She didn't trust herself to speak, so she remained silent.

He rubbed his beard thoughtfully and settled back into his chair, his unblinking gaze never leaving her face. He allowed an uncomfortable and controlling silence to fall between them.

But K.C. didn't speak. Instead, she studied him, the feral glint in his dark eyes, the shadows cast by the nearby table lamp playing across his narrow, wolfish face. He stroked his goatee in mock thoughtfulness as if guessing the substance of her contemplation.

Then her thoughts turned to his flock, the emotionally needy people who were searching for life's meaning, searching for truth in a mixed-up world. This man, a wolf in the same woolly coat as his sheep, stood with them. He promised answers to their questions. He promised them salvation.

Yet what he was doing was far more insidious than one who merely masqueraded as a sheep. He stood at the gate of the fold as their shepherd. Their counterfeit shepherd.

My child, breathed the voice in her heart, *who is the liar?*
It is the man who denies that Jesus is the Christ.
Such a man is the antichrist—he denies the Father and the Son.

And there are many who will lead my sheep astray.
As for you, my child, I have anointed you.
You are mine!
Do not be afraid, my beloved.
Remain in me.

K.C. could no longer stay in the same room with the evil that Rance Randolph represented. She stood abruptly. "I must go," she announced as her handbag fell from her lap to the floor, scattering its contents. She hurried to scoop up the cell phone, nail file, lipsticks, notepad, pens, pencils, and tissues.

"But, dear, you haven't finished your tea." He gave her a pinched smile. "Actually, I don't think you took a sip."

"I must go," she repeated, fighting to remain calm. "I've explained about my need to leave my home only a short while at a time. I'm afraid I've overstayed my comfort level," she said evenly. "I must leave at once!"

"Well, certainly. I'll walk you to your car."

"No," she said, searching the jumbled contents of her handbag for her car keys. "I'll find my way. Thank you, anyway."

"No, no, I insist," he said, taking her arm.

K.C. prayed that Gav had overheard the conversation and would remain in hiding a bit longer.

FIFTEEN

A low coastal fog had moved inland, covering the moon. The air was now damp and cold, and a mist laced through the trees on the estate grounds.

As K.C. and Randolph walked along the pathway to the parking lot, she strained to see through the darkness, searching for Gav but continuing to pray that he would remain out of sight.

"Your chariot awaits," Randolph said when they reached Theo's Buick. He waited while she unlocked the door and stepped in, then closed the door.

K.C. rolled down the window, and Randolph leaned in, one arm resting on the ledge.

"This has been a night to remember," she said honestly. Her Southern sweetness was in place, but she couldn't bring herself to call him "sugar" again. "I appreciate you telling me all about your Fellowship."

"I hope you'll read our literature and return to join us," he said.

"I'll be back. You can count on it," she said sweetly. "Now, I really must go."

"Then, until we meet again."

"Yes, until then," she said, turning the key in the ignition. The engine turned over, then purred to a start, and K.C. backed slowly from the parking space. She gave him a small wave and breathed a sigh of relief just to be out of his presence.

She glanced in the rearview mirror as she pulled away from him. He stood watching her, as if puzzled, then finally turned to walk back to the chateau.

K.C. drove slowly along the winding driveway, searching for places Gav might be hiding. "I'm heading toward the front gate," she said into the microphone still attached to her blouse. "Gav, I can't stop because I'm in full view of the chateau. But I will slow down once I round the last corner before coming into view of the guardhouse. If you see headlights in about ten seconds, jump out from your hiding place, my friend. It will be me. I'm just hoping and praying you'll be there."

She took a deep breath, straining to see through the mist. Still nothing. Only the eerie silhouettes of trees and buildings. She rounded the last curve and rolled to a stop.

Holding her breath, she peered into the darkness, willing the shape of Gav to appear. She waited as long as she dared, then started forward again, slowly. Finally, just before she pulled around the corner, the figure of a man stepped out of the shadows on her side of the car.

He motioned for her to stop, opened the car door, and she stepped out. "Are you all right?" He touched her arm gently. "I lost the transmission about halfway through the evening."

"I'm fine, Gav." She was already removing her wig and hat. She handed them to him, then as he put them on, she wiggled out of the leopardskin coat, grinning at the same time. "You're gorgeous," she whispered. "Leopard skin suits you!"

He gave her a scalding look as he tried to slip one arm into her coat. "It's too small, K.C."

"That's okay, Gav. I think this will work. Let me show you—" She gave him a gentle push into the driver's seat, then wrapped the coat around his shoulders, buttoning the top toggle. "There," she pronounced. "That guard is only going to wave you through anyway." Being so near him unnerved her, and she quickly backed away.

He handed her his V-neck pullover. "Put this on, Kace. It's turned chilly."

She took it gratefully from his hands. "Hurry," she said. "Randolph may have called ahead to tell the guard to expect me."

"Don't forget. We'll meet in front of the cellar."

She nodded. "Just as we planned." She glanced at her watch. "I'll be there."

"Kace—?"

"Hurry, Gav." Hooking her handbag over her shoulder, she waved him on impatiently, afraid they would be seen. "I'll tell you all about Randolph later. Just be careful."

"I was about to say the same thing. Watch for the sensor lights. This place is like a minefield."

An owl hooted mournfully from one of the shadowy trees, and K.C. shivered as she slipped the sweater over her head. At the same time, the sound of approaching footsteps carried toward them from the direction of the chateau. Gav quickly rolled the Buick forward, and K.C. stepped into a mist-shrouded stand of oleanders.

Gav indeed was waved through the electronic gate. He drove down the winding hillside. By the time he reached Calistoga, he'd pulled off the wig and hat and flung the coat into the backseat. Just one mile south of town, a few blocks off Highway 29, he spotted the deserted garage where he and Father Max had planned to meet. He parked behind the ramshackle building and flipped off the headlights.

He'd been waiting only a few minutes when the Morgan, its top up, slowly rounded the corner and pulled in behind him.

"Am I glad to see you!" he said, getting into the Morgan beside Father Max. He reached for a denim jacket he'd earlier left in the backseat.

"Everything go as planned?" The priest's lined face showed

his concern. He immediately headed the Morgan out of the dilapidated garage's parking area and onto Highway 29.

"Like clockwork, except for some bugs in K.C.'s mike. I didn't have time to check it. We can't communicate until we meet at the old cellar." Father Max stopped at the intersection, then turned the Morgan onto the road leading up the hillside to Angels Crest. "You've got the balloon?" Gav asked.

Father Max nodded. "It's in the trunk with the tools." A short time later, he pulled over and parked the Morgan, flipping off the headlights. They were now within a half mile of the compound. Both men stepped out of the car and went around to the trunk. Gav stuffed the partially filled helium party balloon under his jacket, and Father Max grabbed his small tool case.

Worried their voices might carry uphill in the night air, they didn't speak as they stealthily drew closer to the guardhouse. Finally it was in sight. Father Max gave Gav a quick nod, and they headed off the road and into the brush.

Now they slowed their forward movement but continued moving upward and somewhat to the right, away from the guard's line of vision.

Finally, Gav pointed to the place he'd earlier scouted, a hundred yards or so from the front gate. It was well hidden by heavy brush and another of the estate's giant eucalyptus trees, its massive trunk seeming to be a grove in itself, reaching skyward until it disappeared in the veil of mist. Its branches had long ago been lopped off to avoid their use as a way to drop over the electronic fence.

They knelt in the clearing beyond the tree, and Father Max opened the tool case. "You'll have to give me a boost," he whispered, when he'd found the tools he needed: pliers, wire stripper, and a spray bottle of water.

Gav watched the priest with admiration. Who would have

ever thought his talents went so far beyond the pulpit?

"Can you support my weight?" Father Max asked, all business.

Gav nodded and stooped down. Briskly, as if he did this sort of thing daily, the priest stepped onto Gav's shoulders and reached for the support of the eucalyptus as Gav struggled to his feet.

"Okay, now. Steady," Father Max said quietly. "I can almost reach...a lit-tle closer...lit-tle closer. There! Stop." And Gav did, his knees shaking slightly under the strain. He reached for the eucalyptus trunk to steady himself.

Gav couldn't see what miracle the priest was performing. He could only hear the sounds of snipping and wire stripping and Father Max's tense breathing. "How's it going?" Gav whispered.

"Hmm," was the only reply. "Hmm-hmm!" Another snip followed, and then a tool dropped. "Drat! Can you hand me the strippers?"

Gav drew in a deep breath and clung to the tree trunk with one hand while he reached along the ground for the tool until he felt the cold metal handle. By moving ever so slightly, he was able to touch it and scoot it to where he could grasp it.

He handed it to Father Max.

"Good. We're almost there. Al-most..." Another couple of snips and strips and Father Max said, "Okay, it's done. Let me down."

Gav knelt slowly, feeling his way down the tree for support. Father Max stepped down from his shoulders, put down his tools, and brushed off his hands.

"Perfect," he declared, still whispering. It was too dark to see his features, but he sounded triumphant. "I frayed the plastic covering on the wires so slightly that they simply appear to have weathered. As soon as the wet Mylar touches the bare live

177

wires—we'll have quite a show. The surge should give us a blackout of the entire compound."

"For seven seconds—" Gav reminded him. "Not only do I need to get into the compound and hide during those few seconds, you've got to hightail it out of here. Get back to the Morgan, and get away!"

"I know that, son," he said, but Gav could tell he was still preoccupied with the task at hand.

Gav handed him the balloon. "Ah yes. It's perfectly filled— not even halfway. It will appear to have fallen from the sky!" He tied a piece of string to the end, then sprayed the balloon generously with water. "We're ready, son," he said quietly. "As soon as you reach the gate, give me a call with this—" He handed Gav a thimble-sized wooden whistle. "It's an owl call. Picked it up at a sporting-goods store," he whispered. "If all is well, just blow it softly. I'll hear you and let the balloon rise to the top of the fence."

Gav couldn't help smiling. Father Max was a good man to have on a person's team. He nodded, and turned to creep back toward the guardhouse.

"God be with you, son," Father Max whispered.

"And you, Father. Be careful."

Gav reached the foliage at the side of the gate. Inside the small building, the guard glanced up absently, then back to his book. Gav briefly wondered what the man had been reading through the evening that could be so fascinating. Then he reached in his pocket for the owl call and put it to his lips.

Randolph dimmed the lights in his office, and due to the chill in the air, he had Sister Bastancherry light a fire in the large stone fireplace. Strains of a Bach piano concerto filled the room. Crossing to one of the two high-back leather chairs arranged near the crackling fire, he settled into it. A newly uncorked bottle of the estate's finest cabernet sauvignon had been placed on the table between the chairs. A pair of Baccarat crystal wine goblets were beside it.

He poured himself some wine, and set the goblet aside to let the deep red liquid breathe. He laid his head back against the chair and closed his eyes. So many things to consider, to think about, when facing new challenges, especially when those challenges provided such amusement. He smiled to himself, drawing in a deep and satisfying sigh.

A light tap sounded at the door. "Come in," he called. Desirée pushed open the door, and he stood to greet her, taking both her hands in his. "My darling, come sit beside me." He nodded to the chair next to his. He waited until she had settled into the chair, then sat down next to her. "Would you care for some wine?"

"Yes, please," she said. He enjoyed watching Desirée, the elegant tilt of her head, the way she moved across the room. Her beauty and breeding, finishing-schooled and moneyed background were as much a part of her as breathing. She'd come from a life he'd always yearned for. And all she had…and more…would soon be his. He smiled and reached for her hand. Not bad for a man who'd grown up tossed from foster home to foster home, for someone who'd been told so often that he was the devil's child that he believed it even now.

"The private reserve chardonnay?" He squeezed her hand gently. "It's become your favorite in recent days."

"Yes," she said, returning his smile at last. "I—It will have a glass."

He stood and went to his cabinet where he kept the special QmP wines. He uncorked the pale amber chardonnay and poured it into another Baccarat crystal goblet, then carried it across the room to Desirée. Its special qualities always seemed to help relax the rather high-strung woman. It was for her own good that he served it to her nightly.

"To our future," he said, holding up his goblet. She lifted her crystal toward his, and as they clinked, he stared tenderly into her eyes, but she shifted her gaze away from him.

"You seem distracted," he said, taking another sip of wine. "Tell me why."

"It doesn't like doing those things it knows is wrong," she said.

"Such as breaking into the woman's car?"

She met his gaze again, and he could see how troubled she was. "Oh, my darling," he said. "I should have explained. I thought you understood. We are at war against those who would bring us down—outsiders who don't understand our beliefs. It's us against them, Desirée."

Now she watched him intently, and the adoration in her eyes made him reach over and caress her cheek. Adoration from her, from all of them, made his life worth living. He craved it. He rejoiced in it.

"Don't you see?" he continued patiently. "Sometimes we must do what we ordinarily would not. It's worth our efforts in the end if it means saving the Fellowship from those who would seek to destroy it."

She nodded. "It understands, but sometimes..." Her voice broke off with a sigh. "Sometimes it feels paranoid thinking that way."

He laughed lightly. "Oh, my dear! That's from years of listening to psychobabble." He shook his head sadly. "You once told me that you'd spent years in therapy."

"Yes," she whispered as if embarrassed. "For chronic depression."

"Don't you see? Those years of conditioning have *made* you paranoid. There's reality—which I am helping you, helping all our Fellowship members, to find. And there's true paranoia—which you are struggling to overcome." Her eyes were trusting as they met his. "I wouldn't lie to you, my bride and queen! And my darling, you're not alone in your struggles to find truth."

He knew better than to ask her yet for the car's registration. He didn't want to remind her of the break-in, so he said, as he often did to Desirée and many of the others, "Close your eyes, my dearest, and cleanse your mind of all thoughts."

She was conditioned to respond, and after setting down the crystal wineglass, she did as he said.

"Now we are going to walk that path toward truth—toward the light that can only be found in Atara."

Bach played softly in the background, and the fire crackled in the fireplace. He dimmed the light and once again took her hand, caressing her palm with his thumb. The other hand he placed on her forehead, gently massaging her temples.

"You are in the midst of darkness, bleaker and more frightening than anything you can ever imagine. Let yourself go there. It is real, Desirée.

"You are there, now, and cannot leave. Do you understand?"

She nodded, letting out a shaky sigh.

"Breathe deeply. Again. Now again. Faster and faster until you feel light-headed.

"All right, now picture the darkness again. Picture the absence of all things, all emotion, all light. This darkness is but a vast emptiness as big as all the universe.

"It threatens to overtake you, to swallow you so that you will never see light again."

Desirée was now whimpering.

"Place yourself in that darkness, Desirée. Now!"

She wept with fear and reached out to him, trembling, her eyes still closed. Randolph gathered her close and stroked her face, wiping away her tears. She sobbed in his arms.

"Now," he murmured. "Imagine that I'm on the path with you, pulling you from the midnight emptiness. Picture us walking together toward the light of truth...toward Atara...where fear can never touch you...devour you...again."

"Now picture us when we arrive at the light, arrive at our destination—Atara! We are wearing our regal robes, you and I. Hold your head high, my queen. Listen to the chants of adulation. They're for you, my dear, and for me!

"And there is light all around us. We're bathed in it! And we're safe. We're in a place where we'll always be safe!" He almost believed it himself.

She sighed deeply, lovingly, as she stared up at him. For several minutes she couldn't speak.

"Have another sip of wine," he said, handing her the goblet.

She took a sip, watching him adoringly over the crystal rim.

He smiled. "Now for that car registration," he said.

She pulled it from her pocket and handed it to him; he quickly scanned the name and address. Of course. The car was registered to Theodora Whimple. And Satinka could only be K.C. Keegan, the mystery writer's grandniece. He'd seen through her disguise, so it was no great surprise. Yet instead of anger, he felt admiration for her creativity. He only wondered who the young man was who'd posed as her new husband the day before.

No matter, they would make challenging opponents.

Desirée frowned. "Is something wrong?"

"Did you read this?"

"No," she said, looking at him quizzically.

He didn't think she would lie to him, but he couldn't be sure. Leaning toward her chair, he touched her face with his fingertips. What he had to tell her would make everything else fade in comparison—Satinka's visit, the car registration, her own fears.

She turned to him, and he reached for her hand. "Now, my dearest Desirée, settle back and listen."

He smiled warmly into her adoring eyes.

K.C. silently made her way across the compound. Barely visible through the trees and mist was the glow of lights coming from the chateau windows. The grounds themselves were dark except for night watchmen passing by with their flashlights from time to time and for the rare occasions the moon passed from behind the veil of fog.

She arrived at the clearing partway up the hillside. The moon slipped from its shroud again, and she shuddered, looking up at the high stone walls of the old cellar and remembering the tour she and Gav had taken through its limestone caves.

She climbed the stairs to the heavy wooden door, then settled onto the top step in front of it, dropping her leather bag beside her. The estate grounds now seemed too quiet, and she shivered again. Every night bird, cricket, and owl had fallen silent. The only sound was the steady dripping of mist from the trees.

She pressed the button to illumine her watch. It hadn't been a half hour yet, and she thought about Gav and Father Max, wondering if they'd begun working on the security system, wondering, too, how much longer until Gav joined her.

But as always, it was Aunt Theo who occupied most of her waking thoughts and prayers. "Father, send your angels to protect her," she breathed.

Angels, God's magnificent created beings. Not the counterfeit angels espoused by Randolph.

K.C. drew in a deep breath, trying to calm her frazzled

nerves. Waiting was always difficult, and grabbing her bag, she headed back down the steps to pace around the old building. She hugged Gav's sweater close, glad he'd thought to give it to her.

The fog settled closer to the ground, and she squinted into the night. The lights flickering from the turret's windows were now barely visible. She checked her watch again, surprised that only a few minutes had passed since the last time she looked.

She had just moved back up the stairs and leaned against the doorjamb when she heard footsteps approaching…from the road between the chateau and the old cellar. She looked frantically around for a hiding place, but there wasn't time to sprint to the safety of nearby trees.

The footsteps drew nearer, now accompanied by the sound of voices speaking in low tones. K.C. backed against the door, pressing herself into its shadows. The door had been locked when Randolph escorted them on the tour, but it didn't hurt to at least try it now.

She felt for the handle behind her, and carefully pressed her thumb against it. Surprisingly, the door gave way, and she quietly, very slowly, pushed backward until it was open far enough for her to slip in.

Finally, she was inside, and she let out her breath as she pushed the door back into place. She moved to a window and stood to one side to peer out.

Two cloaked figures, one with a flashlight, appeared in the mist. They drew closer, finally stopping near the cellar. The one with the light flashed it around the outer perimeter. K.C. stepped back as the light hit her window and entered the room, raking across the stacks of old barrels, rusty picking trays, and wheeled carts.

Then they started toward the cellar door.

K.C. caught her breath and hid behind a stack of picking trays.

The door opened, and the cloaked figures moved inside. They were laughing and talking and paying little attention to their surroundings. K.C. breathed a little easier when they headed straight for the limestone tunnels and disappeared inside without even a glance around the room.

But still she didn't move. She sensed they would be back.

Just as she expected, minutes later they returned and headed for the door. K.C. pressed her lips together, trying to keep her teeth from chattering. She was cold and miserable. The cellar was giving her the creeps with its smell of sour wine and mildew. And she was frightened that they might lock her inside.

But the two figures exited the building as quickly as they had entered. K.C. crept to the window and peered through again to make certain they had indeed moved away from the cellar.

When they were at last out of sight, she started for the door, then stopped, thinking she heard a voice. Or a moan.

She listened, not daring to breathe. There it was again! Coming from the limestone tunnel the men had just exited.

Again, the low cry carried toward her.

K.C. couldn't ignore it. She moved silently toward the rear of the pitch black room, feeling her way from stacks of trays to wheeled carts to oak barrels. At last, she reached the large, moss-covered opening to the catacombs.

The air inside was indeed sweeter. What was it Desirée had said during the tour? The dark moss kept the air as fresh today as it had a century and a half ago. But it didn't matter. The familiar claustrophobic dread caused K.C.'s heart to thud and her breathing rate to increase. She swallowed hard but kept walking toward the sound, her hands touching one side of the tunnel as she moved further into the earth.

The muffled cry broke into the dark silence. It was a cry for help!

K.C. quickened her pace, now following the tunnel as it twisted and rounded a curve she remembered led to the cave where the barrels were aged. The moaning was louder now, and she knew its source was somewhere inside that cave.

She halted and felt for the door she knew was dead ahead. Surprisingly, it was open, and all she felt was the sides of the opening. Next, she considered whether to switch on the cave's single lightbulb. By doing so, she placed herself at risk, though she reasoned that the person calling out for help was likely to be unguarded—otherwise the cries would have been silenced.

But it didn't hurt to be careful.

Holding her breath, K.C. pressed herself flat against the outside of the doorway, then reached her hand around to the inner wall. Her fingers touched the crude plastic cover plate. A moment later, she flipped the switch.

Heavy, uneven breathing came from the cave as if someone waited expectantly, fearfully.

K.C. breathed a quick prayer and stepped into the room.

SIXTEEN

Her toiletry kit and towel in hand, Theodora moved slowly down the women's dormitory hallway and headed into the community showers and rest-room facilities. The damp night air chilled her, and she gathered the thin cotton robe close.

She had been placed on the third floor of the dormitory in a long room with eight simple but comfortable cots, one cotton blanket on each, and a rather hard pillow that she was told would improve her posture. The walls were bare, as were the wood floors, and there was a single window at the room's far end.

Theodora reached the long row of sinks and placed her toiletries on the shelf in front of her. As she squeezed toothpaste onto her toothbrush, she heard someone else enter the room and looked up to see Desirée's face in the mirror. There were dark circles under her eyes and her face looked drawn.

Theodora placed her toothbrush on the shelf and turned toward the woman. "Desirée, dear, what's wrong?"

"I need to talk with you," Desirée whispered, glancing around the room nervously.

They were alone, but Theodora knew that Randolph's electronic surveillance was far-reaching. The insidious little bugs could be anywhere. But she'd already surveyed the bathroom area and hadn't found even one. Apparently, the leader had some sense of decency.

"Of course, dear. Now?"

Desirée nodded. "But not here." She looked toward the doorway. "Let's go for a walk," she whispered.

Theodora didn't mention to Desirée that the bathroom wasn't bugged. Among other reasons, she didn't want the omission to be remedied. "All right. Can you get us outside?"

Desirée held her finger to her lips and motioned Theodora to follow.

Minutes later they silently moved through the back door, which Desirée unlocked with a keycard, and headed down the outside stairs. Desirée led Theodora away from the plain wooden dormitory structure and onto a path leading up the hillside. The earlier mist still dripped from the trees, but the moon was out, lighting their way as they walked.

Finally Desirée stopped and, obviously still nervous, peered into the surrounding forest of eucalyptus trees. There was a large fallen log nearby and Theodora gratefully settled onto it, then patted the place next to her. "Sit down, dear, and tell me what's wrong. Though I suspect I know."

Desirée nodded and reached for Theodora's hand. "He wants to marry me."

"Randolph." It wasn't a question.

"Yes. He says we will rule Atara together."

"Do you believe him?"

"I do when I'm with him. I look into his eyes, and everything he says seems so plausible. I think about how much I care for him...." Her voice faltered.

"Then later you think it over, and it doesn't make so much sense." Theodora watched for signs that the woman was using the conversation as some sort of ploy. She'd done it before.

"And I can't believe that I've been pulled into this place, pulled into the whole belief system." She released Theodora's hand and stood, walked a few steps away, then turned. In the dusky light of the full moon, the worry lines on her face and her haggard look were even more pronounced.

"I don't know what to do. I've turned over everything to him.

Even my home—the business I started with my husband—is his." Her head was down, and she was wringing her hands.

"Maybe it's not too late."

"I couldn't go back on my word. Besides, I made a decision, for better or worse, to follow him."

"Him or the beliefs?"

"Him. But he's at the center of everything I believe."

Theodora stood and walked across the small clearing to Desirée. "You've given him material things. Though it seems like a lot—your home, your business, your bank accounts—whatever else you've turned over, you haven't given him your life," she said. "It is yours—unless you allow him to take it as well."

"What do you mean?"

"Mass suicide. We've discussed it before."

"He says that people will call it suicide to try to turn us away from our destiny—that of leaving our earthly bodies for another, glorious and forever young. It *is* a journey. He says we will simply fall into a painless sleep, only to wake on the planet Atara."

"And you believe him." Again, it wasn't a question. "You believe that he will feed his followers grape Koolaid laced with cyanide, or whatever poison he's got in mind, and hundreds of people *won't* die?"

There were tears in Desirée's eyes. "When you put it that way, you make him sound like a monster, a mass murderer."

"Last time I mentioned mass murder, you became angry," Theodora said gently. "This time you are weeping. Is it because you know that what I'm saying is true?"

For a moment, Desirée didn't speak. "He overheard our conversation—the day you were planning to leave."

"I assumed he did."

"He said that I handled the situation correctly by encouraging you to stay. He thought I'd done it on his behalf."

"And had you?"

"No. I honestly wanted to know your thoughts. I wanted you to stay." She walked to the log and sat down again. Theodora sat beside her. "He guessed that I was wavering. So he offered me something he knew I wouldn't refuse."

Theodora watched the woman's face. Tears coursed down her cheeks. They seemed sincere.

"He offered me himself. He asked me to marry him here on Earth and rule with him on Atara."

Theodora tilted her head, frowning. "And is this what you want?"

Desirée nodded. "I said yes, thinking it would be a long ways off. You know, so long that I'd have time to adjust to the idea, decide about my beliefs." She wiped at her wet cheeks with her fingers, and Theodora handed her a tissue from her pocket. Desirée dabbed at her eyes.

Theodora put her arm around the other woman. "And now you've changed your mind?"

"It's worse than that." She blew her nose. "He wants to marry soon. He's described the ceremony." She was hiccuping now, and the tears had started flowing again. "Besides the inane way I—make that *it*—" she said, "will refer to *itself* in the vows, the ceremony seems to precede some other momentous occasion."

"You mean the suicide?"

"Maybe. I don't know. Yesterday he began describing everything about it—who will be there—"

"The entire Fellowship?"

"Yes, of course. And what we will serve the guests at the wedding supper."

"Grape Koolaid?"

"No, he is planning to serve our finest estate wine laced

190

with massive doses of something."

"He disclosed this to you?"

"Inadvertently. After we'd discussed the wedding ceremony, he called Brother Dakota and asked for his report." She swallowed hard, then put her face in her hands.

"I couldn't hear Brother Dakota's end of the conversation, but Rance made mention of it being served at the Last Supper. Then they laughed together, and Rance quoted something that sounded like a Bible verse, saying the bridegroom was about to thunder from the skies to take his bride. And together they would leave this earth with their church."

Theodora's heart pounded hard beneath her ribs. She drew in a deep breath. "Did he say when?"

"No. He just said it would be as soon as the wedding ceremony, the food, the wine, were all properly prepared. He also said something about the harvest, mentioning how appropriate for the ceremony to be held this time of year." She turned to look at Theodora. "That means it could be any time."

"And now you want out?"

"I don't know if I can leave him. I—I'm confused. When I'm with him, I feel so relaxed, special."

"Is he any different now than when you first met?"

Desirée nodded again.

"When he took you to plays and wonderful suppers and brought you here as a guest in the chateau—he showed you a different side of himself. He played a role, knowing your loneliness, your emotional needs."

"He still touches a place in my soul," she whispered. "It's as if he knows me better than I know myself. He knows the right words to say." She bit her lip. "Have you ever felt that way about someone?"

Theodora nodded. "His name is Max, and I never knew I would miss him so desperately. He's my soul mate. There's not an hour that passes that I don't think of dozens of things I want to tell him."

"You're married?"

"Oh, no. We've discussed it, but haven't actually planned a wedding. I've had deadlines. And he's busier now than before he retired as an Episcopal priest. I always thought we had all the time in the world. Now..." she sighed, "now, I wonder why we waited. Why we wasted all that time we could have been together." She smiled softly. "But enough about Max and me. Tell me more about your feelings for Rance."

"Maybe what I feel is more infatuation than love, the kind of love you're describing," she said. "I look up to Rance. I love to watch him in action when he's speaking to the Fellowship. And being with him afterward makes me feel special."

"Important," Theodora added.

"Yes, because he's chosen me from among all the hundreds." She paused, and her voice was sad when she continued. "But when I leave him, I feel more empty than ever. He talks about leading me to the light. But when I'm out of his presence, the darkness inside me is deeper than I've ever known before. I want to curl up and die, I'm so frightened."

"He's caused you to feel that way, Desirée," Theodora said. "Don't you see? He wants you to be emotionally dependent on him. That's not love."

"When he talks to me about it, about us and our future, it seems to make sense."

"But then the emptiness settles in."

"Soul famine," Desirée said.

Theodora again circled her arm around Desirée's shoulders. "There is One who loves you with all his heart, dear," she said softly. "His Word—his holy, immutable Word—says, 'I have loved you with an everlasting love. I have drawn you with lovingkindness.'

"His Word is the only thing that satisfies, that will take away that sense of 'soul famine.' He says, 'I will build you up again...you will take up your tambourines and go out with the joyful....'"

Desirée wiped at her tears and blew her nose. "Joyful?" She shook her head slowly. "It's been so long since I've felt any joy."

"Only God can restore your joy because he's the true Source of joy. No matter what you've been through—your husband's death, being taken in by this charlatan, whatever tragedy or sadness you've had in your life, he offers joy in its place. Anything else is counterfeit."

Desirée nodded slowly. "My greatest fear is that I won't be able to stand up to Rance. I've so easily done his bidding. Look how I stopped using *I* in his presence." She looked at Theodora earnestly. "Do you know what he plans next? Starting tomorrow night, his guards will roust us from sleep to trek down to the fountain of Keb-Kaseko Rodolphe to kneel and worship."

She started to weep again. "I hate the thought of doing it, but I don't know if I can go against him."

"God will give you the strength, Desirée, if you'll ask him. He'll work in your heart from the inside out."

"You don't understand what can happen if we disobey."

"And what might that be?" Theodora studied Desirée, wondering if the woman was about to deliver a message of warning from Randolph, and if that warning was the true reason for their conversation. "What can disobedience bring?"

"There was one woman who refused to do his bidding. She disappeared without a word. The only thing we were told was that she'd gone on to Atara to prepare for our coming."

"Why didn't someone stand up for her? Demand an explanation—a real explanation?" Theodora asked, though she knew the answer. Randolph ruled with an iron fist, a fist tempered with a dynamic, charismatic, pseudo-compassionate way of dealing with his followers. From Charles Manson to Jim Jones, they were the same.

"We were afraid," Desirée said. "Though our fear was more of being wrong about the Fellowship than of what he might do to us."

"He's trying to remove your compassion for each other," Theodora said sadly. "Don't you see?" Again, she met Desirée's look. "It started with taking away any love you might have had for yourself. Using *it* in place of *I*."

Desirée didn't speak; she still looked confused.

"Jesus said one of the two greatest commandments is to love others as ourselves. If we don't value who we are in God's eyes, then we can't value others." Desirée frowned as if trying to follow her logic. "Don't you see?" Theodora went on. "By robbing you of your own value, Randolph is ensuring that you look to him for worth. All this talk of ruling with him in Atara is supposed to replace the value that God has bestowed on you as his precious, created child."

Desirée shook her head sadly. "It's too complicated to think about. I can't tell truth from fiction." She shrugged.

"I'll help if you want to escape. But I can't leave until I find out if there are others who want out." Theodora again had the unnerving thought that this might be a trap that Desirée had led her into, a ploy masterminded by Randolph. A setup before arranging her own disappearance. But after studying the other woman's face in the moonlight, she sensed that Desirée's words, her tears, were genuine.

"Loving others as yourself," mused Desirée, sounding sincere. "You're doing just that by not saving yourself."

Theodora smiled. "It's as simple and profound as that."

"What is the other command?"

"That you love the Lord your God with all your heart, mind, and strength. You see, dear, there's no room for worship of any other creature, false angels, or gods. Only the one true God of the universe. The God who loves you as if you were the only one in the world to love." She hesitated. "What I started to say…no matter what happens…remember God's words to you: 'I have loved you with an everlasting love.'"

Desirée nodded and reached for Theodora's hand. "I will," she promised.

After talking a few more minutes, they stood to make their way back to the dormitory.

The words that had haunted Theodora when Desirée first spoke them now drifted back into her mind: *"There was one woman who refused to do his bidding. She disappeared without a word."*

They had now nearly reached the back stairs, and Theodora put her hand on Desirée's arm. "Who was the woman?" she asked. "The one who went against Randolph."

"Her name was Sister Ariel Tilman."

Theodora reached toward Desirée for support. "Oh, my dear. No! Are you certain?"

"Yes, she joined the Fellowship about the same time I did."

"And now she's gone." Ariel, her friend. For decades they'd shared love and laughter and tears and joys. "Maybe," she whispered, "maybe Ariel was sent somewhere. Perhaps she's being held someplace here on the compound."

Desirée shook her head. "I don't see how."

After a moment, Desirée circled her arm around Theodora and the two women began climbing the stairs to the third floor.

They had reached the first landing when Theodora asked Desirée to stop. She was nearly overcome with grief. It washed over her in waves. She closed her eyes for a moment, thinking of Ariel. Finally she nodded. "All right," she said. "Let's go."

SEVENTEEN

K C. stared at the woman seated in front of her. Spiked hair standing in meringuelike peaks. Furious eyes watching from above a crude gag. Marigold Green!

She ran to Marigold's side, knelt, and began unwinding the tangle of rope. Marigold had already worked most of it loose and ranted in anger and disgust at Randolph and his Angels of Fellowship as soon as K.C. untied the gag and finished unwinding the rope.

"My lands," she said. "Am I glad to see you!" She rubbed her ankles. "You have no idea what I've been through. This place is not at all the benign place it would have the world believe. Nor is it democratic! Seems they don't want anyone speaking out against them. Can you believe it? They came right into my home and grabbed me away from my computer! I was still logged on the Internet, posting messages against them as fast as I could! And I have no idea what they intend for me! No one will tell me anything."

Then she blinked at K.C. "But how in the world did you get here?"

"It's a long story," K.C. said. "We can talk about that later. Right now, we've got to leave."

"I couldn't agree more." Marigold unfolded her big-boned body and stretched her torso and legs. "They'll be coming back soon. They're here to check on me at least once an hour."

K.C. stopped abruptly, reasoning through the implications. If Marigold turned up missing, the grounds would be searched. She couldn't let that happen.

"Actually, I assume they'll be back," Marigold went on. "Unless they were just going to leave me in here forever. Now, that's a pleasant thought!"

K.C. remembered Randolph's stories. The wine. The poison. The burial in one of the barrels. "I think you're right—they'll be back. But that presents another problem."

Marigold was partway to the door. She turned around, frowning again. "What?"

"We can't let anyone know you've escaped. They'll be scouring the compound—bringing out the dogs, searchlights, armed security, the works. We can't let them do that."

Marigold looked indignant as she reached up and rearranged her spikes. "If you're thinking that I need to stay here, you've got another think coming, girl! I refuse to remain in this hole one more minute." She turned back to the doorway and flipped on the long, dreary string of lights.

"I understand, believe me," K.C. said hurrying to catch up with Marigold as she strode into the tunnel. "But you absolutely cannot turn up missing. Gav is breaking into the compound as we speak—"

"Gav?" Marigold's face brightened as she turned to look at K.C. "Elliott Gavin?"

"None other," K.C. confirmed.

"Why, I've known him since he was knee-high to a bumblebee. His family lived right down the street—"

"I know. I know," K.C. said impatiently. "But please, let me finish. The only way to find my Aunt Theo is for Gav and me not to be discovered."

"And the search for the missing prisoner will cause your discovery."

"Yes. Exactly."

By now, Marigold had slowed down. "Okay," she sighed at last. "What's the plan—besides go back into the cave? Which, by the way, I absolutely refuse to do. I don't care whose life is at stake. Not even Theodora Whimple's. I never liked her anyway—no offense, dear. It's just she's never once taken up any of my causes. Hasn't come to any of my plays. Not one." She shook her head slowly. "Well, I guess that's no reason to let her languish here in this Angels of Fellowship business. But let me repeat, I absolutely refuse to stay in this cave."

K.C. drew in a deep breath. "All right. Fine. Give me a minute." She stared at the big woman. "I've got an idea," she finally said. "How good an actress are you?"

"I've played some parts in community theater productions around the area. Mostly, though, I volunteer as a drama coach," she added with a hint of pride. "The producers suggested it right after I played Puck in *A Midsummer Night's Dream*. Of course, that was when I was younger and a lot more agile—"

K.C. interrupted. "In just a few minutes, there will be a seven-second blackout." She checked her watch. The hour and a half they'd estimated it would take Gav to break in had nearly passed. "You need to head immediately to the chateau. Did you notice it when they brought you here?"

Marigold nodded.

"Good. Then hurry to the front entrance. By then the lights will be on. It's late, so no one may hear you at first. Bang on the door and scream until someone comes."

"Okay. Got it." She poked her fingers into her spikes once more. "What else?"

"Tell them you're a seeker—"

"A what?"

"Tell them you want to become part of the Angels of Fellowship."

"You're kidding."

"I'm deadly serious, and you've got to convince them you are."

Marigold searched K.C.'s face a moment, then nodded. "I understand."

"All our lives depend on your ability to carry this off."

"How will I convince them that I've undone my own ropes?" But as she spoke, a wide grin spread across her face. "I've got it! How's this? An angel came to my rescue—that's what caused a supernatural power surge—"

"Won't work," K.C. interrupted. "It's going to be caused by a natural-seeming occurrence. A child's balloon."

Marigold stared at her blankly, then went on. "Well, never mind about that. The angel will work, though. I'll make it work. Let me think. Which shall it be of the forty-four? Mozart? Or maybe Shakespeare?" She chuckled. "Maybe I'll make up a new one.

"I've got it! I'll have been visited by a forty-fifth angel from the planet Atara, an angel who set me free and sent me with a message for Rance Randolph."

K.C. was astounded at Marigold's good humor after all she'd been through.

"Aha!" Marigold said, stopping abruptly. They had almost reached the old cellar's large storage room. "Jacques Cousteau! What do you think? He's come to help us save our planet."

K.C. couldn't help grinning. "Of course," she said. "Who else?" Still chuckling, the two women stepped out of the tunnel and into the room. Then K.C. halted and turned to Marigold. "You understand how serious this is, don't you? All our lives are at stake. Randolph is a madman. We can't know what he'll do next."

The humor drained from Marigold's face. "I know that very well, K.C. Believe me."

Suddenly, the lights went out in the tunnel behind them.

"It's time, Marigold," K.C. said, leading her to the door. "Godspeed!"

The big woman raced down the outside stairs and sprinted into the darkness. K.C. followed her out the door, then moved silently toward the forested hillside. Though she and Gav planned to meet at the old cellar, she figured that whoever had brought Marigold Green to the cave probably would return to check on their captive, or worse, to finish the job. K.C. shuddered and hurried to the shelter of a large eucalyptus.

The seven seconds had passed, and K.C. watched the twinkling glow return to the chateau windows, a distance away. It would be only minutes now—providing Gav and Father Max's plan had worked with precision—until Gav joined her. She checked her watch and settled onto a stump to wait.

It was comforting to know that help was at her fingertips if she needed to communicate with the outside world—with Gav, if he didn't make it inside the compound, with law enforcement people, if necessary. She let out a sigh and looked down to the place where she would normally set the handbag with the cell phone tucked snugly inside.

Only the leather bag wasn't there.

Frantically, she thought back to where she'd left it last.

Of course, inside the cave! She'd dropped it when she knelt to untie the ropes that bound Marigold. She had to get to it before someone came to check on Marigold. If she didn't, the handbag would be discovered, complete with her identity. She couldn't wait for Gav. It might be too late. For Aunt Theo, for Marigold Green, for all of them.

K.C. drew in a deep breath and headed back down the hillside as quickly and silently as she could. She opened the door to the old cellar and slipped inside, shutting it behind her. The tunnel was well illumined this time, and when she reached it, she hesitated, not wanting to turn off the lights and face that bleak, frightening darkness again.

But if she left the lights on, she placed herself in greater danger of being seen. She hesitated just long enough to decide that light was much better than darkness, even in this case. It would allow her to make her way more quickly through the maze, retrieve her handbag, and get out.

She swallowed hard and moved tentatively inside, concentrating on her task, trying not to consider that she was heading deeper and deeper into the hillside.

The leather bag was exactly where she'd left it. She quickly scanned the room to make sure it appeared that no one had been there with Marigold. Well, no one but Jacques Cousteau, she thought with a grim smile.

Slinging the bag over her shoulder, she started back inside the tunnel. Then she heard the voices. They were speaking in low but agitated tones, and they were headed toward her.

K.C. glanced around. She didn't have much time. Frantically, she headed toward one of the old barrels in the back of the cave and lifted the lid.

The voices were closer now.

She silently tipped the barrel and stepped in. She folded herself inside and replaced the lid, letting the barrel rock back into place, upright and still. She held her breath, glad she'd remembered her bag this time.

She peered through a crack between the barrel slats, watching as two men entered the cave. She recognized them from her earlier encounter. One man, fairly large, strode through the doorway first; he was followed by a second man, shorter and slighter in build. They were wearing the Fellowship robes, their hoods draped close to their faces. K.C. couldn't read their expressions, but she could clearly hear every word they said. By the sounds of their voices, they were young men, perhaps in their twenties.

"You buy the story?" the first devotee said.

"Nah," the second said. "Jacques Cousteau?" he laughed. "I have a hard enough time believing about the other forty-four."

They poked around some of the barrels, then the first young man spoke again. "Brother Dakota said to check it out. He didn't say we had to decide if there's evidence that an angel has visited the compound."

The second young man laughed. "Yeah, what're we supposed to find? Seaweed or something?"

"Well, we have to tell him something," the first said, stooping down to look at the coils of ropes, the discarded gag. "He'll keep us looking all night if we don't."

"You mean if he thinks there's been an intruder?"

"Yeah."

"You're sayin' we'll get more sleep if we confirm the visit by Cousteau?"

"You got it, brother."

The smaller man chuckled. "You've got a point. We report it really was a supernatural visit, and we get to go back to bed."

"How can we convince him?" The larger man said, standing again. He glanced around the room.

The smaller man shrugged. "We could say there was no way for anyone to break in here. It was exactly as we left it when we brought in the prisoner—locked up tighter than a drum. We could say that the rope was left tied in its original knots." He chuckled and stooped to retie the rope, leaving small hand-sized loops. "Here we are! Her hands just slipped out." He grinned and tied the back of the gag in the same manner. "There!" He stood, and brushed off his hands.

"This time we'd better make sure we do lock up," the bigger man said. "If anyone finds out we forgot to lock that front door, we'll be in a heap of trouble."

"Who's gonna tell?" the second man said. He reached for

the light and flipped it off. "But don't forget to let everyone know we smelled the faint odor of ocean breezes, beach sand, and seaweed in here."

"And saw wet, webbed flipper prints on the concrete floor," laughed the first man.

"One more thing," the second said. He reached up to unscrew the single ceiling light, protecting his fingers from its heat with the edge of his sleeve. "In case anyone comes in to see exactly what we discovered, we'll keep them in the dark a little longer. So to speak."

Still chuckling, they shut the heavy door with a distinct thud. The key turned in the lock, and the voices soon faded.

Silence followed. And complete darkness.

Her heart pounding wildly, K.C. crawled out of the barrel, her leather bag still slung across one shoulder. She fell to the ground, rummaging through the bag's contents, flinging out lipsticks, nail files, a spiral brush, tissues, a bottle of vitamins, a compact…until she at last reached the cell phone.

Frantically, she punched in the number to Aunt Theo's cabin, hoping Father Max might be there. But when she pushed the "send" button, nothing happened. Then she noticed the signal bar on the lighted dial. There was no signal at all. Nada! Nonexistent!

The phone didn't work in underground garages, she remembered. It stood to reason that it didn't work in caves, either. She should have known.

She held the little phone in her lap, keeping the power button pressed for a few seconds longer. The dim green display briefly lit the room. But she and Gav might need the phone later…if there was a later…and she needed to reserve the battery.

Finally, she released the power button, and the room again fell dark.

Gav circled the compound to the old cellar, staying well away from the footpaths and buildings. The access plan had worked like a charm. He'd slipped through the gate just seconds before the auxiliary power kicked in. Then he'd waited while the rather short, stout guard, scratching his head, moved up and down the fence, flashing his light across the top until he spotted the balloon.

The man had then returned to the guardhouse and picked up the telephone. He didn't seem alarmed, which was a good sign. Gav waited until the guard went back to his reading before moving farther away from the entrance.

Just as Gav was skirting the upper parking lot, a panel truck drove out of an outbuilding garage. As it slowly rolled by, a couple of the devotees were visible in the front seat, wearing hard hats instead of hoods, obviously on their way to repair the fence. He only hoped that Father Max's work would be seen as a natural occurrence.

Minutes later, he moved through the eucalyptus grove near the cellar, but when he saw flashlights moving inside, he shrank back into the safety of the trees. Two men, hooded and robed, opened the door and stepped out, laughing lightly.

The larger man turned and locked the door. Then they moved together down the hillside toward the chateau.

Gav let out a breath and looked around for K.C., assuming she'd also hidden in the grove. But when several minutes passed and she didn't show, he became alarmed.

He walked around the perimeter of the old building, not daring to call out K.C.'s name, but keeping a lookout for any trace of her.

There was nothing.

He had now reached the front of the building. The earlier

fog had disappeared, so Gav could easily see the crumbling structure in the moonlight.

He studied the entrance, thought of how the guards had just come through the door. If K.C. was nearby, he reasoned, she would have shown herself as soon as it was safe.

There were only two explanations. She had likely taken cover—just as he'd done—from the same guards. Or she'd been captured. He refused to consider that option.

He looked up at the old building again. If K.C. had been awaiting him here as they'd planned, heard the devotees approaching, and slipped inside...headed for the system of limestone tunnels...perhaps became lost...

By now his heart was pounding. He knew K.C.'s fear of enclosed places, her fear of the dark. He had to get to her!

"Oh, God, help me," he prayed as he rattled the old-fashioned door handle. It was solidly locked. The door didn't budge when he pushed against it. He glanced around and reached into his pocket for a credit card.

K.C. carefully inched her way along the tall stacks of barrels. Some were stacked as high as the ceiling, and she didn't want them to fall. It was so dark that she couldn't make out anything in the room. She moved toward the door, navigating from the memory of what she'd seen during the brief moments the cell phone light had been on.

It helped to know she had the phone in her bag, if she needed it. Making the choice not to use the light gave her a sense of control, and that in turn relieved some of her fear. Besides, if she gave up now and used the light, using up the battery, it meant that she didn't think she'd get out.

So she inched along in the dark, touching the back of the chair where Marigold Green had been bound, then stepping over the coiled ropes and again onto solid ground. As she moved, K.C. tried to keep her mind off where she was, focusing only on the need to find a way out.

At last she reached the door and felt the hard iron of the handle. She rattled it. The old thumb-press was loose in her hand, but the door itself remained shut tight.

She rattled it again, and again, feeling it give somewhat. She swallowed hard, trying to keep her fear at bay.

"The door," she breathed. "Kace, just keep your mind on the door." She tried the handle again. It was so old, it might just give if she forced her weight into it. She pushed and strained, but it remained solidly in place.

She felt the handle again, surprised when her fingers touched a space between the handle and the old wood of the door. She grabbed the phone again and punched the power button, glad for the useful pale green light.

Suddenly it didn't matter anymore about the battery. It only mattered that she get out of the room fast. She held the phone nearer the door handle, examining the inner latch, just visible. With her left hand, she grabbed her nail file and forced the little instrument into the opening.

But before she could lift up on the latch, the handle moved of its own accord. Someone was working on it from the outside.

She backed away from the door, grabbing the first thing she came to—the chair—and prepared to lift it over her head as a weapon.

"Kace—?" Gav said tentatively as he slowly opened the door. The tunnel light behind him cast light into the cave. He stood as a silhouette in the doorway.

K.C. dropped the chair and ran to him with a small cry. "Oh, Gav!"

He pulled her close, folding her in the warmth of his arms.

She could feel the thudding of his heart against her cheek. "Kace," he breathed. "I was so worried." For a moment he just kept her circled in his embrace. Then he pulled back slightly. "Are you all right?"

She nodded. "I've never been so glad to see someone in my whole life."

"Neither have I, Kace," he said, and pulled her close again.

This time, K.C. gave him a gentle push backward and smiled up into his face. "I'm fine, really. And we've got to get to work." She couldn't bear to be this near him.

The expression on his face changed. He was now all business. "The first thing is to get out of here."

"I couldn't agree with you more," she said, grabbing her handbag. But before they exited the cave, she glanced around to make sure she'd scooped up all the contents of her bag.

Gav triggered the lock on the cave door and they hurried down the tunnels, flipped off the light, then left the building for the cover of the eucalyptus grove.

K.C. quickly told him about Marigold Green.

"That puts us in greater danger," he said solemnly.

"I know. But I couldn't leave her in the cave."

"Can we trust her?"

"What do you mean?"

"I've known her all my life. She goes over the top on everything she does. She's never content to simply do as she's told—whether it's obeying city ordinances or reciting a playwright's lines. She even edits Shakespeare."

K.C. stared at Gav. "You think she might take matters into her own hands?" She frowned, knowing it was true.

He nodded slowly. "If I know Marigold Green, and I think I do, I would bet on it."

EIGHTEEN

W e need to find robes," K.C. said to Gav as they discussed their next move. "Have you seen anything that looks like a laundry facility?"

He shook his head. "I did see a ready room."

She frowned. "Ready room?"

"Yeah, where workers go for their daily instructions. This one's probably used for workers who do everything from grape picking to changing lightbulbs."

"How did you find it?"

"After the power went out, I saw the guard call for repairmen. Minutes later, a panel truck pulled out of this area about halfway between here and the main gate. While the garage door was up, I saw the room just to the other side."

"I would think the maintenance might be centered in one building."

"Such as the laundry?"

"That's my bet," K.C. said with a grin.

"Maybe that's the first thing we need to do—get the robes, then try to find Theo."

They started back down the hillside toward the hub of the estate. Though it was now well after midnight, the moon was still high, and the earlier fog hadn't moved back in.

"Watch for the sensor lights," Gav warned in a loud whisper. "I've almost tripped them a couple of times."

K.C. nodded. "Also the night watchmen. Those guys have come too close for comfort more than once tonight." They'd crossed the upper parking lot and were heading for the rear of the maintenance building, when K.C. stopped to listen, then held her finger to her lips.

Gav nodded, and they faded silently into the shadows of some thick foliage. Just beyond them, two robed figures moved briskly along a nearby footpath.

"One's Randolph," K.C. mouthed to Gav. "Who's with him? Can you tell?"

Gav moved aside a large palm frond and peered beneath it. "I would swear it's Marigold Green."

K.C. looked again, and agreed. It was definitely the big woman. Completely engrossed in the conversation, she was gesturing in her usual animated way as if speaking to a neighbor in a supermarket aisle. They headed up the steep hillside to the northwest of the cellar building.

"They appear to be old friends," K.C. muttered. "I suppose if anyone could pull it off, it's Marigold."

Gav frowned. "She won't be content to merely pass as a seeker. She'll try to convince him she's got more inside scoop on this Ataran angel business than Randolph himself."

"She knows the danger we're all in," K.C. reminded him. "I can't believe she'll try anything she can't back up."

Gav shook his head. "She lets it go to her head. Gets caught up in her own performance."

K.C. glanced at the retreating figures, Marigold still gesturing wildly as they moved up the hillside. K.C. aimed a quick prayer toward heaven that Marigold's tongue would be bridled. But at the rate the woman seemed to be speaking, she hoped her prayer wasn't too late.

"The path they're taking leads straight into the grove," Gav said a moment later. "I think we ought to follow."

"Not both of us," K.C. said. "If we're going to mix and mingle come morning we can't be without the robes."

"Right as usual. You want to flip for duty?" He grinned, reaching into his pocket. "Your call."

"Heads," she said, as the coin somersaulted into the air.

"Heads it is," he said. "What's your choice, ma'am?"

The repartee was so easy, just as it always had been. They made a good team. It broke her heart. "I'll go for the robes," she said. "You follow our friends. Maybe we'll get lucky and find out where he hides his followers."

"You want to meet back at the eucalyptus hideout?"

"Hideout?" She grinned again. "You make us sound like some Western gang."

"You are forgettin' somethin', ma'am. I am a sheriff," he reminded her, in his best John Wayne impersonation. "Cain't be part of a gang and be the law, too," he drawled.

She rolled her eyes heavenward and turned to head for the maintenance building.

"Hey, Kace—?"

"Yeah?" She turned.

"You know what I said about being glad to see you? Back at the cave?" She nodded, and he went on, "I realized that if anything had happened to you, I..." His words faltered.

She touched his arm. "Don't, Gav. Please." Then she punched him playfully. "Git down to business, pardner." Then without another word, she hurried toward the maintenance building, and Gav took off up the hillside.

Gav kept to the northwest, where he'd last seen Randolph and Marigold Green disappear into the eucalyptus grove. He figured that Randolph kept his followers well away from the main campus of the estate. The leader wouldn't want them rubbing shoulders with the visitors, at least in an uncontrolled setting.

So Gav wasn't surprised several minutes later when a grouping of a half dozen plain brick buildings loomed in the moonlight.

One building, perhaps an auditorium, was set off to one side and up against the hill. It was striking in its difference from the other, plainer structures. Its roofline spiraled toward the sky, almost as if attempting to touch another world, or perhaps to leave Planet Earth.

Randolph had stopped near the auditorium and was talking with Marigold. She was nodding earnestly, gesturing again, and holding up her hands as if describing someone's size. Probably Jacques Cousteau's.

K.C. had told him about Marigold's visiting angel, and he only hoped that the woman wasn't embellishing her story to the point of total ridicule by Randolph. Then he almost laughed. As if Randolph's belief in forty-four angels wasn't totally ridiculous. If the man believed in forty-four...why not forty-five?

A few minutes later, a robed figure emerged from one of the brick buildings and walked toward Randolph and Marigold.

Randolph stepped forward slightly and reached out to greet the newcomer...a squeeze of the hand...a gentle touch to the cheek. The newcomer's hood fell in folds onto her shoulders, and Gav recognized the face of the woman, Desirée Scott, who'd given K.C. and him their tour.

Then an introduction was made, and Desirée escorted Marigold into the brick building. The door closed behind them, and Randolph turned to walk back down the hill toward the chateau, Gav following at a distance.

Randolph headed through a maze of hedges, into the formal gardens, then down the slope leading to the sweeping lawn at the front of the chateau. Ahead, there was a series of fountains and pools that Gav had only seen from a distance. It was far enough from the entrance gate that visitors might notice it only if they approached the manor house on foot.

A tall statue rose majestically from the center of one of the pools, water spilling from a basket or tray the figure held. Its bronze surface gleamed in the moonlight. And it was directly toward that statue that the Angels Crest CEO moved at a brisk pace, his robe swishing around his ankles.

When Randolph halted in front of the fountain, Gav slipped into the shadows of the gardens.

Randolph stood before the statue in complete silence, staring up at its face. For several minutes he didn't move. Then from the direction of the front gate, a group of six men approached. They were dressed casually but carried themselves as if accustomed to being listened to and obeyed, as if accustomed to wearing Armani suits instead of Dockers, pullover sweaters, and athletic shoes.

Randolph turned toward the men. There was something about his stance, the tilt of his head, that said these were business associates, not seekers or Fellowship members.

Angels Crest board members, perhaps? Gav frowned, dismissing the idea. Why would they meet now...in the dark of night?

The men were speaking in hushed tones. Gav strained to make out the words. They were speaking a foreign language. Perhaps French. The group talked for several minutes, then headed toward the chateau. They passed within a few yards of where Gav was hiding, and he faded back into the shadows once more.

Soon they'd headed up the portico and into the house. Gav wanted to examine the statue more closely but decided it was too dangerous to leave the cover of the foliage. It held some significance, though he had no clue why. He pondered the statue again, then sprinted through the darkness toward the upper parking lot and into the eucalyptus grove.

Minutes later, he entered the clearing where K.C. was waiting. She held up a robe for him.

"Looks about right," she said with a grin. She slipped on her own robe and watched as he pulled the other over his clothing.

The K.C. he loved was back. She'd brushed her hair, removed her contact lenses, and donned the familiar tortoise-shell eyeglasses. She looked beautiful, standing there in the moonlight, even with the ridiculous Angels of Fellowship robe falling in folds from her shoulders.

"Cat got your tongue?" she said, tilting her head in the way he loved. There it was again…that word *loved!* He might as well admit it, he thought, he was discovering anew that he loved everything about K.C. Keegan.

"Wrong again, Satinka-of-the-leopardskin-coat," he countered with a grin. "I was gathering my thoughts." Then his thoughts took a serious turn, and he told her of his discovery of the auditorium, and what appeared to be dormitories, and about Randolph's strange meeting by the statue.

"It will be hard to get into the dormitories undetected," K.C. said, her concern for her aunt taking precedence over Randolph's bizarre activities.

"I agree. There are hundreds of Ataran followers on this compound—most of them living in the dorms. I'm sure any one of them would turn in their own grandmother if it meant saving Randolph from the gentiles."

"Gentiles?"

He gave her a slow smile. "That's what some cults call those outside their fold."

"I can tell by your expression that you've got a plan," she said.

"Most cults have regular times of 'mind-cleansing' activities. Usually mornings and evenings. Sometimes they last for hours, perhaps all day. I'm willing to bet that Randolph keeps a tight hold on his group and holds his gatherings every morning before they meet the public. Maybe other times during the day as well."

"In the auditorium?"

He nodded.

"You're thinking what I am?"

"You want to crash the morning party?" he asked, lifting a brow.

"I'm ready if you are, Sherlock."

Gav checked his watch. "We've got a couple hours until sunrise. I think we should get some rest. It's been a long day, and tomorrow may prove to be even longer."

K.C. yawned and agreed. "I get the presidential suite," she said and headed for one of the larger eucalyptus trees. Moments later, she'd curled up like a cat against the trunk. Her robe was carefully arranged to minimize the wrinkles.

Gav settled his back against another tree, but instead of sleeping, he kept watch over K.C. When a predawn breeze chilled the air, he knelt beside her and gently arranged the soft cotton garment around her neck and shoulders. Unable to resist, he planted a feather-light kiss on her forehead before returning to his own tree to continue his vigil.

Sunlight spilled through the trees, warming K.C.'s face, but it was the scolding of a scrub jay on a branch above her head that woke her. She blinked and rubbed her eyes, reaching around for her eyeglasses.

She finally found them and slid them onto her nose. Gav was nowhere to be found. She stood and stretched, then glanced around again.

Finally, she saw him moving surreptitiously through the grove. He grinned as he drew closer.

"Breakfast, Watson!" He held up two rolls and a couple of cartons of juice.

K.C. stretched her arms again to get out the tree-trunk-for-a-pillow stiffness and smiled as she reached for her roll and drink. "How did you manage this?"

"I was very observant the day we visited the culinary arts school. As you will recall, I asked to see the kitchen—"

"Good thinking, Sherlock. Here I thought you were going to take up gourmet cooking."

"I noticed a large walk-in refrigerator. I also spent quite a bit of time near one of the dining-room windows last night."

"Was it just last night? Seems like a week ago," she said, munching on her roll.

"Anyway, I figured out how the latch worked while I was watching you drink your private reserve cabernet. I returned to the scene of the crime just before dawn, and, well,…the rest is history."

"I think I got the better end of the bargain," she said lightly, lifting her plastic juice container as if in a toast. "Ah, the bouquet. The color. It's exquisite."

"Not to mention the legs," he added with a grin. "Loved those lines, Kace." He lifted his own juice toward her with a nod.

"Gav—?" she said after a minute. "Thanks for helping me laugh." He smiled, understanding, just as she knew he would. "I would either be shaking in my boots because of what we've gotten ourselves into, or I'd be weeping with fear for Aunt Theo."

"I know, Kace," he said simply.

What she didn't say was that their laughter brought its own heartache. It was too familiar, too wonderful. And she didn't want to consider that when this was all over, she'd miss it— miss him—terribly.

It was nearing seven o'clock when they heard voices

through the trees. Though they were a distance from any of the footpaths, they rose quickly and, gathering their things, slipped deeper into the thick eucalyptus grove.

"I wonder if it's time for their meeting." K.C. whispered.

"I was thinking the same thing. Are you ready?"

She nodded, her heart beginning to tap out a nervous dance inside her rib cage. "We've got to be careful, Gav. We've got to look just like them, act like them, do and say what they do…"

"Can you do that?"

"I don't know. You?" She pictured the Israelites' golden calf.

"There are limits—no matter the cause," he said, as if picturing the same idol.

"I know."

"We'll need to split up so we can search for Theo, once we're inside."

"I thought of that, too," she agreed. "It's the only way. Plus we may not stand out quite so readily."

"If one of us gets caught—no word about the other."

"That's understood," she said. "If I'm the one caught, you need to know where I've hidden the phone."

He frowned as if he didn't want to consider the thought. "Where is it?"

"I hid it in the presidential suite," she said, grinning. "There's quite a nice hollow inside that old tree. Also, save my bag if anything happens. I went through quite a lot to retrieve it last night."

"I promise," Gav said and took K.C.'s arm to escort her up the hillside. Just before they reached the top, he halted and turned toward her. He lifted her hood and pulled it close to her face. His touch was tender. So was the look in his eyes.

"Better pull yours up, too, Sherlock," she said lightly as she took a few steps backward.

He arranged his hood, also pulled low to hide his features. "Here we go," he said.

At the top of the hillside the devotees had congregated in the open area between the brick dormitory buildings and the auditorium with its odd spiral design.

She met Gav's gaze, and he gave her a barely perceptible nod. Heads bowed and hands folded piously, they slipped from the grove of trees and, going their separate ways, quickly mingled within the maze created by the crowd.

A bell rang from down the hillside. Probably the chateau, K.C. thought, and the crowd queued before the entrance of the auditorium. Moments later, K.C. filed inside with three other women. They didn't so much as glance her direction, and she breathed a sigh of relief. She only hoped she could quickly find a place and sit down so her shaking knees wouldn't give her away.

But there were no chairs in the long room, and the devotees arranged themselves in long rows, standing. K.C. stepped into an appropriate place toward the back of the room.

As soon as she felt safe to do so, K.C. stole a glimpse of the stained-glass windows that lined the tops of the tall side walls. Designs of angels of every description, in every jeweled color, cast colored light on the pale robes of the devotees. The effect was stunning.

First came a hush, and the devotees bowed their heads. Then came the sounds of drums playing from the rear of the room.

All that could be heard now was a low, rhythmic, pulsating beat.

The volume rose. K.C. tried to keep from turning around and gaping. She could have sworn the drums were straight from some steaming, torrid jungle.

Next came the dramatic entrance of the guru himself, Rance

Randolph, in a pale metallic gold robe similar in design to those worn by his followers. He held up his arms and began to chant. And sway, his eyes closed. His face filled with emotion. "Atara. Atara. Atara."

Voices around K.C. lifted in a silky chorus, chanting to the beat of the drum. Eyes closed. Bodies swaying, dancing.

K.C. lifted her arms to a halfhearted half-staff, and she gently swayed her way through the crowd, heading toward a pillar in the back of the room, hoping she'd be hidden enough not to be obvious.

But she soon discovered she needn't have worried. No one was paying any attention to her. K.C. became bolder and swayed her way up the aisle a few rows, behind some members who were dancing. As she moved, she glanced into the faces of the followers, trying not to be obvious but searching each drooped hood for Aunt Theo's beloved face.

K.C. moved toward the platform where Randolph, eyes closed, was still piously lifting his arms in praise of the Ataran angels. Frantically, she continued searching for Aunt Theo. Every small robed figure with an erect carriage of shoulders and chin caught her attention. But there was no sign of Theodora.

She wondered if Gav was having any success and glanced across the room to see if she could spot him. But he'd disappeared in the crowd.

Just then, Randolph raised his hand to still the drums. K.C. quickly slipped into the row nearest where she was standing. She was too close to the platform for comfort, so she slid her hand discreetly toward her temple and pulled her hood closer to her forehead.

"Brothers and sisters," Randolph said, his voice adopting a tone that seemed to K.C. a practiced mix of reverence and power. "We have an extraordinary visitor with us this morning."

Again, a hush of expectation fell across the room.

He smiled, nodding at a few individuals in the congregation as his gaze skirted several rows from the front of the room to the back. K.C. held her breath as he turned her direction.

His gaze seemed to linger on her face for an instant before moving on to others in her row.

"Dear ones," he continued. "We have had a miraculous visit by an angel of Atara." There were gasps of wonder throughout the room. He smiled again and nodded. "Yes, it's true," he said. "But rather than a secondhand report, let me introduce you to the unlikely visitor in our midst—a woman whose life has been radically changed by what she saw, by what she experienced."

He looked to the right of the platform, offstage, and nodded; at the same time, he lifted one hand dramatically. "Sister Marigold," he said in an awe-filled voice. "Dear Sister, please, come tell your new brothers and sisters about your encounter...and about your new quest for higher consciousness."

Marigold Green, dressed in a shimmering white robe, rushed onto the stage, smiling and bobbing her head toward the audience. She too wore the practiced beatific smile that seemed to afflict most of the fellowship members. Surprising how quickly she picked up Randolph's affectations.

Marigold lifted her arms and tilted her face skyward. For a moment she didn't utter a word, just stood, looking for the life of her like an angel with a message.

Marigold's gaze moved across the devotees until she spotted K.C. After an almost imperceptible nod, she folded her hands and stepped into a shaft of sunlight streaming onto the platform. Her robe, made from some synthetic gossamer material, shimmered and danced as if on fire.

When she finally spoke it was in a fervent tone. "Brothers

and sisters," she said quietly and as if perfectly sincere, "listen to this miracle…this message from Atara.

"Once it was on a mission to destroy the Angels of Fellowship. It was so certain your leader was a fraud, that it was relentless in its pursuit to expose his wicked ways. It posted messages on the Internet. It told everyone it knew." Marigold laughed lightly, shaking her head as if in awe at her own ignorance. A top performance, K.C. thought, though still nervous that the woman might get caught up in her own acting success and go over the top, as Gav had so appropriately put it.

"But my dears, as often is the case," Marigold continued, "those who shout the loudest against something they don't understand later make the most sincere converts."

Her voice dropped, and she lifted her folded hands into place beneath her chin. It was a pose calculated to express deep earnestness. "You see, it was visited last night by an angel, an Ataran angel."

There was a buzz of speculation among the devotees. Marigold held up a hand to quiet the group. "There is a forty-fifth angel, an angel who's been sent to save our planet from destruction."

Marigold launched into a tirade against pollution. K.C. thought of Gav's warning as Marigold's voice rose to a fevered pitch, and she shook her fist at the sky. But no one sensed anything was amiss; her audience was completely engrossed.

"You see," she concluded, "it was told that it's because of the way we've treated our earth and our seas that the meteorite is heading our direction. The angel, the forty-fifth angel, Jacques-Yves Cousteau, visited this humble being just last night." She went on to describe in great detail everything about the angel's appearance, his demeanor, his voice, his words—even his French accent.

She paused dramatically, taking a deep breath. "His message

to each of us, devoted Angels of Fellowship, is to become hypervigilant in our watch for the end times. The millennium is coming. We must pay attention to what we are told."

Nicely done, K.C. thought. Marigold didn't dare say anything negative about Randolph, but she may have planted thoughts some of the devotees might later consider.

Just as K.C. let out a sigh, relieved the woman had nearly finished carrying off her mission, Marigold stood tall, her chin in the air, her broad shoulders back; she let her hood fall away from her spiked hair.

"Now that it has said all that," she said, her voice carrying through the large room, "let me tell you what it really thinks."

From where he was standing slightly to one side and behind Marigold, Randolph looked up in surprise. He started forward as if to stop her from speaking, then seemed to think better of it. Arms crossed at his chest, he stroked his beard with one hand, his vulpine eyes on Marigold's back. His narrow face wore the thin-lipped, frightening look that K.C. remembered from her evening with him.

"Let me tell you what it really thinks!" Marigold repeated in a loud cry. Her face was flushed now and alive with animation.

This time, Randolph didn't wait. He stepped to one side of Marigold. The guard from the front gate entered the platform from the other side.

Marigold glanced from one to the other, then, smiling, held up her hand. "Let this humble being finish," she said.

NINETEEN

The hundreds of devotees glanced at each other as if alarmed by Marigold's announcement, and there was some uneasy shuffling about.

In a heartbeat, Gav was standing next to K.C. He glanced toward the exit, a silent signal that they needed to leave as quickly as possible. K.C. was poised and ready to move, but she remained as still as a statue, watching the interaction on the platform. Gav was doing the same.

Marigold was still planted in the shaft of sunlight, a smile of rapture on her broad face, her hand held skyward. Even Randolph stood quietly to one side, allowing her to go on, though his pale eyes were watchful.

"You see, this Ataran believes that the angel Jacques Cousteau came to tell me the secret for saving our planet." There was murmuring among the devotees, and K.C. held her breath, afraid to consider what might next fall from Marigold's mouth. "Yes, yes," she went on excitedly, "our planet can avoid disaster if each of us will return to our homes to pay attention to the ecology of our neighborhoods…if we will work to save our live oaks from bark beetles…if we will use biodegradable detergents…if we will separate our trash…if we will use cloth diapers." She launched into a tirade against the use of disposable diapers, citing the tons of refuse they generated each day and the thousands of years it would take the plastics to disintegrate.

K.C. fought to keep from meeting Gav's glance and rolling her eyes. All around them, however, the devotees looked at each other, puzzled, and their voices soon rose in a muffled hubbub. Beside K.C., Gav groaned under his breath. "I knew she would shoot herself in the foot," he muttered.

"She's trying to get people out of the compound," K.C. whispered. "It's probably the only way she could think of."

"More likely, she was hoping to get help for her 'save-the-earth' projects back in Pelican Cove."

"That, too," K.C. shot back, picturing the robed devotees holding tape measures around live oaks while Marigold snapped pictures, documenting their growth.

Now, very smoothly, with a fixed smile above the goatee, Randolph stepped forward. "These are wonderful considerations, Sister Marigold," he said. "But they're not exactly what the angel told you, is that correct?"

"It believes our deity wants us to have minds of our own," she countered.

Ignoring her, Randolph looked out at the followers, clearly taking charge. "Sisters and brothers," he said. "Our novice clearly has much to learn about our place on Earth, where we are but sojourners.

"Sometimes in our exuberance we misread our mission. We misunderstand the message." His smile faded. "Make no mistake, my friends, in the deep heavens of Atara, where the angels await our arrival, there has been no error. There is no saving our planet. It is too late."

K.C. shuddered, aware of his true message. There would be no deterring this maniac, not even Marigold's communication from an Ataran angel, in which he claimed to believe.

Randolph continued talking, convincing his followers of the coming "journey of joy," and, while pretending to listen, K.C. considered what Marigold had attempted. Then her thoughts settled on the leader and his motivations.

As K.C. watched this master manipulator perform, she

became convinced that he didn't believe one bit of what he was expounding to his followers.

Why would he allow a newcomer to speak in front of the group? Did he really believe her story? Did he think her conjured-up visit from Jacques Cousteau would help him convince the group of some convoluted truth?

It was more likely, K.C. decided, that he didn't believe her story. If that was the case, why did he allow her to tell his devotees a story he knew to be fabricated? How did he think she had escaped from the caves?

Suddenly, it occurred to her that perhaps he was aware of Gav's and her presence. A cold, raw fear crept up her spine. Had he known all along?

She licked her dry lips and let out a deep cleansing breath, trying to calm her pounding heart. She tried not to consider that they were in much greater danger than she'd thought.

Randolph's eyes seemed to bore into her soul. He knew her! She was sure of it.

In a sudden burst of clarity, she understood him. He was playing a game, a dangerous game, with them all. He was king; his followers, even she and Gav, were his pawns.

Her attention turned back to his words as he discussed the day's business of dealing with the chateau's visitors and the new wines they were to introduce, and finally he went over the details of the grape harvest.

"This is our time of year to celebrate," he said, his voice heavy with meaning. "When the harvest of the first vineyard is completed, we will celebrate in a way we've never celebrated before."

There were murmurs of speculation, but he held up his hand to silence the group.

"You see," he said, smiling broadly. "I have an announcement to make." Then he looked down at a woman in one of the front rows. "Sister Desirée," he said, "Would you join me?" The same woman, K.C. remembered, had escorted Gav and her to Randolph's office.

The woman moved down the row of standing robed figures and stepped onto the raised platform. When she turned, K.C. was surprised at the look on her face. She seemed drawn and pale, almost fearful. But she smiled up into Randolph's face. It was as if she had no choice.

He took her hand and kissed her fingertips. "Sisters and brothers, at this year's harvest celebration, we will also celebrate the occasion of my marriage to Sister Desirée Scott." The king had taken a queen, and their pawns broke out in applause. Randolph's narrow face again twisted into a smile. "It will indeed be a time to rejoice!" he said to them all, but it was K.C.'s upturned face on which his gaze rested. "There will be further disclosures as we approach that day of celebration," he said as if speaking to K.C. alone.

K.C. was almost afraid to breathe.

Finally, he began a closing chant, this time without the accompaniment of beating drums, and Desirée lifted her voice with his. Soon the others joined in and the room reverberated with the low, mellow chorus of voices. After a few minutes, Randolph ceremoniously swept down the center aisle. In a place of honor at his side was Desirée Scott.

Walking directly behind them was Marigold Green, chin tilted skyward, eyelids piously half-closed.

The field workers were the first to be dismissed, then row by row, the others were allowed to file from the auditorium. At the rear doors, Randolph and Desirée stood to one side, greeting followers with a handshake. Opposite was a serene-looking Marigold, greeting those queued on her side.

Still shaken by the wordless encounter with Randolph, K.C. inched her way forward, being careful to keep to the right side of the double line. Finally, she was standing before Marigold. Ever the actress, the woman didn't change her expression. She just reached for K.C.'s hands, squeezed them sincerely. But when Marigold pulled back her hand to greet Gav who was standing directly behind K.C., she'd left a small piece of paper in K.C.'s palm.

As they mingled with the crowd outside, K.C. and Gav made their way toward the grove of eucalyptus trees. Still sheltered by the robed followers who were scurrying to their jobs in the fields or in the chateau, K.C. chanced a glimpse at the small, torn piece of paper.

Go to the vineyard in the northernmost part of the property. Be there within the next fifteen minutes, prepared to work. You must first pick up a grape tray and gloves from the truck parked nearby. Avoid the supervisor who will be at the far end of the vineyard.

It was signed with a scrawling "MG."

K.C. and Gav had now moved into the cover of the thick grove, and she handed the paper to Gav.

"Do you think it has to do with Theo?" he asked after scanning it.

She nodded. "I can't imagine why else Marigold would take the trouble."

"Then you'd better go," he said, touching her shoulder.

She could see his worry. "Our search may be over," she said. "We can get to Aunt Theo, grab Marigold, and be out of here."

He met her eyes without comment.

"You're thinking what I am, aren't you?" She could see it in his face.

"If you're thinking we can't leave the rest here to blindly follow Randolph to their deaths—then yes, as usual, we're on the same wavelength." He didn't look away from her. "But K.C., you saw them in there today. He's got them so convinced that he's right."

"Yet there's something wrong with his reasoning..." she began.

Gav let out a short laugh. "There's a lot wrong with his reasoning."

"No, I don't mean the obvious," K.C. said. "There's something else. It's as if he doesn't believe his own doctrine. I could see it when Marigold spoke. He didn't believe her story any more than you or I did."

"So there was some other reason for him to put her on stage."

K.C. agreed. "But I can't figure out why—unless he's playing some bizarre game with us."

"Game?"

"I think he knows we're here, Gav. I sense it. The way he seemed to be watching me..."

He looked thoughtful. "I noticed it, too. But we have no evidence. Besides, if he knows we're here, why wouldn't he come after us...search the compound? Be done with it."

"Have you ever seen a cat tease a June bug...play with it until it's dead?"

"I don't know, Kace. Why would he jeopardize his plans for the Angels of Fellowship?"

"Megalomaniacs are like that. They don't think anyone, anything, can take away their power. In fact, he may be getting a rush out of the chase."

"The one thing I did figure out," Gav said, "was his timetable. He may be taunting us with the information—daring us to try to stop him."

"The wedding...the harvest celebration...is the date he's chosen—"K.C. choked on the words, thinking how he watched her—"for the mass suicide. And, if we're right, he's counting on us to lose the game. We'll be part of the 'celebration.'"

"There's too much that ties it together," Gav said, again frowning. "There's just one thing I can't figure out."

"The wedding?"

"Right, again, Watson." Gav grinned, attempting to cheer her up. "Why would he marry if he's planning to die with the rest?"

The realization struck K.C. at the same time Gav spoke the words. "Of course," she said. "That's what hasn't made sense. You're right. He's not planning to die. It's not in his eyes...that look of hopelessness...the way it is in the others'."

"I'll do some snooping around his office while you're gone, Kace. See if I can find something that will give us a clue." He hesitated. "I think the men I saw him meet last night have something to do with all this."

"Be careful, Gav." She resisted the urge to touch his cheek. "Remember the phone's in the tree, if you need it—though its battery may be running low by now." She started up the hillside, then hesitated, looking back. "I'm as dedicated to getting everyone out as you are," she called out in a loud whisper. "I'm here for the duration—game or not, pawn or not."

He gave her a half-smile and a salute. "Be on your way now, Watson. If it's Theo you're about to meet—"

"—I'll give her your love, Gav," she finished.

"You always did finish my sentences," he muttered good-naturedly.

Still smiling, she gave him a wave, then headed through the eucalyptus trees.

~ ~ ~ ~ ~

Theodora bent low over the vine, pulled back a glossy leaf, and carefully clipped off a thick cluster of grapes from underneath. The sun beat on her shoulders as she worked, and she prayed, just as she did every day while she labored in the vineyard.

This morning she lifted Desirée before God and prayed for her continued strength of spirit. Though Theodora still feared that Desirée might betray her, she had placed Desirée in God's hands. Theodora's prayer was that her every word and action would be God-breathed…and that the needy woman would see a glimpse of her Savior in Theodora's life.

Amazingly, since Theodora's arrival, Desirée hadn't been the only devotee to notice her spirit of love. Others had sought her out to talk, and often just to spend time in her presence. Every morning she prayed for each by name. Especially she prayed that the day would come when they would walk away from Angels Crest free of the spirit of captivity that bound them.

But it would take a miracle, she acknowledged, because evil was strong in this place. She was fully aware that if her Lord asked her to sacrifice her life on behalf of the others, she would give her life. Though she would tremble, she would do whatever her Lord required.

Father, thank you for bringing me here, she prayed as she snipped another clump of grapes. She lifted her face to the sun, and for a moment, breathed in the fragrance of the rich soil and the sweet fruit. *This is not a place I would have chosen, yet you have sent me and have equipped me with the power of your deep love for each of these, your children.*

Give me strength for today. Equip me with wisdom to help those who will cross my path. Let me love them with your love, your heart, your hands, your voice. She cut off another long cluster of grapes, placed it in the tray, then reached for another. She let her thoughts rest on each woman, each man she'd met at Angels Crest. She mentioned them by name to her Savior, thinking how he'd known them—and loved them—since the beginning of time.

Again, she pulled back a thicket of leaves and reached for the grape cluster beneath it. She looked at her tanned forearm, glad it had become stronger and no longer ached as it did during her first few days.

"I am yours, my Father," she breathed. "I give you this day!"

Theodora was so intent in her prayers and meditations that she didn't glance up as a robed figure moved into the row opposite her. She heard only the snipping of clusters being removed from their vines and the ruffling of leaves in the morning breeze, almost a background chorus for the words she was lifting heavenward.

"Aunt Theo!" came the loud whisper.

Theodora looked up, blinking in surprise. "K.C.—?" There was her grandniece's sweet grinning face with its beautiful tortoiseshell eyeglasses atop that pixie nose. "Oh, my!" was about all she could manage as she stared lovingly at K.C.

Then she caught herself, and glanced around to make sure they weren't being watched. Sister Vesta was a distance away and busy harassing some of the other workers.

"How in the world did you get here?" Theodora asked. "How did you know where I'd gone?"

K.C. laughed lightly, though she quickly stooped to lop off another large cluster of grapes. "It wasn't easy, Aunt Theo! You didn't leave us much of a trail," she whispered.

"Us?"

"Gav and me."

"Aha." In spite of all the danger, Theodora felt like dancing.

"No, not 'aha,' in the way you think," K.C. whispered quickly with a scowl. "You've just got all the people who love you working together—even Father Max."

"Max is here?" Theodora pushed aside some leaves, then tenderly lifted a long clump of grapes into place for cutting. What she wouldn't give for just a glimpse of his merry eyes or to hear the musical cadence of his voice.

"He's at your cabin—but he helped Gav break in here last night." K.C. paused, working furiously as Sister Vesta strolled by the end of the row. When the woman had passed, K.C. said, "We've got to get you out, Aunt Theo. Tonight. Gav's got a plan."

Theodora shook her head quickly. "I can't leave, sweetie. Do you know what Randolph's leading his group toward?"

"Yes. It's pretty evident," K.C. said, her hooded head still bent over the vines. "How long do you think we've got until he tries to pull it off?"

"The rumor is that it will take place when this harvest is over. And that will be soon," Theodora whispered back.

"He's a time bomb, Aunt Theo. He may act immediately if he thinks we're on to him. Or if he senses that the authorities might become involved."

Sister Vesta strolled nearby once again, and the two women bent over their work, deftly and quickly cutting the grape clusters from the vines and laying them in the trays.

K.C.'s voice turned solemn. "Hundreds of people could lose their lives if he gives the signal."

Theodora nodded sadly. "That's why I can't leave. I must do what I can to get others out."

"Are there people here we can trust?" K.C. asked, snipping away a small branch so she could better reach the grapes beyond. The women moved a few feet down the row, and began their cutting again.

"A few," she said. "Desirée Scott is one who has access to a lot of information."

K.C. looked alarmed. "I heard the announcement of their marriage this morning. Can you trust her?"

"I'm not sure. She's torn between what she knows is right and what she thinks her heart is telling her to do."

K.C. looked thoughtful. "You're in a dangerous position, aren't you, Aunt Theo? Not knowing whom to trust, who might turn against you?"

"God is with me, K.C.—as much here as he is at home. Although sometimes he feels even closer," she mused. "I feel his touch in every breeze, hear his voice in the rustling trees or in the call of a bird." She laughed lightly. "Now you'll think I've gone batty."

But K.C.'s look told her she didn't think that at all. "He knows you need him here more than ever. Nothing batty about that at all."

"I can't help thinking he's brought me to Angels Crest for a purpose. That's another reason for not leaving. It's where he wants me to be." She smiled gently, not wanting K.C. to think she was ungrateful for the daring rescue attempt.

K.C. nodded, clearly understanding. "Gav and I were talking about the same thing a few minutes ago," she said. "We've decided we can't leave either."

A deep and sudden fear stabbed at Theodora's heart. It was one thing to be willing to sacrifice her own life. But her precious grandniece's life? Gav's? That's where her commitment faltered, though she didn't let on.

"Welcome to Angels Crest, K.C.," she said after a moment, and she reached through the heavy-laden vines to touch her niece's fingertips. For a moment, the two women stood without moving, gazing at each other. "I know it's selfish of me, sweetie...but I'm so glad you're here."

"I wouldn't have it any other way, Aunt Theo. Neither would Gav."

We're so alike, thought Theodora, with pride, noting the stubborn set of K.C.'s chin, the determined gleam in her eyes. *Nothing—no one—can deter us from the course we've set. Not even Rance Randolph.*

TWENTY

Gav removed his robe and stuffed it in K.C.'s tree, then trailed a group of visitors taking the Angels Crest tour. Minutes later, he joined still another group, walked with them into the chateau as far as Angels Repose. He asked the tour guide if the group might be privileged to meet the CEO, and feigned disappointment when they were told that unfortunately Rance Randolph was speaking to a group of distinguished restaurateurs at the culinary arts center.

So as his group milled about at Angels Repose, sampling fine wines and perusing Angels of Fellowship propaganda, he slipped from the room and back toward the entrance hall, then headed toward the stairs at the rear of the manor.

Gav was growing more suspicious by the hour at the ease with which he and K.C. were able to move about the compound. K.C.'s worries about Randolph and his games were not so far-fetched. He supposed the chateau was as heavily guarded as Fort Knox, yet here he was, climbing empty stairs to the third floor and striding down a deserted hall to Randolph's office. Even the CEO's outer office was vacant.

Many of the Fellowship members were giving tours, he reasoned, and others were busy with the harvest. As he moved down the hallway a strange notion came over him that he was indeed being watched. Perhaps baited.

He tried the door, found it locked, and pulled a credit card from his wallet. After a glance around, he determined there were no surveillance cameras, at least that he could see, and certainly no devotees lurking about. He inserted the plastic card into the space between the door and its jamb, clicked it once, twice, then on the third try the door swung open.

Gav glanced about the room, quickly assessing the business end of the large room. He didn't flip on the lights; sunlight streamed into the office through the French doors, spilling onto the highly polished wood floors and Chinese rugs.

He strode to the desk and riffled through the papers on top. He was acutely aware of the trouble he'd be in should he be discovered—not only from Randolph, but also from his peers. Essentially, he was conducting a search without a warrant.

But hundreds of lives were at stake. The clock continued to tick. This was no time to worry about protocol.

He found nothing incriminating on Randolph's desk, though he hadn't expected to. Next he slid open the drawers, one at a time, rapidly thumbing through files and legal-size notepads. Still nothing.

He heard voices in the hall and froze, listening carefully until they passed. When it was quiet again, he opened another drawer. Nothing. At right angles to the desk was a matching oak credenza. He quickly slid open the slim doors and checked the contents. More folders were arranged in a very precise manner in slotted polished oak drawers, two deep in three rows.

Gav pulled out the first drawer, scanning the file names. Everything from résumés for culinary arts academy chefs to recommendations for wine label designers.

He tried the second drawer. Then the third, quickly scanning, aware that Rance Randolph could return at any moment. He riffled through the tops of the folders with his fingertips and had almost reached the end, when a file name caught his attention: *Keb-Kaseko Rodolphe*. It might not tell him anything about the men who'd met Randolph at the fountain, but nonetheless he was curious about the supposedly world-acclaimed vintner and his connection to Angels Crest.

He lifted the thick manila folder from the drawer and started to scan its contents.

Just then, the sound of approaching voices carried toward him from the hallway. They drew closer, and Gav caught his breath, wondering if this time they were headed into the office.

He couldn't take the chance that they might pass by. He quickly pushed in the drawers and closed the credenza's sliding doors. Keeping to the quiet of the Chinese carpet, he hurried past the plush sitting area to the French doors at the far end of the room.

The voices were louder now. He recognized Randolph's pious tones. A higher-pitched female voice was talking with him.

Gav tried the brass handle. It seemed to be locked from the outside. He pushed harder. Still it wouldn't budge. He glanced frantically around for another place to hide. There was nothing.

The voices were closer. He heard the door to the outer office open and footsteps approaching Randolph's inner sanctum.

His heart beating rapidly, Gav tried the door once more. This time he pressed the handle downward with his thumb, jiggled it slightly to the left, and the lock released. He moved silently through the doorway, closing it behind him.

Pressing his body flat against the outside wall, Gav breathed a prayer that Randolph would not pick this time to catch a bit of fresh air on his balcony. He also hoped that the CEO wouldn't suddenly find need of the Rodolphe folder Gav still clutched in his hand.

The voices drew close enough for Gav to overhear snatches of conversation, but Randolph and his guest seemed to have stopped at the sitting area. Gav sidled closer to the glass doors.

"It is certain the woman is the one you're looking for," said the female voice. Randolph said something in reply that Gav couldn't catch, then the woman spoke again. "She was picking opposite Theodora Whimple."

"You let them speak?" Randolph asked.

"Of course, it thought you said..." Again, Gav couldn't make out the words.

"Was the man anywhere near?" At least Randolph didn't expect Gav to be in his office.

There was a mumbling reply, then Randolph asked, "Is the woman now in the vineyard?"

"Yes," the woman said clearly. "She was still conversing with the Whimple woman..."

"I want you to return immediately," Randolph said, then his voice dropped. Gav leaned closer to the door but was unable to hear the rest. If he was a cursing man, now would be the time for it, he thought grimly. Instead, he glanced around, trying to remain calm as he looked for a way of escape. He had to get to K.C.!

The balcony overlooked the formal English gardens on one side, and on the other, the estate's century oak, an ancient, gnarled tree that leaned precariously toward the chateau.

Narrowing his eyes, he calculated the distance. If he could slip past the glass doors, he might be able to swing onto one of the branches and shimmy down the tree. A great plan if he wasn't seen either from Randolph's office or from the ground.

The sounds of voices inside continued. Gav could hear only faint murmurings now; mostly it was Randolph speaking, and he sounded agitated. It seemed they might be moving away from the sitting area, possibly toward the desk and credenza. Again, he hoped that Randolph wouldn't notice anything amiss on his desk or in his files.

Finally it was quiet, and he heard the soft thud of the office door as it closed. He waited several minutes before moving closer to the French doors. When at last he thought it was safe, he peered through. The room was empty.

Breathing a sigh of relief, he opened the glass-paned door, only to hear the murmuring of voices continuing in the outer office.

He quickly stepped backwards onto the balcony, this time to the opposite side of the French doors—across from the century oak. A quick glance at the grounds told him no one strolled nearby. He tucked the file folder into his shirt, then hoisted himself to the balcony railing.

Seconds later, he was scrambling downward from branch to heavy branch, hiding in the thick foliage and keeping to the outside of the tree away from the scrutiny of anyone inside the chateau who might happen to glance out the windows.

Finally he sprang to the ground. He quickly rounded the corner and strolled into the formal gardens just as a new group of tourists arrived. With a benign smile plastered on his face and a few interested nods, he trailed along as they headed to the old cellar and underground caves. When they were lined up and ready to move inside, he stepped into a nearby oleander thicket. As soon as the door of the cellar banged shut, Gav moved into the eucalyptus grove and sprinted to the area where he and K.C. had agreed to meet.

K.C. looked up as Gav headed through the trees, his face etched with worry.

"Thank God," he said, coming toward her, "You're safe!" Without hesitation he folded her into his arms. "Oh, K.C.," he murmured into her hair.

Her heart beat wildly from his nearness, but she gently pushed away from him. His face was pale, and she sensed his fear for her. "What's wrong, Gav? What did you think had happened?"

He explained about what he'd overheard from the chateau balcony. "I don't know what he's got planned, Kace. But from the snatches of conversation, I think he's about to start a search for you. He sent the woman back to the vineyard to get you."

K.C. took a deep breath, feeling her knees giving out, and settled onto a nearby stump. "So, we were right. Randolph not only knows we're here, we've let him pull us into some bizarre game."

"A deadly game. And from what I picked up, he also knows your—*our*—connection to Theo."

K.C. told him what Theodora had heard about the security guard's stash of weapons. "Even in the shadow of the Waco tragedy, should we call for help—your deputy, the FBI?" She paused, considering their options. "Father Max?" she added, thinking of his wisdom and courage. How they could use his help right now!

Gav leaned against a tree across from her, his eyes narrowed in thought. "As long as there's a chance to save even one of the Fellowship members, maybe we should wait." His eyes met hers, and the depth of emotion she saw in them caught her off guard. "It's you I worry about, though, Kace. You and Theo."

Looking away from his face before his expression of love melted her resolve, melted her heart, K.C. thought about what her aunt had said about being where God wanted her.

"I've had such a skewed idea of ministry," she mused after a moment, speaking more to herself than to Gav. "Aunt Theo said she's exactly where God wants her to be. She says he brought her here."

K.C. turned back to Gav, again meeting his eyes. "She said she's never felt more alive—even in the face of the danger, the threat of losing her own life."

"That's what ministry should be," Gav added softly. "Giving your life for others."

"My motivation was to come here to find Theo. But now I've decided if she can't leave, neither can I."

"Or call in the troops for help?"

She shook her head. "He's as crazy—or crazier—than David Koresh. None of his followers would have a chance to escape."

"None of *us*, K.C.," he corrected gently. "Because of his crazy, deadly sport, we're his prey; we're also part of this Fellowship. If they die—"

"—we die," she finished. "Unless we beat him at his own game."

He gave her a halfhearted grin. "There you go again—"

"—finishing your sentences?" she said, attempting to raise his spirits.

"I'd love to give you a hug," he said, standing and opening his arms. "Will you let me?"

This time K.C. took the few steps toward him and circled her arms around his neck; they stood holding each other as if tomorrow's dawn might not come. She closed her eyes and shut out the world and everything in it, good and bad, except for the wonder of being held by the man she had loved, it seemed, forever.

Suddenly she pulled back, frowning up at him and tapping her fingernail against something beneath his shirt that felt like cardboard.

"I wasn't able to find exactly what I was looking for," Gav explained, pulling out a file folder. "There wasn't time. But I did come across this file. I hadn't planned to take it, but there wasn't time to put it back."

K.C. settled onto the stump again and Gav sat next to her, opening the folder.

"Keb-Kaseko Rodolphe," she read aloud, scanning the file name over his shoulder. "World-famous vintner, and the man who got us all involved in this cat-and-mouse game."

The moment she said the words, she looked up at Gav in wonder. "That's it!" she said, then added, "I think."

Gav frowned. "That's what?"

"Rodolphe. I don't know why I didn't think of it before. Isn't that the French version of Randolph?"

"Not exactly, but they've got the same Latin root."

"How do you know all this stuff?" K.C. said with admiration.

"Latin was required in seminary, as you remember."

The earlier moments that had opened her heart to let in warmth and light suddenly vaporized. "I remember," she muttered.

He ignored her comment. "Anyway, they're from the same root. Randolph is Old English, meaning 'shield-wolf,' and Rodolphe is the French version of the Old German word for 'famous wolf,' Rudolph."

She put aside her personal feelings and instead concentrated on what he was saying. "Could that be a clue?"

"You're thinking it's one and the same. He's both individuals."

"I am indeed," she said. She stood and paced as she spoke. "Think of it, Gav. He can be anyone he wants on the Internet. He can put out any information he'd like as this world-famous vintner. Either of his identities can give the other acclaim...acclaim that strikes the casual observer as legitimate." She was thinking out loud. "And right now, wine is a hot commodity. The industry has grown tremendously in the last few years."

She could see in Gav's eyes that he was right there with her. She hurried on. "It's the yuppies and Generation X'ers who get pulled into materialistic fads—from requiring a cappuccino bar on every corner to attending designer wine and cheese parties. We're also the ones who have lost our moral moorings. The world seems a desperate place, and we're desperate for answers.

"What better place to offer solutions? What better place than right here?" She gestured toward the chateau grounds. "It's beautiful. It's part of a culture that these generations understand—the love of gourmet food, fine wines, classical music, and the intellectual pursuit of life's meaning—all right here. It's a place where crime and poverty can be shut outside the gates, almost as if they no longer matter, or perhaps don't even exist."

She frowned in thought. "Once they're here, he manipulates them by using their fears of all that's outside these gates, also of what he tells them is coming. The meteorite is probably only one of many fears." She shook her head slowly. "I can't help thinking it's like shut-ins who watch nothing but the local news or airplane disasters and use that 'reality' as their measure of life. A very frightening life outside the confines of their home."

She walked back toward Gav. "And this guru, this Keb-Kaseko Rodolphe, is part of this pseudo-culture Randolph is holding out as his net." She sat next to him again. "He's a father-figure who offers safety behind his gates. That's part of the net, too."

Gav nodded slowly. "The net that pulls in his prey."

"For his game," K.C. said, shuddering.

"But we're back to why," Gav said thoughtfully. "We've already determined that he doesn't intend to die with the others." He paused. "Yet he's duped them into believing in another universe, the planet Atara, its angels." He shook his head. "These are intelligent people. It's one thing to come to the Fellowship for this culture or safety he offers. But I don't understand how they can believe this other idiocy."

"Other major cults believe people will become gods in another life. It's not unusual for intelligent people to put aside their ability to reason—just because their egos can't pass up the opportunity to someday shine like the stars." K.C. took a deep breath. "But we come back to the question...*why?* Why is Randolph—or Rodolphe—going to all this trouble? For what gain...aside from the sport of it?"

"Maybe this will tell us." Gav had been thumbing through the papers in the file as they talked, but now gave them his full attention.

He handed half the stack to K.C., and she began scanning each handwritten or computer-printed sheet. Most were drafts of articles supposedly written by Rodolphe, covering everything from making traditional Spanish sherries to determining the proper time to harvest grapes by testing their sugar-to-acid ratio.

"Anything?" Gav asked absently.

"Nah, just a fascinating article on how they make sherries the old-fashioned way in Spain."

Gav shook his head as he came to the bottom of his stack of papers. "I really wasn't expecting miracles here, but I'd hoped for something. Anything. A clue. No matter how obscure."

"Wait a minute, Gav," K.C. said as one of the handwritten legal sheets caught her attention. "Take a look at this."

Gav scanned the paper she handed him. "It's in Spanish."

"So's this one. And this..." she held up a few more hand-written pages, all toward the bottom of the stack. According to their dates, they were the most recent additions to the folder.

"I don't read Spanish, Kace. Last I remembered, neither do you."

"That's not the point, Sherlock," she said. "Maybe I'm grasping at straws here, but what are the reasons someone might suddenly start writing in Spanish?"

He raised an eyebrow. "To use it as a code? Or maybe to keep prying eyes from knowing what's written here?" He gave her a half grin. "Hey, I'm reaching. Give me a clue, Watson. What're you thinking?"

"Well, first of all, we're in California. Just about every person in the state knows some Spanish. Even I could probably figure out some of what's written here—just from my two years of high-school classes. So I don't think he's attempting to hide anything, in code, or otherwise."

"Then what do you think his reasons are?"

"It's actually very simple—though not conclusive." She grinned, glad she'd been the one to think of it.

"Kace, just tell me what you're talking about." She loved it when he got exasperated.

"If I were planning to visit—or perhaps live in—a foreign country, I believe I would brush up on the language of that country."

"Spain?"

She laughed. "You're still pondering how to make those old-fashioned sherries." Then she frowned, and her voice was serious as she continued. "I know this may seem obscure, Gav. But what if he's planning to leave the country? Maybe he's planning to head someplace like Mexico or South America." She shrugged. "I know it's far-fetched, but…"

"It's not far-fetched at all, Kace." He paused, obviously considering the notion. "The Fellowship members turn over their life savings, their homes, cars, bank accounts, CDs, stocks and bonds, to Randolph—"

"—or Rodolphe, perhaps?"

He let her sentence completion go without comment. "You've got something K.C. This could be what we're looking for."

"His motive."

Gav nodded. "Big-time."

"He convinces his followers to accompany him to Atara—"

"—with his new bride," K.C. finished for him. "Which, I might add, is a nice touch."

"After the mass suicide, he skips the country, a millionaire…" Gav grabbed her hands. "If we're right, he'll have put the funds in overseas accounts."

K.C. shook her head. "Talk about a needle in a haystack, Gav. We're definitely going to need help from the authorities on this."

"Not necessarily. If I can get into his computer system, maybe I can find his account numbers. That will be the proof we need to put him away."

"Gav, even that might be dangerous, to the others, I mean."

"Putting him away?" Then he nodded. "You're right. He may have programmed them to go through with the deed if anything happens to him."

"I'd bet my life on it."

He gave her a half-smile. "Again, we've concluded that we need to act alone."

"I know, Gav. As Aunt Theo said, God's put us here for a purpose. We need to see it through."

"No matter the outcome?" He took her hand and held it in his.

She raised a brow. "Just to be on the safe side, why don't we call Father Max? Let him know we've found Theo. Ask him to pray for us."

"Maybe it's time," Gav said as he stood. "It is comforting to know we've got contact with the outside world if we need it." He turned when he'd almost reached the tree where the cellular phone was hidden. "There's one more thing, Kace, that you should know."

K.C. noticed his face was once again drawn with worry. "What is it?"

"You know when we were talking about the Latin root of *wolf* earlier?"

She thought he was going to refer to her taking offense at his mention of seminary. "Yeah?" she said tentatively.

"Something's been bothering me since I first saw his name. I didn't figure out why until a few minutes ago when we were discussing Latin words." He bit at his lip, a habit he'd had since childhood when lost in thought. "Somewhere along the line— maybe in Hebrew class—I also picked up some Egyptian root words."

"We'd be better off if you'd taken Spanish," she quipped, but Gav didn't smile.

"The name Keb—" he began, his voice suddenly very serious. "Even now I hesitate to tell you...."

She nodded. "Go on."

"It's from the ancient Egyptian Book of the Dead. And Kaseko..." His expression said he would rather spare her the knowledge, yet wanted her to know.

She nodded again. "I can only imagine," she said, though her words came out in a whisper.

"Kaseko means 'to mock' or 'to ridicule.'"

"Hmm. So Randolph believes himself to be the wolf-god who mocks death. Nice combination." She paused, shaking her head. "Gav, the man is sick."

"Yes," Gav agreed. "He is."

"Get the cell phone," K.C. said, and Gav turned again to the tree. "I'm beginning to think it's time to call in the cavalry."

A moment later, he turned back to her. "It's not here," he said. "I tucked it under my robe before I left for the chateau. I remember specifically." He turned to search again the hollow in the trunk. Finally he looked up, his eyes meeting hers. "The robe's still here, Kace," he said, "but the phone is definitely gone."

TWENTY-ONE

Theodora awoke with a start. Disoriented, she glanced around the still dark dormitory room. The Fellowship members who shared the facility, rubbing eyes and yawning, were complaining about being disturbed in the middle of the night.

"What time is it, anyway?" someone asked from one of the iron beds near the window.

"Two o'clock," was the yawning reply from the woman who bunked by Theodora. "In the morning!" Others in the room added sleepy remarks as they rose and donned their robes.

Desirée and Marigold appeared at the doorway, hesitated for a moment to let their eyes adjust to the dim light, then moved toward Theodora.

"We thought you might like some company," Desirée said with a smile.

Theodora nodded. The two had become as thick as thieves since Marigold's arrival. She'd hoped that Marigold had come to help, but so far the big woman seemed too enchanted with Desirée, probably because of her former riches or maybe her elevated position within the Fellowship as Randolph's future bride.

Theodora reached into the upright locker near her bed and pulled out her robe, slipped it on, and adjusted the hood. When she was finished, she walked with the other two women into the hallway where the others were standing in a double line.

"It knows how hard this all is on you," Desirée said to

249

Theodora. "It has never forgotten that it was because of me that you stayed."

"It-it-it," Marigold said, shaking her head good-naturedly. "It has never heard of anything so ridiculous in all its life!"

But Theodora stopped and touched Desirée's arm. "Dear, you don't have to pretend with us."

Desirée touched her hood, seeming both nervous and embarrassed. "What do you mean?"

"Lately, you've slipped into using *it* more often than *I*."

"I'm sorry. It seems that Rance wants me with him every spare minute." Theodora noticed even in the dimly lit hallway, her face wore a pleased expression. "It—I—just slip into forgetting the dreaded pronoun without thinking." She laughed lightly.

Marigold raised a brow and exchanged glances with Theodora.

Theodora felt sorry for Desirée. She was still so vulnerable. Theodora had thought Desirée was making progress in seeing Rance Randolph for who he was. Now the girlish crush on the leader seemed to have returned—probably due to a calculated move on his part. But before she could comment, Sister Vesta, standing at the head of the group, gave the signal to move forward.

The long line of women inched toward the doorway leading down the back stairs. Once Theodora was outside, the damp breeze bringing in a thin night fog hit her face, causing her to wince. Her temple throbbed, and she yearned to return to bed. But instead she drew in a deep breath and moved down the stairs with the others.

Even before she reached the first landing, she'd looked across the clearing between the auditorium and the other dormitories. Lines of devotees were coming together in one snake-like throng. Each person had been given a candle, and in the dark mist, the sight was dramatic: Hundreds of worshippers, already lifting their voices in a chant to Atara and its angels, were slowly moving onto the pathway that skirted the edge of the eucalyptus forest.

"Hurry, now," Sister Vesta called from the bottom of the stairs.

Theodora gathered the robe with her left hand and started down the remaining stairs, carefully holding the handrail with her right. At the foot of the stairs, she was given a thick candle and a small book of matches. Marigold and Desirée had already received theirs and now were mingling with the group of worshippers.

Sister Vesta watched, making sure the candle was lit. Moments after Theodora moved into the crowd, she extinguished her light. Desirée had warned her about the night to come, and Theodora wanted nothing to do with the ceremony; she would not light even the weakest flame in its honor.

She drew in a deep breath as she walked, knowing that this time there would be no pretense. Each morning in the auditorium she meditated on God's Word while the others chanted their praises to Ataran angels. She prayed for her Savior's presence to surround her while Randolph ranted about the life to come. And she hid behind the room's thick pillars while everyone else swayed and danced to the beating drums.

Tonight there would be no place to hide.

The sounds of murmuring chants rose around her, the smell of candle smoke burnt her nostrils, her knees quaked, and a nauseous bile flamed in her throat.

Oh, Lord, she prayed as she walked. *You've brought me here. Me, of all people! I'm not worthy. I have failed. I have done nothing to help anyone find their way out of this place. You obviously should have sent someone else.*

I am surely the weakest of all your children! So why have you called me to this task? Why me, Lord?

She was suddenly so filled with fear, she could no longer pray. Around her, praises rose to false gods. She could do nothing to stop it.

She wanted to shout to them all to stop their rantings. She wanted to tell them it was all a sham. But her great fear had turned her mute.

Hot tears filled her eyes, and she bit her lips together to keep from weeping. Suddenly she doubted the strength of her resolve. Would she really be able to stand up for her God?

Wouldn't it be simpler, easier, to bow to the statue? To keep her heart focused on God, yet give lip service to the Ataran gods?

Such a weakling I am, Lord. It's a good thing I wasn't present at the Crucifixion. I might have denied you, too.

A soft breeze lifted the edges of her hood, and she gazed into the misty skies. Barely visible were the stars and moon. They appeared to be hidden behind a veil, or a shroud. But they were there nonetheless. As solidly in place as ever.

God's world hadn't changed. Neither had he. Her fear had nothing to do with him or who he was. Her fear didn't lessen his power, his omniscience, his faithfulness.

They were nearing the chateau now, and she could see the stone fountain beyond it. Torches had been placed around the statue of Keb-Kaseko Rodolphe, probably so Randolph could clearly see those who worshipped his statue—and those who didn't. The flames leapt and danced, creating a flickering red orange glow in the heavy air.

It's a good thing I wasn't at the Crucifixion. I would have denied you, too.

Peter! Of course.

It came to her with such sudden clarity that she was momentarily stunned. It had been Peter, disciple and powerful man of God upon whom Christ built his church, yet a man so filled with fear that he denied his Savior on the night he needed him most.

Fear. A common emotion, even among God's chosen.

The breeze touched her hot face again, and her tears evaporated. She drew in a deep breath, feeling strangely comforted.

My beloved child, I am with you.

Do not allow your fears to separate you from my love.

I am here!

Do not be ashamed. Give your fears to me, my child.

I am your shield. I am the lifter of your head.

Keep your eyes on me, my beloved.

Theodora lifted her gaze from the burning torches, the gleaming metallic statue, to the deep, mist-shrouded heavens. *I am here!*

"Kace!"

K.C. squinted into the darkness. Gav was standing over her, near the tree where she had been sleeping. They had earlier moved to a new area further up the hillside.

"What's wrong?" She sat up and looked around. A strange glow off in the distance showed through the eucalyptus leaves. It seemed to come from the direction of the chateau.

"Can you hear that?"

K.C. stood and stretched her limbs, then her back. Sleeping on the ground was taking its toll. She shook her head, still yawning.

"Listen!" He held his finger to his lips. K.C. listened more carefully; now she could hear the faint sounds of chanting in the distance. "It started a few minutes ago—from near the dormitories. Then the group seemed to march by as if in some sort of parade."

"A very somber parade, judging from the sound of it."

"Shall we go see?"

"I'm game if you are," she said.

"Don't use the word *game*," Gav reminded her with a grimace.

They donned their robes and pulled their hoods low. Then creeping through the eucalyptus grove, they followed the sounds of chanting, down the hillside, past the old cellar building, along the winding road leading first to the upper parking level, and finally to the chateau grounds themselves.

A few minutes later, K.C. let out a low whistle as they caught up with the group near the parking lot. Candles— scores of them—flickered as the pale hooded figures who carried them moved as one massive, living beast along the road. The faces of the devotees were illumined by candlelight, but the shadows cast by their features made each to appear to be wearing some grotesque mask. The chanting continued without pause: "Atara-Atara-Atara. Come for us, angels of Atara. Come for us. Save us. Take us from this world. Take us to Atara. Atara-Atara-Atara."

"He's not very creative," K.C. whispered to Gav. "Even I could have come up with something a bit more poetic."

Gav rolled his eyes. "Is that your new mission? Writing chants for mad gurus?"

"Merely an attempt at levity, my dear!" She turned back to the mass of robed figures.

"I like that," Gav murmured as they started moving through the trees again.

"My attempt at levity?"

"No," he said, then paused and met her eyes. "The 'my dear' part."

This time K.C. rolled her eyes. "There—look where they're heading," she said after a moment. "Straight for the chateau."

"Actually, my guess is they're heading to the front lawn—out by the fountain. Look, he's got torches set up around it."

"The guy's nuts," K.C. said as they reached the edge of the grove near the parking lot. A distance ahead, the devotees were moving along the roadway just to the side of the gardens near the chateau. They could now clearly make out the flickering and dancing flames around the fountain. "Did you ever go back to see the statue—find out whose likeness it is?"

Gav shook his head. "It's in the open. Too risky."

"I suppose we'll find out soon enough," she said. "Probably one of the Ataran angels. Maybe Abraham Lincoln?"

"I vote for Winston Churchill. Or maybe Johann Sebastian Bach."

"Or the greatest of them all—Keb-Kaseko Rodolphe," she said, half joking.

Gav turned to her, his face serious. "You may be right, Kace."

"Mr. Wolf-god-who-mocks-death himself," she murmured with a shudder. "It does make sense. And these, his followers, are coming to worship." Then her gaze flew to Gav's. "Oh, no! Aunt Theo! She'll not put up with this. I know her."

He didn't answer but caught her hand and held it fast. His touch comforted her. He didn't let go of her hand until they headed into the gardens and slipped into the foliage near the chateau.

The grounds in front of the house were now teeming with Fellowship members. Randolph, dressed in his pale gold robe, stood at the base of the massive statue. He lifted his arms and began to sway. His followers did the same. From the rear of the group, the drums began their heavy, seductive rhythm. Deeper and louder they beat, and the devotees' voices joined the cadence in a chorus of low, whispering chants. The volume gradually increased until it was frenzied, wild, and burning with intensity.

Candles now out, they danced with eyes closed. Swaying, hands waving in the air, flames licking skyward from the torches. Perspiration shining on ghostly faces.

"Atara-Atara-Atara. Come for us, angels of Atara. Come for us. Save us. Take us from this world. Take us to Atara. Atara-Atara-Atara."

K.C. turned to Gav. "'Take us to Atara,'" she said, frowning. "Think of its meaning. You don't suppose this is when he's planned the suicide?" Her voice faltered, and she couldn't finish.

"This may be something he requires of his followers every night, Kace. We don't know. Besides, it's the same chant we heard in the morning meeting."

But as she watched with both horror and fascination, K.C. wondered. In her short time with Theodora in the vineyards, her aunt had said nothing about such a ceremony, only that Randolph required odd behaviors of his members, almost as if he were determined to rob them of their humanity.

Now watching them, she considered the notion that she and Gav had often discussed since their arrival at Angels Crest. Cult leaders chipped away at people's humanity—their self-esteem, their creativity, their sense of belonging to humankind, their relationship to the God who had created them—and what was left?

Nothing. Cleared minds. Empty spirits. Ready to be filled with whatever garbage the guru might choose.

She watched the macabre dance in front of her. Without

their candles, the robed figures seemed more shadow than sub-stance, pale shadows dancing in the firelight. Led by the feral-eyed, bearded lunatic who masqueraded as an angel of light.

A chill spidered down her spine.

Since the beginning of time, evil had not come up with a more creative way to ensnare his prey…or a more effective way. His was a promise of everything a soul could want…except the One who would stop its longing, quench its thirst, fill that God-shaped vacuum inside.

Mad dancers with empty souls. She watched their aimless dance in the torchlight.

And she pictured Christ, who at time's beginning had writ-ten their names in his palm. He had laid this earth's foundation for them while the morning stars sang together and the angels shouted for joy.

He knew each one of these hundreds by name. He gave his life in exchange for theirs—as if each had been the only one in the world to love.

But they didn't know. They didn't know!

"Oh, Lord," she breathed, thinking of Aunt Theo who was hidden somewhere in the throng. "Oh, Father, give her strength! Wrap her now with your power, your love! Shelter her with your faithfulness."

And the chant went on: "Atara-Atara-Atara. Come for us, angels of Atara."

Gav reached again for K.C.'s hand, and she turned to him. His eyes were filled with the same soul-anguish she felt. He seemed unable to speak, perhaps feeling his words inadequate.

Finally, Randolph signaled the drums to stop their rhythmic beating and the followers to halt their dancing. All was quiet except the sounds of crackling torch flames.

"My children," he called out in a sonorous voice. "The one whose image is before us is worthy of our adoration. It is he who rules Atara. It is he who will welcome us there when we arrive."

K.C. cast a nervous glance at Gav. He squeezed her hand, and they turned again to watch and listen to Randolph.

"From this day forward, we will be required to bow down before this, the greatest of all Ataran angels!"

K.C. examined the body language of Fellowship members nearest where she and Gav hid, wondering if they were bothered by his words or the new proclamation. But, judging from their expressions, she could see they were still caught up in the frenzy brought on by the dance, drums, and firelight—and, of course, their revered leader's voice crying out in the night.

"You will move forward in groups of ten, forming rows of thirty abreast," Randolph said to the group. "You will approach Keb-Kaseko with absolute reverence, bow down and worship, touching your faces on the ground. You will remain prostrate until all have knelt."

"Keb-Kaseko..." K.C. murmured, exchanging a glance with Gav. "God of the dead. You were right." She watched as the first row of ten worshippers approached the statue. They lifted faces and arms in praise to Keb-Kaseko while reverently murmuring the now familiar Ataran chant.

"And he knows very well the ridicule, the mocking he's subjecting his followers to," Gav added.

"He's stealing their dignity."

"He's robbing them of more than that, Kace," Gav whispered. "Most people who get caught up in cults—even when they come out—turn away from any thought of supernatural intervention in their lives."

"Including God." K.C. knew it was true. She thought of friends who had gone into groups they thought were mainstream Christianity, then discovered the bizarre doctrine and history behind the veil first presented to them. They'd become so disillusioned that they'd completely turned away from God.

She watched the rows come forward and bow before the statue. Then as each remained prone, the next group moved forward, lifted their arms and voices in praise, then knelt face-down before the still chanting assemblage.

Whispering a prayer for her aunt's strength and protection, K.C. tried to find Theodora's face among the throng. But row by row, the devotees moved forward, repeating the ritual of the former group. Her aunt wasn't among them.

Randolph stood to one side of the statue, arms held out over the Fellowship members and nodding slowly, almost as if receiving the praise himself. K.C. noticed how he was orches-trating the event for maximum emotion, moving each group very slowly into place, murmuring words of encouragement and praise to Keb-Kaseko.

Finally, only three rows remained, two of ten people, and one of seven. These were probably among the most reluctant to obey Randolph's edict. Judging from Randoph's attentive, narrow-eyed stance, he assumed the same.

The next row moved forward and stood hesitantly before the statue. For a moment it seemed they would not obey. Two or three of the robed figures shuffled nervously, and some of the others exchanged glances, then one by one, they lifted their arms, though without much fervor, and knelt. A moment later, they stiffly bent toward the ground until their faces touched the grassy lawn.

Then the following row inched forward. Even more hesitant than the previous group, these followers halted and stared at the statue, then moved their gaze to Randolph as if weighing their decision.

"Need I remind you," he said, "that disobedience is not an option? Friends," he continued, adopting an intimate tone. "Our place on Atara is secured, yes, even enhanced, by proof of our devotion here tonight. You see, my friends, the end is near. Very near.

"Everything we have learned about Atara and its angelic beings has prepared us for the final victory—overcoming an inflated sense of self in order to become instruments for the Ataran angels. Tonight we worship them completely because someday, my friends, we will rule with them, and—joy of all joys—someday we will be worshipped just as they are!

"Through this act of homage, proof will be provided that you are ready for the final journey. And I have a secret to share with you…" he leaned forward, his voice dropping. "It is *you*, my friends, *you* who need the proof that you are indeed ready to shed the last vestiges of your earthly selves and take this decisive step to higher consciousness."

Randolph's voice now rose to an emotional pitch as he continued his plea with the remaining seventeen people. "Leave your apprehensions and fears behind. Step toward me, my Ataran friends—" he reached a hand toward them, his golden robe shimmering in the firelight, his feral eyes glinting. "Come, now, oh mighty rulers of Atara. Bow. Worship with me. Lift your praises to Keb-Kaseko."

Suddenly, one of the robed figures stepped forward. She allowed her hood to fall to her shoulders. K.C. caught her hand to her mouth.

It was Theodora.

K.C. held her breath as her aunt lifted her face toward the heavens, closed her eyes a moment, then moved her calm gaze back to Randolph.

"Rance Randolph," she called out in a clear voice, "I will not bow.

"There is one God and Creator of our world and of our universe. To him only will I give my allegiance. I am his child." K.C. could see her aunt's hands trembling as she gestured heavenward.

For a moment Randolph didn't speak. The chanting stopped, the drums fell silent. Everyone stared at Randolph, awaiting his response.

"We have understood from the first day you joined us that you are—how shall I put it?—the product of a deluded society," Randolph said with an impatient tone. Then he laughed lightly. "That you have grandiose delusions of a personal God." He practically spat the words. There were sizzling sounds as moths were incinerated by the torch flames. "Where is your proof of this personal God, Sister? Do you think he'll swoop down from the skies to save you from us?"

When she didn't answer, he laughed. "You see, Sister Theodora, you can offer no more proof of your God than I can of the Ataran angels." There was a titter from the crowd.

"Stop! All of you!" shouted a loud female voice from the row behind Theodora. The hooded figure quickly made her way to Theodora's side. "I am another who will not bow to any statue, especially one that so resembles you!" There was no mistaking the voice.

Gav and K.C. exchanged glances. It was Marigold Green.

"People!" she cried out. "I wanted to tell you yesterday morning that the visit by the angel was false. That Jacques Cousteau didn't really appear to me, but I was afraid for my life. I thought I could go along with your practices, your beliefs. But ladies and gentlemen, what can you be thinking? Don't you think this is going just a little bit too far?"

Security guards prepared to rush forward, but Randolph held up his hand to stop them. Obviously, he wasn't concerned with losing control. He chuckled and shook his head slowly.

"My, my, what have we here? A deluded mystery writer *and*

a self-acknowledged liar?" He laughed again, still shaking his head. "I'm sorry, Sisters, that you chose this particular time to release your venom. You see, these moments are sacred.

"Nothing will be allowed to interfere. Not you. Not anyone who is unwilling to join us in this hallowed occasion. Therefore, I will need to remove you from our midst."

K.C. moved slightly, preparing to go to her aunt's aid, but Gav reached out to restrain her. "Wait," he mouthed. "We can't help her if we're caught."

Biting her lip nervously, she watched her aunt's face. It was amazingly peaceful.

Theodora seemed to draw in a deep breath, and when she spoke again, her voice was strong and calm. "Perhaps you should see if there are others who will stand against you and this Keb-Kaseko," she said, throwing out a challenge. "Why don't you ask—then let us go in peace—those of us who want no part in this?"

Randolph's narrow face twisted into a smile. On either side of where he stood, security guards had moved into position, poised, catlike, ready to pounce.

"Yes, perhaps I should," Randolph said. He looked down at those rows still standing and nervously shuffling about. "You heard this...this woman...and her brilliant solution. I, on behalf of all Atarans, am interested in the outcome." He fixed his gaze on the faces of the robed figures.

For a moment, no one moved.

Then a young man stepped forward. "I will not bow down," he said, moving to stand beside Theodora and Marigold.

"Nor will I," another man said, his voice low and solemn.

They were followed by a middle-aged couple, then three older women and another man, all holding their heads high as they stepped forward. Then the others squared their shoulders and voiced their decisions.

Finally, a single robed figure stood alone, the only person remaining from the row where Theodora and Marigold had earlier been standing. She let her hood drop back onto her shoulders, and her blond hair shone in the glow from the torches.

"Sister Desirée, my bride and future queen of Atara," Randolph said quietly. There was great triumph in his tone. "And where do your passions lie?" A glint of firelight reflected in his eyes as he awaited her answer.

Desirée lifted her face to him, paused, then her voice rang out. "It chooses you, my lord and king," she said with a regal bow. She shot a defiant look at Theodora before moving her gaze back to Randolph, her face alight with adoration.

Without another word, she knelt before the statue, chanting, "Atara-Atara-Atara. Keb-Kaseko is our king! Let us worship our king!"

Around her the devotees took up the chorus until the heavy night air was filled with the sound of it. A very pleased-looking Randolph signaled his guards, and they moved toward those who had dared to defy him.

TWENTY-TWO

It was now nearly dawn. Randolph, who stood on his office balcony looking out over the Angels Crest grounds, scarcely considered the beauty of the morning, the mist that twisted among the live oaks on the Angels Crest grounds, or even the vineyards that spread across the distant hillsides.

From his vantage point, through the leafy foliage of the hillside, he could just make out the roof of the old cellar where the dissidents had been taken. Outside, the guards were at their posts.

He pictured Theodora Wimple's grandniece and the young man accompanying her and smiled to himself.

It wouldn't be long now. The trap was set.

All he needed to do was wait.

An hour later, a knock sounded on his office door.

"Come in," he called, and Dakota hurried inside, robe swishing around his ankles. "You've prepared the *QmP* formula, Brother?" he asked as soon as the man had settled his round body into a chair in front of the desk.

Dakota nodded. "The delivery truck arrived just moments ago. The formula is ready. The wine is ready to be uncorked." He smiled. "All that's necessary is to administer a small amount in each glass as it is served. It's odorless and tasteless. The result is immediate." He went on to explain the scientific formulation.

"Well done, Brother," Randolph said. "You will be in charge of the distribution. You will have twenty Fellowship leaders working for you—all trusted security people."

"It's to take place after the wedding ceremony?"

"Yes, yes, of course." He paused. "And you understand the order in which we will proceed?"

The round man nodded again. "Everyone will drink together. Groups of ten."

"With the exception of a few. Some will abstain so they may attend to the arrangement of the physical bodies."

"I—it—will be one of those who take care of those duties?"

"Yes," Randolph smiled. "Finally, only one will remain to see to the arrangement of the other."

"Who will that one be, Brother Randolph?"

"It's only appropriate that I be the last to leave on this most miraculous of all life's journeys," said Randolph. He paused, frowning. "I have one more request to make of you."

"What is it?"

"Because we have only three days until our journey, I want to be absolutely certain that no one leaves these premises."

Dakota frowned. "We already have a system in place."

"Apparently that system wasn't quite secure enough." Randolph was talking about K.C. Keegan and the young man. Dakota knew it.

"To be absolutely certain, the Fellowship members should be kept in a secure place within the compound until their...ah...journey."

"As in the auditorium?"

"Yes."

Randolph smiled. "My thinking exactly." He paused. "You'll make the arrangements?"

"Of course."

"Good, then. We'll put this into action immediately."

"Will there be others who will join those in the auditorium during the next three days?"

"You can count on it, my friend," Randolph said solemnly. "You can count on it."

~ ~ ~ ~ ~

It was a subdued assemblage that entered the auditorium a short time later. Randolph immediately sensed that the previous night's activities made some doubt his leadership, perhaps doubt the doctrine of the Fellowship.

A piece of rotten fruit in the barrel. That's what Theodora Whimple had been last night.

A flash of a painful memory caused him to wince. His foster mother had also called him that when she was angry; she'd said he was a piece of decaying fruit whose evil ways were harming her other, natural, children. Her words always preceded the beatings, beatings that left him too bruised to attend school.

When he was five she'd told him that God was watching his every move. She said God wrote down every bad thought, every evil deed he even considered committing. And that he would someday be punished. The woman marched him to Sunday school each week, pinching his ear as she escorted him the several blocks to church. As he passed the neighborhood children, they laughed and went back to their play.

He remembered how, when he was seven, the same woman stood piously before the congregation and spoke of the trials of foster parenting, saying that she knew God would reward her for reaching down to care for the most indigent and backward members of society. She'd said the words with such disgust that for years the boy equated indigent and backward with ugly and bad.

As a child, he had been rotten to the core, or so he had been told. And now? He laughed to himself as he considered his plan; he supposed he was fulfilling a prophecy.

His thoughts returned to the group in front of him, raising their arms in halfhearted worship. The drums continued to beat, and the Ataran chant rose skyward.

How quickly the rotten can spoil the good. Just as had been evidenced at the statue. But the spoilers—Theodora Whimple, her crazy sidekick Marigold Green, and the others who stood with them—had already begun to influence his followers' thoughts. He could see it in their faces, hear it in their voices. It was time for his counter move.

"My friends," he intoned, signaling to the drummers and calling a halt to the dancing and chanting. "My friends, gather closer. I have something important to reveal to you." They moved forward, glancing at each other and frowning. Yes, he could see their doubts written clearly on their faces.

"Please, come closer," he said, his expression serious, caring, compassionate. "What I am about to tell you will be difficult. Very difficult. Please, sit down. This may take some time, and I want you to feel comfortable to ask questions."

There was some general hubbub as they settled onto the floor. He stepped from the platform and adopted an intimate yet professorial stance, leaning against a tall stool in front of them. "Dear friends, the world's end, as I predicted, is about to happen."

The devotees exchanged worried looks, many of their expressions stricken.

"It's amazing to me how we are directed by outside forces—in this case, our beloved Ataran angels—so that our timing is impeccable." He smiled slightly. "For you see, we were directed to begin the final stages of Ataran worship last night. And now—according to scientists around the world—the meteorite is hurtling toward earth."

He stopped, allowing them to react.

"Because of this event, and because, as you know, we will soon be embarking on our final journey, from now on, we will not be leaving this place." He saw their looks of confusion and hurried on. "I don't mean the compound. I mean this auditorium."

A few devotees showed their alarm, and he held up his hand. "I have told you from the beginning that this compound will be our safe haven when this day arrives. We can assume the rest of the world will quickly move into a state of panic.

"But we are safe here, my friends. From today forward, our doors are closed to the public. There is no need to continue with our harvest. We will allow the fruit to rot on the vines.

"For there is no need to gather it in for wine.

"The wine we drink when we arrive in Atara will put Angels Crest wines to shame—even the best of our reserves.

"To be certain of our safety, I am sealing the auditorium doors. We will sing and dance and lift our voices in praise to Atara until the hour comes for our journey."

The faces of his followers were now pale and still. They seemed unsure of him.

He smiled and dropped his voice intimately. "Friends. We have long awaited this day. Do not be afraid. Those outside our compound are filled with fear because of what's ahead. But we are safe. Do you understand? We are safe!"

He searched their faces. "Are there any questions?"

A young woman raised her hand, and he nodded to her. "Can we call our families...tell them good-bye?"

"When you came here, you broke all ties to family and friends. Do you remember?"

She nodded.

"Do you remember why?"

"So that we could channel our thoughts and energies on Atara," she answered. "You said all of our being must focus on moving toward our ultimate destiny."

He smiled and nodded, showing her how pleased he was

with the response. "Yes, exactly. And that hasn't changed." He walked over to where she sat, stooped down, and took her hand. "I know it's hard to understand," he said gently. "But it's better this way. You told me how your family rejected you when you said you were going to join our Fellowship."

She nodded.

"They haven't changed their minds, and they might try to change yours. We can't weaken, my dear. We absolutely cannot."

He stood again, looking around at the upturned faces. So trusting. So believing they were. He gave them a loving smile. He was feeling stronger again. They believed in him whole-heartedly once more. Their adoration made him feel invincible. It hardened his resolve. It gave him strength. He would miss that adoration when they were gone.

"Are there any other questions?"

One of the drummers raised his hand.

"Yes, Joshua?"

"How long do we have, I mean, until the journey?"

"No more than three days." Randolph raised his hands in delight, looking skyward as if toward Atara. "Three days!" He threw back his head and burst out in what he hoped would pass for joyous laughter. "Think of it, my friends! We have waited and planned and anticipated this event. And now it is almost upon us."

Then he moved his gaze back to their faces, an expression of joy still on his face. "If ever there was a time to celebrate, this is it!"

He held out his hands. "Please, stand."

The group did as they were bade.

"Brothers and sisters, today—because we celebrate the coming events—I am going to allow a toast with our finest reserve wine. It is the first glass of many we'll be sampling during our remaining hours on Earth."

Brother Dakota arrived with three other robed guards. Some of the students from the culinary arts school wheeled in silver carts filled with bottles of wine, both red and white, and Baccarat crystal stemware. On the platform, long tables had been set, almost communionlike, Randolph thought proudly, with the finest linen cloths, sterling chalices, and candles for use at the end of the celebration service.

The first mournful tones of Mozart's *Requiem, Laudate Dominum,* carried from the sound system. The music swelled, filling the large room as the sunlight filtered through the jeweled windows.

Mozart's last and unfinished work, Randolph thought. It was his favorite of all. So appropriate for the Angels of Fellowship on this day. So appropriate.

When all had been served, Randolph lifted his crystal glass in a toast.

"To Atara!" he declared in a joyful voice.

"Atara-Atara-Atara!" was the chorused reply.

"Gav, I'm scared. I think we should go for help."

The two were now hiding in an abandoned gardening shed they'd discovered at the northernmost boundary of the Angels Crest property in a stand of cottonwoods. Rusted tools hung on hooks, and cobwebs laced the corners of the room. The early morning sunlight filtered through the room's one small, dirty window, and dust particles hung in the heavy, dank air.

K.C. was sitting on an overturned pail, and Gav stood near the door. It was open a crack, and he watched for signs of anyone approaching through the tall, golden grass, live oaks, and cottonwoods lining this far edge of the property.

Nearby a small bubbling stream had provided them with fresh water and a way to wash and refresh themselves in a cover of thick ferns. They were at least one mile from the chateau and, K.C. hoped, off the regular rounds of guards and other Fellowship members.

"There's no guarantee we can get out—or get back in with help that won't set off a Waco or a Jonestown. I still think the best way to help is from inside."

K.C. rubbed her head. She'd been distraught since Aunt Theo had been led away from the statue with the others last night. "So far our efforts have amounted to zero. Zilch. *Nada.*"

"We could have gotten Theo out—if she'd allowed it, Kace. Keep that in mind. It was her decision to stay." His voice was gentle. "I know it's terrifying to consider that now she's being held captive in the caves. But Kace, what she did last night may have made the difference in getting some of the others out— those people who stood up with her."

Tears threatened to fill her eyes, and K.C. swallowed the sting in her throat. "I know, Gav. But we've got to get to her. Get her out. There's not much time left." She took a shaky breath. "I worry that after what happened last night, Randolph may step up his timetable."

Gav opened the small paper sack he'd just brought up the hillside from the culinary arts center and handed her a wheat roll. She quickly brushed away her tears and gratefully took a bite.

Gav pealed off the top of his orange-juice carton. "Time to regroup," he said after a long swig. "Decide our next move."

"I know it's better to concentrate on the task at hand, rather than the 'what ifs,'" K.C. said, speaking to herself, rather than to Gav. "So tell me your ideas, Sherlock. Then I'll tell you mine."

He was chewing a bite of his roll. "You first, Watson."

"The group has been taken into the tunnels. We know there's ammunition inside."

"And guards who know how to use it," Gav added, taking another swig of juice.

K.C. nibbled on her roll, her forehead creased in thought. "He's expecting us to go after them."

Gav nodded. "You bet."

"So it's a trap of some kind."

"Right again."

"So we need to do the opposite of what he expects," she said and took a drink of juice.

"I agree. But there's only one problem," he said with a halfhearted grin. "Exactly what is that?"

She frowned, reaching for another roll. "Leave? Or pretend to?"

"So he lets down his guard."

K.C. nodded slowly. "The only worry is that he'll think we've called for help." She walked to the window, looking out at the wild landscape. She nibbled on the roll and watched a scrub jay hop along the branch of an oak tree. A gray squirrel scrambled up the trunk and gave the bird a warning bark. A hummingbird swooped and dove and tumbled gracefully in the morning sun. How strange that this group hid under the guise of God's beauty.

"Okay, I've got an idea." Gav interrupted her thoughts and she turned toward him again.

"I knew you would, Sherlock," she said.

Gav checked his watch. "Randolph's meeting with his Followers in the auditorium right now. That means the compound is empty."

"Except for the security guards."

"And they're probably concentrated around the old wine cellar."

She agreed. "So where is it they won't be?"

"His office. I've been in there once. We'll slip in, get into his

273

computer system, find out what we can about the group who met with him the other night—"

K.C. interrupted, frowning. "That's not going to help us rescue Theo and the others."

He held up a hand. "Let me finish, please, dearest?"

"Dearest?"

He raised a brow. "A figure of speech, my dear," he said, quoting her words.

"Go ahead," she sighed.

"We'll also send an e-mail to Father Max."

"Aha," she said, a smile spreading across her face. "Randolph will see the e-mail. We can let him believe we're leaving."

"Of course."

"What about Father Max? If he thinks we're on our way home, he won't try to get help to us if anything goes wrong."

"That's the flip side of the coin," Gav said. "We're on our own."

"With God's help," K.C. reminded him.

"Why don't we ask him to be with us?" Gav said.

"I know he's here," K.C. said. "But my knees might stop their shaking if you say a prayer. To hear someone else pray aloud makes his presence more tangible somehow."

Gav took both her hands in his, and they stood together, heads bowed in the pool of sunlight spilling through the dusty window. "Father," he prayed. "We come to you in need of your guidance, your power, and your comfort. We ask not just for ourselves, but especially on behalf of Theo, Marigold, and the others."

"Let them feel your presence—as real as if you were in the room with them," K.C. prayed. It felt natural to join her voice and heart with his, just as they'd always prayed together through the years. "Take away their fears, our Father. Protect their hearts and spirits."

"And be with us, Lord," Gav continued. "Go before us as our shield—"

"Our rock," added K.C. "Hem us in—behind and before; lay your hand on us," she prayed from Psalm 139.

Gav continued the passage, his voice low. "'Where can I go from your Spirit?'" he said. "'Where can I flee from your presence?

"'If I go up to the heavens, you are there; if I make my bed in the depths, you are there.'"

K.C. joined her voice with his, and they spoke the next verses together.

"'If I rise on the wings of the dawn, if I settle on the far side of the sea, even there your hand will guide me, your right hand will hold me fast.

"'If I say, "Surely the darkness will hide me and the Light become night around me," even the darkness will not be dark to you; the night will shine like the day, for darkness is as light to you,'" they finished, their voices blending in soft unison.

"Father," Gav said, "may we be aware of your light."

"Today and through all our tomorrows," K.C. said, then lifted her face and gave Gav a gentle smile.

They donned their robes once more and scrambled down the hillside, staying well out of sight in the cover of trees and thick brush. A few minutes later, they reached the center of the compound and moved briskly along the pathway, wending their way to the chateau. The entrance had been left open, and they exchanged alarmed expressions, wondering if they were falling into a trap after all.

"It was left open last time," Gav whispered as they moved

inside, "and I don't think I was expected."

"Then lead the way, Sherlock," she whispered back.

They climbed the wide, winding staircase and moved along the carpeted hallway. As he'd done once before, Gav unlocked Randolph's office door with a credit card. After a quick glance inside to make sure they were alone, he held open the door for her to enter.

"Okay, over here—" Gav led the way to the computer and flipped the switch to turn on the power. They pulled up chairs and quickly sat down in front of the computer.

"He's on the same Internet connector I am," K.C. said, "I found that out when we were exchanging e-mails, so that means I can log on as a guest and send a message under my code name."

"Satinka?" he murmured, sitting very near her, his eyes on the monitor screen.

"Yep, we're back to that wily feline again," she said absently, looking for the correct program in the hard drive folder. "Aha! Here it is!" she pronounced a moment later. "And...we're now logged on."

"Quickly," Gav said. "Send a message to Father Max. Let's say—"

"How about, 'Father Max: We're on our way out. Meet us as planned at the rendezvous. DO NOT notify authorities.'"

"Rendezvous?" Gav lifted a brow. "There was none discussed."

"He'll know that," K.C. said, typing the last sentence. "Okay, what do you think?"

Gav read the message over her shoulder. "Send it," he said, then he touched her hand as she reached for the mouse. "No, wait. Is there a code of any kind that you can think of to let him know we are staying, that we need his fervent prayers."

K.C. thought for a moment, then smiled. "Yes, I think I've

got it. Let's add Psalm 139:5." She typed in the reference. "Our code."

"'You hem me in—behind and before,'" he quoted. "Do you think he'll get it?"

"Father Max?" she said. "Are you kidding?" But her words sounded more confident than she felt. She clicked the 'send' button.

"All right, one more thing," Gav said, checking his watch. "Open the files on the hard drive. Look for anything that references Keb-Kaseko Rodolphe."

K.C. scrolled down through the lists. Nothing. She shook her head.

"Okay, try some of the file folders, maybe under chateau operations, or Angels Crest operations." She clicked a few open, then shook her head. Still nothing. "This is like looking for a pine needle in a giant redwood forest," she said.

Gav gave her a quick grin. "Except redwoods aren't pines. They're of the *Taxodiaceae* family. You won't find a pine needle among 'em."

"Exactly!" she countered, rolling her eyes. Then staring again at the monitor, she clicked open the folder icons, one after the other. She stopped suddenly. "How about something in Spanish?"

"Open it, quickly." He nervously checked his watch again.

"Drat!"

"What?" Gav scooted closer.

"It's not opening. The file's not opening. I think it's locked."

"You can do that on one of these?"

She sighed, clicking open the control panel. "Yeah, unfortunately for us."

"What are you doing?"

"Trying to get around his security system. If I can find the right extension folder, I can unlock the file."

"I have no idea what you're talking about," Gav said. "But we don't have much time. Their meeting may be over any minute."

"I know, I know," K.C. breathed, hurrying through the massive extension folder. "Whew," she finally sighed. "Here it is. One more lit-tle click—waa-lah!—'tis done! We're back in business." She quickly closed the control panel and went back to the Spanish file.

"Here it is, Gav!" she said a moment later. "Read this!"

He let out a low whistle, reading over her shoulder.

"This is the proof we need to show to his Followers." He smiled and gave her the thumbs-up sign. "We've done it, K.C.! Print it out, and let's get out of here."

"Here it comes. All five beautiful little pages!" K.C. said, clicking the printer icon. They waited for the printer to spew out the document.

But nothing happened.

The printer light didn't so much as blink with the announcement of a document on its way.

"Try it again," Gav whispered. "Hurry." He checked his watch, then looked to the exterior office. "We've got to get out of here."

A message flashed on the screen, and she groaned. "It's out of paper!"

Gav searched Randolph's desk, then moved to the credenza and poked around inside. "Okay. Here it is!" He ripped open the package and handed her a bundle of paper. She rammed it into the paper tray.

"Okay, okay…" she muttered to the computer. "Come on, baby. Do your job!"

The green printer light blinked and the whir of the coming document rose from its interior. Just as the first page rolled out, there was a noise from the outer hallway.

Gav's frantic gaze met hers. "Someone's coming. Quick! Close the computer files."

She clicked the appropriate icons, and the files closed. Page two of the report rolled out of the printer.

"Three to go!"

"We'll have to leave from the balcony!" he said. "I'll make sure the French door's unlocked while you get the document. Hurry!"

"Go on. I'll be right there." Page three rolled out.

He strode across the room and worked with the temperamental door lock while K.C. grabbed page four. One to go!

Her heart thudded wildly beneath her ribs, and she awaited the next page, poised and ready to run.

The office door slowly opened. Before she could react, Rance Randolph stepped inside.

"Well, well, well," he said, his narrow face twisting into a smile as she stood and turned toward him. "What have we here?" He strode to the printer and pulled out the last page of the document. Then he turned to her and reached for the other four pages.

His expression told her she had no choice but to turn them over. Once he had the whole document in hand, he placed the papers in a nearby shredder and flipped the switch. Then locking his gaze on her face, he smiled. "So good to see you again, Satinka."

TWENTY-THREE

Gav immediately stepped back into the room, trying to remain calm. His only thought was for K.C.'s safety. "Leave her alone," he demanded.

"Ah, we have still another guest at the chateau," Randolph said smoothly. He reached into his desk drawer and removed a gun, then held it loosely in his hand. "Let me see if I recall...yes, yes, of course. The young newlyweds—Elliott and Katherine Gavin, I believe it was."

Gav glanced at K.C. Her face was white.

"Or was it Satinka?" he stepped closer and, pulling back her hood, touched her red hair. K.C. jerked her head away from him, and Gav stepped forward threateningly. "I do miss those long, black curls, my dear," he went on without so much as a blink toward Gav. "And the leopardskin coat."

"Okay, so you know who we are," Gav said. "Just let us go. We'll leave you in peace." He moved closer to K.C., though knowing his mere presence would offer little protection. The gun in Randolph's hand glinted as he gestured with it.

"Do you really think I've led you here only to let you go?" Randolph laughed, shaking his head. "Now, really, I would think by now you know me better than that." He laughed again. "I must say, though, that you two have provided endless entertainment. Better than C-Span." He walked to the entertainment center and flipped on a monitor, made a few adjustments, then motioned with the gun for Gav and K.C. to join him.

He chuckled, watching their faces, as the tape began to play.

It was the two of them, slinking about the compound, beginning with Gav's climbing out of the trunk of Theodora's car to their hideout in the eucalyptus grove. He fast-forwarded the action, and now their shadows could be seen slipping into the culinary arts center, then into the cellar, even their last hideout at the old gardener's shed.

"My dears, you should have looked to the beautiful Napa Valley skies," he said, laughing. "The cameras were hidden in the trees."

"There were no wires," Gav said.

"Since when do we need wires for such devices?" he said. "Or light? We simply use infrared."

"You've known about our every move," K.C. said, turning on him, furious, after he'd clicked off the monitor.

"Not every move," Randolph said. "But enough."

"Why didn't you just capture us at the beginning and be done with it?" she said. "What was the point?"

"There was no point, my dear," he said. "As I said, you were better than C-Span. I had only hoped that you'd be more of a challenge. That's all. You were, in the end, simply a disappointment—especially to find you here." He shook his head sadly. "No imagination at all."

"So the game's over," Gav said. "Let us go."

"Who said it's over?" Randolph said. "An important ceremony is about to take place at Angels Crest. I don't want you to miss it." He laughed.

"The execution of hundreds of people? Is that part of your ceremony?" Gav asked.

"Execution?" He let out a deep sigh, as if about to explain something to a child. "My followers are about to embark on a journey to the beautiful planet Atara. What they will find there is far better than any life they've got here. Earth is but a melting pot of sorrow, pain, frustration, and disappointment. Nothing more." A shadow of intense pain crossed his face as he spoke, and K.C. realized he believed it.

"What about the meteorite?" K.C. asked. "Isn't that part of the melting pot?"

"It is predicted," he said almost indignantly. "Biblical cryptologists—"

Gav interrupted. "You know as well as we do, there's no truth to their predictions. People can find anything they want to in any document—even in the Declaration of Independence."

"Besides," added K.C., "you don't intend to participate in the suicide. We know all about your plans, and the way I see it, you've acquired quite some wealth at the expense of your organization. You used some for the running of this place. You invested other funds and reaped huge benefits from those investments."

Bingo. She was guessing now, but there was an expression of pride in his eyes that told her she was hitting the mark. He made no move to stop her from speaking. It was as if he wanted them to know of his success, his brilliance.

"Along the way," she continued, "you brought in other investors. But now you're greedy, and you don't want to give up what you've acquired—not even to pay them what you owe.

"So, you plan to sell Angels Crest to the investors in place of their return." He winced slightly, and she knew she'd struck a nerve. "But what you hadn't counted on was your unwillingness to let it go—for any amount of money. After all, you built this place from near ruin. You want it all."

Gav watched her, astounded. He'd had no idea that she had spent those sleepless nights on the rock-hard ground, putting herself in Randolph's shoes, trying to figure his motives, his plans.

"So after the mass suicide, you'll fake your death—who knows how?—but in reality, you'll leave the country, probably head straight for Buenos Aires and that pile of money.

"I also noticed in the report you so quickly shredded that an insurance company was listed. You've been paying massive premiums on Angels Crest.

"A terrible, swift-moving brush fire, not all that uncommon in California this time of year. What a shame that it should strike immediately following the deaths of your followers.

"But in the end, Randolph, you would indeed have it all. And hundreds of dead bodies would never whisper a word about what you did to them or where you've gone."

Gav gave her another incredulous look.

"You're very clever, my dear. Too clever," Randolph said. "It's too bad you won't live long enough to know if you're correct or not."

K.C. took a deep breath. She'd known the risks from the beginning, but to hear him say the words made her mouth go dry and her heart pound.

Randolph stepped to his desk and picked up the phone. "Sister Bastancherry, please call Brother Dakota. Tell him to bring two guards immediately to my office."

Then he turned again to Gav and K.C. "A nice scenario you've painted with a very creative mind, my dear, but I would have thought you'd spend your spare time in a more productive manner." He laughed. "The rewards would have been greater if you'd figured a way out of the compound."

He stepped closer to her. "For you see, now it's too late." He touched her cheek with the cold metal of the barrel and held her gaze with his own. Her heart thudded harder now, and she fought to keep from showing her fear. "You're a newspaper reporter, I understand," he continued. "So you'll be especially interested in our ceremony.

"As I recall, it was a reporter who touched off the Jonestown affair, was it not? I can still see his limp body sprawled on the tarmac of that airport in the Guyana jungle. Just think, he was the first to leave on that particular journey—just as you will be on ours."

Gav signaled K.C. with his eyes. She knew he meant for her to head for the French doors. He was about to make a move to save them. But just as Gav lunged for the gun, the office door flew open, and three armed guards rushed in. The revolver tumbled to the floor, out of reach.

It was quickly assessed that K.C. carried no valuables, not even her purse or cell phone. Gav was frisked, then relieved of his wallet, keys, everything in his pockets. Without another word, K.C. and Gav were led from the chateau.

As soon as his office was cleared, Randolph buzzed Sister Bastancherry. "Are they here yet?"

"No. But Sister Desirée just arrived."

He sighed impatiently. He wondered how she'd convinced the guards to let her leave the auditorium. Of course, it was probably her status as his intended that made the others bow and scrape, even the guards. He would have to remedy the oversight. "Send her in," he said. "But let me know the minute the others arrive. Show them into the conference room. I'll join them there."

A moment later, Desirée swept into the office, looking radiant.

"Darling!" he said, rising and stepping toward her. "I thought you were to remain with the others."

She smiled sweetly and tilted her chin in a way that spoke of refinement and coquetry. It melted his heart and he couldn't be angry with her. "I wanted to be with you," she said. "We need to discuss our wedding vows."

He chuckled, reached for her hand, and drew her nearer. "Now, that's a wonderful thought."

Desirée was looking up at him so innocently. She lifted her hand and lightly, lovingly, stroked his goatee with her fingertips. "You see, this ceremony is very meaningful to me. Once I seriously doubted you, Rance. But lately, something's happening to me." There was an ethereal glow on her face. "I can't explain it, but it's made all the difference in my acceptance of our journey to Atara.

"You've led me in my thoughts away from the darkness and on the path leading toward the light. These moments have become some of the most significant in my life." She touched his face. "Because of you, Rance. All because of you.

"I know I've held myself in reserve around you in the past, but now..." She let out a loving sigh. "...now, I feel regenerated. Almost as if I've only just begun to live."

"Desirée," he murmured, overcome. His voice was husky when he continued. "My darling, I had no idea." He pressed her close, feeling the steady beating of her heart. Then he pulled back slightly and looked into her lovely eyes. "I've noticed you've dropped the use of 'it.'"

She laughed. "I was wondering how long it would take for you to notice." She tilted her chin upward again. "After all, how can I rule Atara with you, my king, and call myself 'it'?"

He laughed with her and pulled her close. How right she was! And, oh, how he would miss her when the time came. He held her for a moment, then she smiled up at him again.

"You've opened my eyes to a whole new world—literally," she said. "And for that I'll always be grateful."

Sister Bastancherry opened the door a crack and looked in. "Brother Randolph, your appointment is waiting. They've been seated in the conference room."

"I'll be right there," he said, then looked back to Desirée. "Will you wait for me?" he said, kissing her fingertips.

"Of course, my darling," she said. "I'll just busy myself at the computer—working on the wedding vows."

"The first draft!" he added, realizing that he was surely going to have to rethink his plans for her. "I want to help with the final draft. After all, this is my wedding, too."

As he slipped from the room, Desirée gave him a small wave and seated herself at his desk.

K.C. and Gav were escorted into the old cellar by the security guards. Without a word, the men gave them a rough shove through the storage room and into the dark moss-lined tunnel leading to the caves.

K.C. glanced back at Gav, and she could see the secret message of reassurance in his eyes. He was with her. He knew her fears. He gave her an almost imperceptible nod as one of the guards nearest her gave her another push to keep her moving forward.

They wound through the tunnel, past the room where K.C. had found Marigold, around a corner and deeper into the earth. The air was chilly, and she shivered, partly from the cold, partly from fear.

She nibbled at her lip as they moved onward. The tunnel appeared to be narrowing, its ceiling height shrinking, and somewhere in the distance a slow, loud drip could be heard falling into a body of water. She shivered as they wound still deeper into the mountainside.

K.C. wished that she could feel Gav's reassuring touch…the touch of someone who loved her…in this terrifying labyrinth that with each new twist and turn spoke of deception, danger, and death.

Gav? Did she just think to herself that she needed Gav's touch because he loved her?

K.C. swallowed hard, forgetting her fear for a moment. The touch of someone who loved her? Gav's reassuring touch? There was no doubt he'd been attentive, even affectionate at times, during their last few days together. But when had she begun to consider that he might love her?

The tunnel seemed to shrink even more. Now K.C. stooped to keep from bumping her head on the moss-covered ceiling. She shivered as her hair caught in the tangle of dark moss and wondered if spiders and roaches might have found the environment a suitable habitat. She grimaced. This certainly wasn't the time or place to dwell on whether Gav still loved her. But strange as it was, that glimmer of hope, that precious spark of love, right now seemed her only light in the terrifying darkness.

The light grew dimmer as working light bulbs grew scarcer, and it seemed harder to breathe. She tried to calm her fears, telling herself it was probably her imagination or simple hyperventilation.

Finally another of the thick wooden doors loomed ahead, barely visible in the dim light. One of the guards pulled out a key and opened it. At first K.C. thought the room was empty. But after her eyes became accustomed to the light of one mere candle on some sort of a box, she caught a glimpse of a few of the faces. These were the people who'd stood against Rance Randolph!

Her guard shoved her inside. Gav was pushed in just behind her and the door closed, the handle turning and clicking until it locked.

"K.C.!" came the welcoming voice from somewhere in the darkness.

"Aunt Theo?"

A moment later, her aunt grabbed K.C. and hugged her close. "Oh, my sweet darlin'," she whispered. "It's good to hold you in my arms again."

Next, she grabbed hold of Gav. "Young man," she said. "K.C. told me you were here! Thank you for coming."

"It's good to know you're all right, Theo," Gav said. "I've missed you." He held her close for a moment before releasing her.

"Folks," Theodora said, "I'd like to introduce my grand-niece, Katherine Cassandra Keegan...." K.C. groaned audibly, and several of the group laughed. "Actually, we call her K.C.," her aunt corrected. "And this is Gav, Sheriff Elliott Gavin from Sugarloaf Ridge."

"These kids and their names," Marigold Green called out from somewhere in the middle of the group. "I think Katherine is such a nice name. So's Elliott. I have no idea why you'd want to change two perfectly sound names to Gav, a name I've never heard of before, and to K.C., two initials, for heaven's sake. It's like having an acronym for a name!"

Several of the others joked with Marigold about her own name, and there was laughter here and there across the room.

K.C. looked at Gav. Levity was the last thing she'd expected from this imprisoned group. They surely knew there was no escape, and that the chances of dying with the others were great. Yet here they were chitchatting as if attending a neighborhood tea.

"Are you okay?" K.C. asked her aunt after a moment.

Her aunt sighed deeply. "Yes," she said, her voice strong. "We've been brought food today, and the guards come by to take us a few at a time to some rest-room facilities in another cave. We're fine. Really."

"Has Randolph been to see you? Said anything about how long he'll keep you?"

Theodora guided K.C. and Gav away from the rest of the group. "He came to talk with us right after he'd sent us away from the ceremony—did you see it?" K.C. and Gav nodded, and she went on. "It was very odd. He didn't hand out the ultimatum I thought he would—"

"Such as 'bow down or die'?" Gav said.

"Exactly. Strangely, there was none of that. He just said we would be here for a short time and then released."

"Do you believe him?" K.C. asked.

Theodora shook her head. "No." And she told them what had happened to her friend Ariel Tilman.

"I think he'll take us in with the rest when the time comes," Gav said.

"Do you have any idea how long?" Theodora asked, and again, K.C. was struck by the strength in her voice. Especially when she was feeling so weak in comparison. "And my next question is obvious, I think," continued her aunt. "Is there any way out?"

"I don't know yet, but I won't stop trying to find a way," Gav said, moving to the door and inspecting the dead bolt again. "We've broken through several doors already, so maybe one more's not so unthinkable." He shook his head as he twisted and turned the mechanism. It held fast. "How about tools? Has anyone here searched the room for anything that might work?" he asked.

"We've done little else but look," said one of the men.

"There's nothing in here. Not even a lightbulb in the socket," said another. "They scoured this place clean before we were brought in."

"They wanted to make good and sure we didn't get out," added Marigold Green. "Guess Randolph figured I'd escaped once, and I might do it again." She giggled. "Where's Jacques Cousteau when you need him the most?"

Gav lifted the candle toward the barren walls of the cave, examining every crevice and nook. Several murmured disappointed words about the fruitless search, but Gav skirted the room twice more before putting the candle back on its stand, then headed again to where K.C. and Theodora stood talking.

"I think we should tell the folks what we discovered, Kace, don't you?"

She nodded. "I agree. We don't have the proof we need, but maybe if we're taken into the auditorium with the others, we could all spread the word—let them know he's merely an opportunist."

"And mass murderer, if he goes through with his plan," Gav added. Then he called for everyone's attention, and when they had looked up, he told them about the computer file.

"But it won't make any difference whether he's a charlatan or not, unless we can stop him," Marigold said. "And I for one do not intend to go down without a fight."

"Hear, hear!" called out some of the others. Others voiced the brave actions they had planned.

"They've got guns," an older woman said quietly.

After a moment, they went on discussing possible ways out of their dilemma, and Theodora turned to K.C., slipping her arm around her niece's waist. "You know, honey, I haven't stopped believing that God brought us here."

"Aunt Theo, it just seems all this has gone from bad to worse. We had finally found the proof we needed. Then suddenly we were caught and brought here. A place where we can't do you or any of the others any good."

She looked around nervously, feeling the old, familiar sensation squeezing the breath right out of her. "And now we're trapped—" She bit her lip, trying to push from her mind the fear of being in this dark, enclosed place. She had kept the sensation bottled up since they were first shoved into the room.

Now it threatened to spill over.

"I find that talking to the others gets my mind off my own anxieties," her aunt said softly, watching K.C. with understanding eyes.

"You're afraid?" K.C. was surprised.

"I've never been so scared in my life—practically every moment since I arrived at Angels Crest," she said with a half-smile.

K.C. found her aunt's hand and pressed it. "I didn't know."

"We're human, honey. Fear is a very human emotion. But it doesn't mean God isn't with us. It simply means we can't feel his presence because fear is in the way.

"And most of us are feeling the same way right now. I don't know how many hours we've been in here, or how many we've got left to go, but we're all struggling with our fears."

"Yet you said that you're still sure God led you—and Gav and me—here."

For a moment, Theodora didn't speak. When she did, her voice was so low that only K.C. and Gav could hear her words. "We may be facing death. All of us. And soon."

K.C. didn't want to consider it, but she nodded.

"God has already done a mighty work to snatch these souls straight from the jaws of hell. They stood up against unbelievable pressure to obey, to bow, to worship a false god. God's already at work in their lives."

"And you're saying he's brought us here purposely to be with them in this dark place…during what might be their final hours?" K.C. mused, knowing the answer.

"I'm sure of it, sweetie," Theodora said, then she looked up at Gav. "And you, son, you who have a soul yearning to minister, to serve. God's placed you here to do just that. These people are in need of healing. Soul, body, and spirit healing. We are his instruments—his hands, his heart, his voice, his physicians."

Gav nodded, and Theodora touched his arm. "None of us knows how long we've got on Earth. But when you think the time might be sooner than we expected, it's amazing how our perspectives change."

"And priorities," K.C. added, understanding.

"It's true. He's led us here! Think of it!" She gestured to the others in the dark room. "He's here with us! Among us!"

K.C. swallowed hard. "St. Francis of Assisi's prayer has never had more meaning, has it?" She reached for their hands, and they bowed their heads together. Her voice was barely a whisper as she prayed:

"Lord, make us instruments of your peace.
Where there is hatred, let us sow love.
Where there is injury, pardon.
Where there is doubt, faith.
Where there is despair, hope.
Where there is darkness, light.
Where there is sadness, joy."

Gav released their hands, then circled his arms around them both as she continued.

"O Divine Master," K.C. whispered, "grant that we may not so much seek
To be consoled, as to console,
To be understood, as to understand,
To be loved, as to love.
It is in giving that we receive,
It is in pardoning that we are pardoned."

She swallowed hard, and blinked back her tears as she said the final words: "It is in dying that we are born to eternal life."

"Blessings, my precious ones," Theodora said, embracing them each quietly and letting the silence speak and comfort them. After a moment, they each moved into the group.

K.C. sat down with a group of three women. Gav did the

same with two of the young men. Others gathered near each of them, until all were engaged in conversation. Theodora sat with Marigold and several others. Questions were asked, and opinions were openly encouraged. Deep conversations about family pain and childhood sorrows, rejection and defeat and failure, continued through the night.

Tears flowed, of yesterday's sorrow and of a new and present joy.

Throughout the night, the murmuring of voices filled the cave. But no longer was there the spirit of fear. The spirit of love and healing began to flicker brighter than the light of the single candle on its stand.

A peaceful silence, followed by sleep, finally blanketed the group. Gav leaned his back against the side of the cave close to K.C. Still wide awake with the wonder of all that had happened, she propped herself up beside him. Theodora and Marigold Green had fallen silent nearby, and soon their even breathing told K.C. that even they were sleeping.

"Kace," Gav said.

"Yeah?" she whispered back.

"There are some things I've needed to tell you for a long time."

K.C. started to protest, just as she had many times before, knowing his words had to do with their past, with a pain she didn't want to face. But here in this place, knowing that there might never be another chance, she had to listen.

"It's time to speak from our hearts, Kace," he whispered. "We can't put it off any longer."

She swallowed hard and reached for his hand.

TWENTY-FOUR

K C. relished the feel of Gav's strong hand around hers and the comfort of his nearness in the darkness. According to his watch, it was early morning, but the room remained midnight black except for the light from a single candle, this one half spent. Each lasted only a few hours, but with a supply of only a few dozen, the group had unanimously decided to burn only one at a time.

Gav moved closer to K.C. and when he turned toward her, his face was visible in the soft candlelight. She sighed deeply. "Before you begin, may I tell you what I'm feeling? Why I've stopped you when you've tried to explain what happened three years ago?"

He nodded and tightened the grip on her hand, wrapping his long, tapered fingers securely around hers. He was as nervous about this conversation as she was, and she suspected she knew why. It seemed strange that only a few days ago even the thought of his indiscretion had sliced through her heart like a knife. Now, in light of all they'd been through, the pain had lessened. It was still there, but it no longer threatened to overwhelm her.

"When you broke our engagement," she said, "and left seminary, then disappeared from my life, I can't begin to describe to you what I felt.

"Suddenly, circumstances have thrown us together again, and it's as if those three years simply melted away." She shook her head slowly. "I can't pretend to understand why you did what you did. And it still hurts after all this time. I know it will be difficult for you to tell me about the other woman. But it's even more difficult for me to hear it. And for that reason, I haven't wanted you to—"

"Another woman?" Gav croaked. "Is that what you think?"

"Well, yes. What other explanation could there be? To leave me and seminary at the same time. I assumed you couldn't go into church ministry because of some..." Her words faltered, ending in a soft sigh. "...some unfaithfulness."

"Oh, K.C.!" For a moment he didn't say anything more. He looked heavenward and swallowed hard, then closed his eyes. When he looked at her again, his pain for her feelings was etched deep in his face. "Oh, what I've put you through!"

"Then it's true?" She had hoped he would dispute her words.

"Oh, no! It's not true, Kace. Not only would I never do that to you, I could never love anyone but you."

"Maybe love didn't have anything to do with it," she persisted.

He suddenly cupped her face with both his palms and tilted it gently until she was looking straight into his eyes. She could see the truth in them and felt the sudden welling of tears. "There was no one else?" she breathed.

He shook his head slowly. "Never, Kace. Never!"

"Then, why, Gav? Why did you run from me?"

He dropped his hands. "That's what I've been wanting to tell you...for days now. I prayed for God's perfect timing, but each time I started to lead into the conversation—"

"I stopped you," she finished, lifting a brow.

"I love the way you do that, you know."

She smiled into his eyes. "Go on," she said. "I'll try to restrain myself, no matter how much you love it. I do want to hear the rest of this."

"It's hard to explain, and though I've gone over it in my

mind, even imagined how I would someday tell you, I still feel inadequate and ashamed."

"Gav," she whispered. "What is it?"

"First, I need to ask your forgiveness, Kace."

"Me forgive you? When I believed that you'd been unfaithful?"

"But I did something even worse, I think."

"What, Gav? What could have been so bad?"

"I blamed you for my own inability to be honest before God. That's why I left."

K.C. was stunned. She pulled her hand away from his and stared at the candle's flickering flame, trying to understand.

"Kace?"

She turned back to him.

"I chose to go into the ministry because of you. I thought that's what you wanted."

He had been right. She had wanted that for him...for them both. She'd pictured them serving God together in some little village church. She nodded, understanding. "I thought we'd both received the call to serve God," she said softly, looking into his eyes. "I remember the church service when it happened. We both felt God's touch—at least I did. We saw Father Max afterward. We told him what had happened. Then we knelt and prayed with him. I thought it was real...that God had called us to serve him together."

"I did, too, Kace. But it wasn't until later that I realized serving God doesn't always mean becoming a pastor." He swallowed hard. "While I was busy trying to sort all this out, I was marching closer and closer to ministry in a little church somewhere, performing weddings and funerals, attending teas, and I couldn't bear the thought of that kind of ministry. I'm sorry.

"It is a calling for some, for many. And it's a wonderful calling, but it wasn't for me. And as commencement neared—" His words broke off. "—I realized I was falling headlong into priesthood because of my love for you, not my love for God. I knew it was what you wanted. I wasn't sure what God wanted."

She started to protest, but he touched her lips with his fingertips. "Let me finish," he said gently. "The worst part was that as time passed and I became more despondent, I started blaming you for my wrong turn."

"Oh, Gav, why didn't you tell me?"

"I couldn't. Or wouldn't. I thought I was doing the right thing, or maybe the righteous thing. Perhaps the stoic thing, by giving you up at the same time I gave up the priesthood. I thought if you'd been truly called to serve God in a pastorate, he would provide you with the proper mate."

"The proper mate?" She shook her head, incredulous. "Gav, you make it sound like God's got some sort of production line going in heaven. Picks up pairs of humans, sorts them out, pairs them together in this career or that. If one mate doesn't work out, he picks out another, tossing the first one aside." She let out an exasperated sigh. "Come on, Gav, didn't our love count for anything? How about our friendship? Didn't it count?"

"It didn't take me long to figure out what a fool I'd been. By the time I sorted everything out, I didn't think you'd ever forgive me."

She held his hand in her lap, rubbing the soft hair on the backs of his fingers with her thumb. Then she lifted his hand and kissed his fingers. "You could have at least asked," she said, smiling up at him.

He chuckled softly. "As difficult as it's been to have this conversation—even though we've been thrown together, nonstop, for the past few days—you really can't blame me, can you? I can only imagine what would've happened if I'd shown up on your doorstep."

"So God sealed us in a dark, windowless room to get us to talk," K.C. pointed out with a grin.

"Pretty drastic measures," Gav said, touching her cheek. "But well worth it," he murmured, pulling her closer.

But her eyes were serious as she looked up at him. "Gav, we may not have any more time together than this…"

He didn't let her finish but bent his head and covered her mouth with his. His kiss was both tender and passionate, familiar yet as new as the springtime sun after a long dark winter. K.C.'s heart danced beneath her ribs, and despite the terror of the dark place, despite their unknown tomorrows, she relaxed in Gav's arms, thinking only of her love for him.

After a moment, she pulled back. She smiled into his eyes and let out a contented sigh, completely forgetting where they were, the dangers they faced. All that mattered was Gav, her precious Gav. She reached up to touch his face, marveling at the strength, the love, she saw in it. She traced the line of his jaw, his lips, with a butterfly-soft touch, then kissed the corners of his mouth.

Her hand rested lightly on his chest, and she could feel his heart pounding. For an endless moment, neither of them moved.

Then their lips met again.

"Kace," he whispered huskily after a moment. She looked up and caught her breath at the emotion she saw in his eyes. "Kace, I love you. I always have." He kissed her again.

She reached for his hand again and held it to her cheek. "Oh, Gav…" she breathed, closing her eyes.

He lifted her chin gently with his fingertips, tilting her face toward him. "What's wrong, K.C.?"

"It's hard to release all the pain of the past, and to think about starting all over again."

"You've forgiven but not forgotten?" There was no bitterness in his voice, just simple understanding.

"The love is still there, Gav, as strong as ever. But when I think about what happened before, I feel so uncertain about our future."

"For now we can only consider today, K.C.," he said solemnly, and she understood his meaning.

This moment may be all we have anyway, she added silently as she studied his face. She nodded. "No matter what happens, God has given us the gift of finding each other, discovering our love before…" Her voice faltered, and she bit her lip to keep tears from forming. They traced down her cheeks anyway, and Gav wiped them away with his fingertips.

"For today, Elliott Gavin," she said softly, "my heart is yours. Today and always." She paused. "No matter what our future holds, I love you!"

He bent his head down and kissed her again.

K.C. pulled back after a moment and let out a shaky sigh. "You haven't told me about your career plans now, Gav. I know you're taking psych and sociology classes, but what are you planning to do with them?" She smiled sadly. "That's, of course, assuming we have a future."

"Let's not consider that we won't, Kace," Gav said softly. He stared at the burning candle for a moment. "I wish I'd known a few years ago what I know now—that serving God doesn't have to be from a pulpit." He folded his arms around her shoulders as she leaned her back against his chest. "What we've been through the past few days is ministry. What your parents are doing in the Romanian orphanage is ministry."

"Giving a cup of water to a child…" she said softly.

"Yes, especially that," he said. "This experience has made

me wonder about working with kids, high school and college age, who are especially vulnerable to cult leaders. They know just how to snare the most emotionally needy. They promise the world to these kids, a world of love, acceptance, and structure that some of these students have never known."

"Just as Randolph has done here, though to adults."

He nodded. "I can't help thinking that the cult recruiters on campuses need to be exposed. These kids need to be taught awareness of cult entrapment, taught the truth about what they're getting into."

She turned to look up at him. "Aren't there experts—detectives, actually—who're hired by parents and others to get their kids away from cults and communes?"

He nodded and gave her a small grin. "Yes, there are."

She suddenly sat up. "You're already planning this, aren't you? That's what you're training to be!" It all made sense. The police academy, sheriff's training, psychology classes, sociology classes. "That's it, isn't it?"

He chuckled lightly. "I won't make a very good detective if I'm that transparent."

"Gav, that's wonderful!" she whispered, still aware of the sleeping people scattered throughout the room. "It's perfect for you! And is it ministry? Wow! Of course it is." She placed her hands on either side of his face and kissed him again on the lips. "I'm so proud of you, Gav."

But even as she said the words, her spirits fell. He'd chosen a single man's ministry. There could no family life. No children. How could there be? He would be traveling around the country, working undercover as a cult member, or lecturing on high-school and college campuses. Deprogramming the brainwashed ex-cult members.

But then she was taking God out of the equation. Gav hadn't merely picked out a career like some people pick out a new pair of running shoes. God had chosen him, called him, to serve him in this way. Both their futures were in God's hands, whether that future on Earth ended in a matter of hours, or fifty years hence.

He touched her cheek as if he knew her thoughts. She smiled up at him. "I'm so proud of you, Gav," she repeated.

They whispered in the darkness, catching up on all they'd missed in each other's lives during the past years. Finally, sighing deeply, K.C. snuggled against Gav, her cheek against his chest. Still propped against the wall of the cave, he bent over her protectively, his cheek resting on the top of her head. "I love you, Kace," he breathed into her hair. "I've never stopped loving you!"

She closed her eyes, shutting out everything except the feel of his arms circling her and the sound of his husky voice whispering her name.

"I don't know what's ahead for us," he murmured a short time later. "But this one thing I know, Katherine Cassandra Keegan, I will love you until the last breath I take."

Finally she slept.

When she awoke it was to dark confusion, voices shouting orders, and the ex-cult members scrambling about the room. The candle had melted to a puddle of wax while they slept, and now the only light came from the guards' flashlights, casting harsh beams across the frightened faces.

"Line up. Now!" shouted a robed guard, a big, burly man K.C. had seen before. "It's time to go!"

At first words of delight were exchanged. Someone called out that they were being released at last, but K.C. glanced at Gav. His face told her what her heart already knew. Her hands grew clammy; she wiped them on her robe and tried not to notice that they were trembling.

The group formed a double line in the hallway, all still wearing the robes in which they'd been brought to the caves. Then the men and women were led separately to the rest-room facilities and given a bottle of water and a small wheat roll to take with them as they walked from the tunnel.

Finally they were led through the passageway, armed guards flanking each pair, and together they moved through the winding, twisting corridors, sometimes almost crawling through the maze of tunnels and caves. At last, the wine cellar was at the end of the tunnel and, beyond that, early morning daylight streaming into the big storage room through the tall windows.

As soon as they were led from the cellar door, K.C. drew in gulps of fresh air, closing her eyes as they walked. Her knees were now as shaky as her hands were earlier, and with each step, she wondered how she could possibly take another.

The group moved along, their faces grim. Marigold Green was K.C.'s partner in the double line.

Theodora was directly behind Marigold, and K.C. glanced back. Her aunt gave her a brave smile, but K.C. could see the alarm in her eyes. Theodora smiled softly, as if to calm her niece, and K.C. gave her a return nod, then turned back to face the front of the small parade.

She'd tried to find Gav, but he must have been assigned a place at the rear of the group, she decided, because she couldn't spot him without craning around. A quick glance at her armed guard told her she had better keep marching along, face forward.

They were now on the footpath that skirted the edge of the eucalyptus grove and were heading up the hillside. Soon the rectangular brick dormitory buildings loomed ahead, and the shadow of the spiraled auditorium fell across the ground where they walked.

It was obvious now that the auditorium was their destination. K.C. swallowed hard. All along, she'd thought there would be a way to escape. And now here they were, marching like lambs to the slaughter.

Perhaps if they all rushed their guards at once, she thought, or grabbed for their weapons. Anything! Anything but going along docilely to their deaths.

Marigold Green must have had the same thought, for at that very moment, she turned to her guard, gave him a big smile, then stuck out her foot to trip him, at the same time socking him in the face with her bottled water.

He quickly outmaneuvered her, but in the process, struck the big woman across the side of her head with the back of his hand. She crumpled to the ground, water bottle and wheat roll flying. K.C. quickly moved to kneel beside her.

But her guard grabbed K.C.'s arm, twisted it, and pushed her back into line. He kept her arm in the painful position as they walked. She bit her lip in anger and to keep from crying out in pain.

Suddenly, there was a commotion from the rear of the group, and she looked back to see Gav lunge for his guard. The guard grunted, almost knocked off balance.

But he reacted in time to slice the rock-hard side of his palm into Gav's esophagus. Gav fell limply to the ground, coughing and groaning. He then ordered Gav to kneel before him.

Gav shook his head and again tried to stand. The guard shoved him down. Gav was now holding his neck and choking.

K.C. caught her breath. The guard suddenly pointed his weapon at Gav's forehead.

She wildly struggled to free herself but couldn't get loose from her guard's grasp. He merely tightened his hold. She yelped and fell to the ground. Around her the earth seemed to spin in a whirl of darkness and pain. Her arm was still pinned by the guard in a helpless twist, its position keeping her in a head-down, kneeling position.

The group was silent now, and she sensed, rather than saw, that everyone's attention was on Gav.

She tried once more to stand, only to hear the guard laugh and tighten his painful grasp. So she remained perfectly still, breathing a prayer for Gav.

A heartbeat later, she heard the hammer click. Gav's guard had cocked his revolver. But she couldn't lift her head to watch.

All she could see were the tears that dropped in the dirt beneath her face.

TWENTY-FIVE

L et them up!" a female voice said with regal authority. "Now! Step back. Weapons down. Let them up!" The hold on her arm suddenly lessened, and K.C. drew in a deep breath and stood, her knees shaky. She brushed herself off, and looked back to see Gav standing. Their eyes met, and he nodded slightly, indicating he was all right.

"There's no need for such violent behavior," said the voice again, from the top of the stairs at the entrance to the auditorium. K.C. looked up to see that it was the Scott woman, the same who wouldn't stand against Rance Randolph at the Keb-Kaseko statue.

She now filled her new role with dignity, as if having practiced this, her destiny, for a lifetime. She stood, arms outstretched, her gown falling in soft folds to the ground, her hood resting over her shoulders like a mantle. Her hair hung gracefully, its color nearly matching the pale gold robe. She seemed to shimmer in the morning sun.

K.C. blinked, astounded by the change in the once-timid woman. She now seemed ageless, bigger than life, almost as if at any moment fire would blaze from her eyes, lightning bolts from her hands. She lifted her chin upward, regarding the group standing below her. Her manner was almost haughty.

"These dissidents will meet their reward soon enough," Desirée said with a voice of stern authority. "You do not need to concern yourself with hurrying the process."

The guards seemed to shrink in her presence and backed away a few steps from the group. She gave them a curt nod, and the double line began to move forward once again.

At the auditorium's entrance, K.C. moved with the others into single file, and they entered the doors of the large room. It looked much as it had when she and Gav had seen it before, stained-glass windows casting rainbows of light across the Fellowship members' robes, the cathedral-like feel of the high-beamed ceilings, the huge marble pillars that lined both sides of the room.

The only difference was the arrangement on the platform: A series of long cloth-covered tables were spread into one long row. Placed on them were silver chalices and crystal bowls on sterling pedestals, linen napkins, and tall candelabras blazing with lighted tapers.

The hundreds of Fellowship members, looking emotionally and physically depleted, sat around in groups, their faces pale with bruise-colored circles under their eyes, perhaps from hours of frenzied pseudo-worship, or from the wine that had obviously been freely flowing. Or perhaps they were subdued, K.C. thought, because somewhere in their glazed minds, a small kernel of truth told them what was ahead.

Some sort of preparation was taking place near the platform with robed Fellowship members and guards speaking to each other, and the group that had just been escorted in seemed to have been forgotten.

K.C. looked around for the others and spotted Gav making his way toward her. Theodora, Marigold, and the rest of the group had already disappeared into the crowd, as planned. They would spread the word about the computer file. K.C. only hoped some parts of the devotees' minds were still open, had even the smallest reasoning ability, so that they could hear the truth…and perhaps believe it.

Gav touched her hand. "K.C., are you hurt?"

"No, not a bit," she said with a small smile. "How about you? I heard that revolver hammer click back…"

"And thought, 'I'm glad you're gone, you rascal, you.'"
Grinning, he quoted the words from an old Louis Armstrong tune.

"It's not funny," she said.

"Gallows humor," he defended. "They teach it at the academy." Then he reached for her arm and guided her toward one of the wide marble pillars, out of sight of those working up by the platform.

His face was deadly serious when they reached the pillar and he turned to face her. "K.C., if anything goes wrong, I just need to know that we're okay. I mean, that you know what I said to you last night wasn't just because of what we face today. What I'm trying very hard to say, Kace, is that I didn't say I loved you just because I thought we might—"

"Die here today?"

"There you go again, finishing my sentences."

K.C. reached up and touched his lips to silence him. "You don't have to say this, Gav. I know you meant everything you said last night. That you would have said it in a moonlit garden with a thousand tomorrows stretching into eternity—if you'd had the chance."

"I couldn't have said it better myself." He gave her a quick kiss on the nose.

"And I didn't say I love you just because of all this." She gestured around the auditorium. "I said it because I meant it. I would have said it—"

"In a moonlit garden," he finished for her.

She grinned up at him. "It's catching."

"We think alike," he said, arching one brow. "We always have."

She rolled her eyes heavenward. "It's actually a rude habit I learned from you in fourth grade."

"Yeah, right."

Just then there was a scramble of more activity from the platform. Rance Randolph's voice boomed over the sound system, and he called for the attention of everyone in the room.

Gav reached for K.C., folding her into his arms. Then pulling back, he looked into her face. "K.C., I love you!" he whispered. "If there are no tomorrows…"

Tears filled her eyes, and she gazed into his eyes. "That's one sentence neither of us should finish," she said. "Our tomorrows are in God's hands, my beloved. No matter what happens here today."

Then they walked from behind the pillar and joined Theodora, Marigold, and the others. Together they moved to the outer fringes of the assemblage.

Rance Randolph glanced at the beautiful woman who stood next to him, Desirée Scott, who would soon become his bride.

"You look absolutely radiant," he said.

"It's my wedding day, dearest," she answered, her face aglow, her voice bubbling with affection.

He basked in her adoration, just as he always did, even though he was still at war with himself as to whether he should bring her into his plan. The only thing stopping him was the fear that once she knew about the Argentine funds—which included those she'd turned over to the Angels of Fellowship—she might turn against him.

And he didn't think he could bear that kind of disapproval. It would be better for her to die believing in him, in Atara and her own deity, than for her to lose faith in him.

Disapproval was abhorrent to him, whether from Desirée or from any of his congregation. His gaze took in the robed figures standing before him, then it rested on the faces of the dissidents. He could see stark disapproval in their expressions. How dare they oppose him?

Even in childhood it seemed everyone had disapproved of him. He was the child of the devil, according to his foster mother, the one who'd disapproved the most.

But no more! Once he had experienced the power of leadership in his Haight-Ashbury days, he soon craved it. Power ensured approval on demand. Opposition was no longer an issue because behavior and action could be dictated.

And now he was adding money to the heady elixir of that power. Money and power together would bring him everything he yearned for, along with a new identity, new friends, and a new life.

His eyes met those of K.C. Keegan. She didn't blink or flinch. Neither did the man who stood beside her, the man who had lied and said he was her husband. And then there were the calm, cool eyes of Theodora Whimple. She'd started all this trouble with her snooping, making the dissidents think he might be wrong.

How dare she?

And the big-shouldered, silly, frumpy woman, Marigold Green, standing there watching him with her air of superiority. How he loathed her spirited ways. People with minds of their own always rubbed him against the grain.

Ha! These and the others who thought they could stand against him would certainly pay for their folly. Pay dearly. Soon they would drink of the sacred cup, and he would be done with them. He laughed to himself. Sacred indeed. The only thing sacred about it was that it symbolized their passage from this life to the next. If there was such a thing.

He turned and smiled into Desirée's eyes, reaching for her hands. "Are you ready, my love?" he asked.

She nodded. "I am." She said the *I* proudly, and he squeezed her fingertips affectionately. One of the most rewarding aspects of his leadership was to completely cleanse a person of all they'd once been, only to see that self be rebuilt, as in sweet Desirée's case, into a radiant, confident, even majestic being.

Hand in hand they stepped to the microphone. "Brothers and sisters," he said with emotion. "Our waiting is almost over. Our last hours on this earth are about to pass. But this is a time to celebrate, not to mourn. Before our journey, Sister Desirée and I will wed. We will taste our final supper, and we will partake of our final elixir of life that will send us on our journey to Atara.

"This, my brothers and sisters, is a time to dance and be happy!"

He gave the signal for the drummers to began their throbbing, pulsating rhythm. He lifted his hands and began the chant.

"Angels of Atara. Come for us. Save us. Take us from this world. Take us to Atara. Atara-Atara-Atara."

His conditioned flock raised their arms in devotion to the Ataran pantheon. They swayed to the music, just as always. Robes flowing and swinging, dancing lights from the jeweled windows splashing them with color.

He closed his eyes, feeling the vibrations of the beating drums. These were the last hours he would hear them. The voices lifted the chant. "Atara-Atara-Atara."

Louder and louder, now they cried the words. "Come for us. Save us. Take us from this world. Take us to Atara. Atara-Atara-Atara."

For hours now they had been in this semiconscious state. They would follow his leading as docile little lambs. They trusted him, their Ataran leader, to take them from this world to the next.

And trust him they should. For they were in pain. He had listened to their stories of sorrow in all the mass-cleansing sessions, and those in which he counseled them individually. He was about to take that pain from them.

They would find rest at last.

"Angels of Atara. Come for us. Save us. Take us from this world. Take us to Atara. Atara-Atara-Atara." They lifted their arms and whirled about the room, following his lead. "Atara-Atara-Atara."

Suddenly, his eyes opened, and his gaze rested on those few who stood sullenly at the back of the room.

They were not raising their arms to the Ataran host. They were not moving their lips, even pretending to offer their voices in praise. Arms folded across their chests, they met his gaze.

He held up his hand, a signal for the drums to halt.

There was silence in the room.

Randolph stared at the dissidents. "Come here!" he said. "I order you to come forward."

They exchanged glances, then slowly, the group walked to the front of the auditorium until they stood just below him in front of the platform.

Suddenly, Sister Desirée touched his arm. She wore a look of regal wisdom, inclining her head ever so slightly toward him. She made him feel like a king! He only wished the Ataran myth were true. What a reign they would have had together.

"My darling," she said, leaning away from the microphone, "I have an idea for our amusement."

"What is that, my queen?"

"I know how you love the challenge of games," she said. "Why not allow these fools to speak their minds?" She laughed, a bell-like, musical sound. "I for one would be so amused to hear another story like that of Jacques Cousteau, the forty-fifth angel." She was right, of course. It had been since the crazy woman, Marigold Green, arrived that he'd seen an almost miraculous change in Desirée. She'd been amused, she said. Perhaps that's what had caused the metamorphosis.

He chuckled. "It was very entertaining," he agreed. Amusement, he thought, was the stuff of royalty. Court jesters and musicians. Board games. The hunt.

He thought of the game he had played with the so-called newlyweds. Yes, his darling Desirée was right. He would end the game now, after one final move on his part.

"You—newlyweds," he said pointing to K.C. and Gav. "Come, join me on the platform."

K.C. reached for Gav's hand. He squeezed hers gently, as they climbed the stairs to stand between Rance Randolph and Desirée Scott. K.C. thought she might be sick, so great was her fear.

In a flash, it was not her life that passed before her eyes. Rather, it was a picture of the early church, the Christians who had been sacrificed to the lions for the sport of the Romans.

They'd been given the opportunity to deny their faith, deny their belief in Jesus Christ, the Son of God. But even knowing they faced the most terrible of deaths, they stood firm.

She'd heard that some went singing into the arena to face the hungry beasts, knowing the terror and pain ahead.

K.C. had always wondered if she could stand up for her God in the face of a terrible death. But it had always been a philosophical question. Until this day, she'd never dreamed it could ever happen.

From her first hour on the compound, events had unfolded

so gradually that until the moment she and Gav were man-handled by the guards, she had kept alive the hope of rescue.

Now, her gaze rested on the cloth-covered tables, just beside where they stood. Crystal bowls of poisoned wine rested atop pedestals on either end, sterling chalices in the center, arranged around an elegant candelabra.

Poisoned wine. She wondered how Randolph and his guards could force someone to drink. She shuddered, trying not to picture the spectacle. She would find out soon enough.

Images of the early Christians came to her mind. Many had faced death for their beliefs. They, too, had refused to bow to false gods.

Instead they had chosen death, and the terror of being eaten alive by ravenous beasts in a stadium. As a sport for thousands to watch. As a game for the rulers to bet on.

Death. K.C. considered it now as a reality, maybe for the first time in her life. Death!

Then another thought followed rapidly, almost unbidden, at least by her: Death had been conquered. Christ died an agonizing death on the cross to bring life.

Death was not the victor—Christ was!

K.C. felt hope and joy burst forth inside her heart. He was alive! Christ was alive! That had been the hope of the early Christians. They knew that no death, no matter how terrible, would claim victory over them!

Their Lord was with them as they walked in to face the lions. But even the reality of his presence was only a reflection of the real joy they would know when they saw him face to face. *Now we see but a poor reflection as in a mirror, but then we shall see face to face.*

She lifted her gaze heavenward, looking beyond the curious faces of the crowd, beyond temporal walls that imprisoned her and Gav and Theodora and the others. She breathed in the deep peace brought by Christ's presence.

It is in dying, my beloved child, that you are born to eternal life!

Peace filled her being, a sweet and precious fragrance that left no room for fear.

"This question is the last of the game we've been playing," Randolph was saying. "And we might call this a *Pit and the Pendulum* question." He laughed, and beside him Desirée tittered.

"You will each answer separately." He looked pointedly at K.C. "I think we'll start with you, my little Satinka."

K.C. stepped closer to the microphone.

"Your question, my dear, is this: If you were given the choice to bow before the Ataran deity or die, which would you choose and why?"

K.C. felt surprisingly calm. She smiled at the sea of faces before her, breathing a prayer for them even as she began to speak. Then her gaze rested on Theodora. She remembered her aunt's words from the night she refused to bow. What a model of strength and commitment. She smiled softly into Theodora's eyes, wishing she could tell her how much she loved her.

"My aunt said it so eloquently the other night," she finally said, her heart pounding. She knew she was sealing her fate. "I bow to the only God and King, the God of Abraham and Isaac, the God of the Bible, who sent his only Son, Jesus, to redeem us from sin. He is the one true, living God. I cannot, I will not, bow to any other."

There was not a sound in the room.

"The game is over," Randolph said. He immediately searched the crowd for Brother Dakota, his guard, and when he spotted him standing near a side door, said, "Prepare the chalice." The guard moved up the stairs to the tables. He poured wine into one of the sterling chalices.

"And now," he gave Gav a challenging look, "it's your turn to answer the same question."

The room was filled with silence. Gav took a deep breath and when he spoke his voice was clear and loud. "I will not bow down, and my reasons are many."

"Give us just one," challenged Randolph.

"All right. But will you hear me out to the end of my reasoning?"

Randolph studied him for a moment, then glanced at Desirée. She lifted a regal eyebrow and nodded.

"Yes, go ahead and speak your piece," he said.

Gav stepped closer to the microphone and looked out at the upturned faces. "I will give my reasons to all of you," he said. Behind him, K.C. prayed harder than she'd ever prayed in her life.

"Because," he continued, "you deserve to hear them. You must hear them. I will not bow down to Rance Randolph, in his words, a representative of Ataran deity on Earth. I will not bow because, very simply, he is a fraud."

There was murmuring, and most of the Fellowship members looked at each other, their eyes unfocused, their thought processes dulled. But K.C. noticed that sprinkled throughout the massive group there were some who seemed alert. Those few moved closer to hear Gav's words.

"I came here to search for truth," he continued. "I won't lie to you—I'm a sheriff from a nearby community. I came also to search for people who'd been reported missing.

"First I want to tell you, there is no meteorite on its way to Earth." Several voices lifted in protest, calling him a liar. Others watched dully, as if he made no sense. Only the same few alert individuals remained attentive.

Randolph started forward, but when he saw the loud

317

protest against Gav's words, he smiled, and waved him on to continue.

"There is no meteorite," Gav repeated. "So you need not fear that the world is coming to an end.

"But there's something else that makes me loath to bow before this man."

Again, there was silence.

"He does not plan to travel to Atara with you! He has already deposited your money—those gifts you gave him of property, homes, businesses—into an account in a foreign bank! It's *your* money he plans to use to flee from this place once you are dead. Are you listening?"

K.C. saw Randolph start to bolt toward Gav, but Desirée gave him another of her calm, queenly smiles and touched his arm. He clamped his mouth shut and let Gav speak. But K.C. knew it was only a matter of time till Gav was given the same sentence as hers.

"I've seen the proof," he said quietly. "I saw the printout from the computer! I know this man is a fraud!"

At first there was no reaction. Gav's shoulders slumped forward, as if he knew he was defeated. The devotees stared at him in silence.

Then suddenly, someone from the back of the room called out. "I want proof!" Others said the same thing, and K.C. watched in amazement as their dulled expressions changed to anger and surprise and interest.

"Yes, we want proof, otherwise you're just another outsider looking to destroy our truth," said a loud voice near the front of the assemblage. Other voices rose in spirited discourse.

Rance Randolph, looking smug, stepped forward. "Yes," he said with a tight, triumphant smile, "where is your proof?"

Again, silence fell, almost as if a shadow, across the people.

Then with her head tilted regally upward and a majestic

318

smile on her face, Desirée took three graceful steps to the microphone and lifted it close to her lips.

Before the stunned and confused Randolph could say a word, she spoke, her voice ringing across the ocean of robed figures.

"I can provide that proof," she said.

TWENTY-SIX

Desirée Scott pulled several sheets of paper from a pocket in her robe. From K.C.'s vantage point, they looked to be from the same file that she and Gav had found on Randolph's computer. Columns of names, numbered accounts, and dollar amounts. Desirée waved them at the crowd.

"You'll want to take a close look at this. I've provided a copy for each of you." Her tone was now clipped, businesslike. Shades of a woman who'd once partnered with her husband in running a multimillion-dollar company. She nodded to Brother Dakota, who quickly began distributing the documents.

K.C. and Gav stared at each other, astounded. In front of them, hundreds of hands reached for the papers which now seemed to be flying across the group as they were distributed. Those cult members in the front rows, the first to scan the printout, were already crying out in anger and dismay, trying to stampede the stairs to get to Randolph on the platform. His guards clumsily tried to keep them back, looking to Randolph for direction.

But he seemed confused, powerless—as if he'd been so sure of his control that he was now unsure how to handle his followers. So he did nothing.

Desirée was still clearly in charge. "Look at column one," she called out. The hubbub quieted somewhat as the group listened. "You will see a list of each of our names, with a number next to each. That number matches our net worth when we came into the Fellowship.

"Then turn to page three. In column one you'll see a list of the Angels Crest assets.

"Now turn with me to page four." She waited as pages were flipped. "Here you'll see that these assets have been electronically transferred to a bank in Buenos Aires. The date of the final transfer was this morning at nine o'clock—just before Rance Randolph joined us here. Just before he came to join us…to journey with us…to Atara."

She paused, letting the realization sink in. The room was now silent. Even the most groggy of the followers were now at full attention.

"Don't you think it's convenient," she continued, "for us to leave on a journey, a journey that would surely cause our certain deaths…leaving Randolph with our millions?

"We die, he jumps on a plane for South America."

Now there were shouts of anger, and Randolph seemed to cower as his devotees turned against him, shouted at him, again tried to stampede the platform.

"Flip the page again," Desirée commanded and they quieted momentarily, doing her bidding.

"Randolph sold Angels Crest—for six million dollars—to a group of French investors." She shook her head slowly. "Conveniently, escrow closed yesterday.

"This makes me wonder, my friends, about the timing of the so-called meteorite. Isn't it interesting that its collision with Earth coincides so nearly with the close of escrow?"

K.C. looked at Gav. "The men you saw at the fountain?"

He nodded. "The buyers. I wonder if they knew his plans. Perhaps that's why the secrecy of the meeting."

They turned their attention to Desirée, who was now gazing out at the Fellowship members, a satisfied smile on her face. Finally, she took the microphone again and called out to

Brother Dakota. "Open the doors, my friend. I think it's time to include some interested bystanders."

Before Randolph could react, Dakota opened the doors, and to K.C.'s amazement, law enforcement officers poured inside, weapons pointed.

Randolph glanced wildly about, then bolted for the crystal bowl of tainted wines. He grabbed a chalice and dipped it into the crimson liquid, then raised it to his mouth. Gav dove for him, knocking the cup from his hands. The red wine sloshed across the linen cloth and dripped to the floor.

"Let him drink," growled Brother Dakota who had catapulted his round body onto the platform with surprising agility. He now held his weapon to Randolph's head. Then he reached under his robe, pulled out a pair of handcuffs, and quickly locked them into place on Randolph's wrists.

"You think you've outsmarted everyone here. Well, esteemed Ataran Master," he muttered, "there are some things about Angels Crest that will surprise *you*. The real property of *QmP* is one of them. It never contained poison. It never contained anything but water." He shoved Randolph down the stairs. Minutes later, Randolph stood against the far wall, head down, a spattering of light from the jeweled windows falling across his gold robe.

Clearly in charge, Dakota now shouted instructions to the other officers who continued to pour through the open doors. K.C. heard the blare of sirens and caught glimpses of the arriving ambulances, fire trucks, black-and-whites, emergency vehicles of every description, pulling to the front of the auditorium.

Randolph's remaining guards were rounded up, their guns removed. They were handcuffed and lined against the wall with their leader.

In the center of the auditorium many of the remaining

followers milled about as if dazed, shaking their heads and reading the documents. Some had broken into smaller groups and were talking to the dissidents.

Gav, brushing himself off from his scuffle with Randolph, walked back to stand near K.C. The amazement on his face matched hers. By now, Marigold and Theodora had rushed onto the platform so they could watch the activity with Gav, K.C., and Desirée.

"Do you think he's FBI?" K.C. asked Gav as they watched Dakota in action. "Somehow he doesn't look the part. You know, the image you usually think of."

"Maybe that's why he was so successful," Gav said.

"Is anyone who we thought they were?" K. C asked.

"What a mass of tangled webs it's turned out to be." He chuckled.

"Make that tangled vines," K.C. said with a grin.

"Brother Dakota's the greatest surprise," Gav said.

"The award for finest performance goes to Desirée," K.C. said, turning to the woman who now stood grinning, arm in arm with Marigold Green. "How in the world did you pull this off?"

Desirée laughed and gave Marigold a hug. "This woman reminded me of my acting skills. Did you know we worked together in a performance quite some time ago? She was my drama coach."

K.C. remembered. "Right after you played Puck in *A Midsummer Night's Dream*?" she said to Marigold.

"Ah yes. My Shakespeare debut!" Marigold said, licking her hands, then arranging her spikes. She couldn't have been happier if she'd won the Academy Award for best director.

"You fooled Randolph," Gav said to Desirée, shaking his head appreciatively. "We all tried—unsuccessfully, I might add. But you're the only one who managed the impossible."

Desirée reached over and put her arm around Theodora. "I wouldn't have if not for this dear woman. I came here so confused. I'd given up everything because of my despair. If Theodora hadn't come, then stayed—even when she knew she was risking her life—and talked some sense into me..." Her voice broke off. "I don't know what would have happened."

"But the computer file? How'd you find it?" Gav asked.

She smiled. "That part was easy. I was in Randolph's office right after you two were there. I found your e-mail. You'd logged on as Satinka, a guest, and it was addressed to someone named Max—" She turned to Theodora. "I remembered what you said about him. It had to be the same man, so I sent him a message, asking him to meet us here today, to bring the law with him."

She laughed. "I didn't realize until Brother Dakota broke into the room and caught me in the act, that he was FBI, working undercover. He'd come to the office to find the same information.

"I did a search by date and time, and the same file you'd discovered came up. We knew we had the proof we needed. We planned the rest of this before Rance Randolph came back to his office to write our wedding vows." A shadow of sadness crossed her face.

"You asked Max to meet us?" Theodora asked, looking anxiously toward the door. There was still a crowd of emergency crew workers, firemen, and policemen blocking the doorway.

"Yes, and he must have gotten the message because he certainly called in the troops," Desirée said with a grin. "I do believe he's called every law enforcement and emergency crew this side of the Rockies." She paused, and K.C. followed her gaze to where it rested on Dakota. The short round man was rushing around, still robed in his Angels of Fellowship attire. "Of course," she continued, "I think Dakota had something to do with the coordinated efforts of the FBI."

She gave the others a small smile. "He's asked me to go out to dinner with him once this is over."

Everyone looked back to her, surprised, and Marigold said, "Well, if you want my opinion, he's as cute as a bug. I'd take him over Efrem Zimbalist Jr., anytime."

K.C. wrinkled her nose. "Efrem who?"

"Before our time," Gav said. "He played an FBI agent on TV, back in the sixties."

"Not just any FBI agent," corrected Marigold, shaking her head. "The agent of all agents. But this guy…" She waggled one eyebrow toward Dakota, who was now escorting Randolph to the doorway. "…has Efrem beat all the way to Sunday."

Gav rolled his eyes and K.C. giggled. It seemed good to laugh after all the tension. Without realizing it—or maybe she did—Marigold had helped them all with her offbeat humor.

As soon as Randolph and his guards had been taken outdoors, the hubbub around the doorway lessened, and K.C. looked to Gav, then to her aunt. She circled her arm around Theodora's waist. "Why don't we go see who might be waiting outside—trying to get in?"

Theodora smiled. "I'd like that," she said.

The three moved down the stairs and headed through the crowd. Before they'd reached the back door, Father Max poked in his head and looked around.

A smile lit his face when he saw the three walking toward him.

Without hesitation, he moved to Theodora and took her hands in his. "Oh, my dear," he said, his eyes searching hers. "Are you all right?"

"I've never been better," she said. "Just hearing your voice, Max. And seeing your face once more." She reached up and patted his cheek. "Oh, how I've missed you!"

After a moment, he turned to K.C. and Gav. He took their hands, his days of concern and—more than likely—sleepless nights showing in his face. "And you two? You're not hurt?"

"We could feel your prayers, Father," Gav said. "God was right here with us."

"It was he who had hemmed you in," Father Max said. "Not Randolph."

K.C. and Gav nodded. "You got our message." K.C. said.

"Yes, but I was puzzled—until I received the second post from Desirée Scott. I was suspicious until I remembered that Marigold Green had mentioned her to you. I prayed about it, attempted to put the puzzle pieces together, and finally felt at peace. Then I simply picked up the phone to do as she asked."

Then he turned again to Theodora. "Dear, about the ballet…"

Theodora smiled. "Well, at least we can still go. It's tomorrow night, isn't it? I've thought about it all week."

"It was last week," Father Max said gently. "That's how we knew something was wrong."

Theodora narrowed her eyes in thought. Then she brought her hand to her mouth as she realized her mistake. "Oh my, I had two things written on the calendar for this week—Bubba's grooming appointment and our date for the ballet." She looked up at Max. "Does that mean they were both last week?"

K.C. asked, "Does Bubba's groomer drive a white van and pick up his furry clients?"

"The groomer is a female, actually, but why do you ask?"

K.C. laughed again. "Well, it seems Marigold saw what she thought was a catnapping."

"A catnapping?"

K.C. explained.

Theodora shook her head slowly. "I'm sure it was Sally of Sally's Grooming Service. Poor Bubba. He must be wondering why I haven't picked him up." She smiled. "And Sally too. Though she often boards him when I'm away. She probably thought I forgot to ask her this time."

She turned to Father Max. "I'm so sorry about the ballet."

He took her hand. "All I really care about is being with you. We have so little time alone."

"That's one thing I'd like to remedy, dearest," Theodora said, her eyes bright as she gazed into his. "Our time alone."

"I couldn't agree more," Father Max said. Without embarrassment, he folded Theodora into his arms and held her close. For a long time, they stood, arms wrapped around each other, seeming oblivious to the hundreds of people still milling around them.

Gav and K.C. looked at each other and smiled.

"Do you think it's love?" K.C. said, raising a brow.

"Definitely. Love of the truest sort," Gav said. But he was looking at K.C., not the older couple. He caught her hand. "Don't you think it's time we go home?" When she nodded, he circled his arm around her shoulders, and turned her gently toward the door.

Theodora and Father Max followed, and when K.C. looked back, she wondered how they were managing to navigate their way around obstacles and people.

They had eyes only for each other.

TWENTY-SEVEN

K.C. leaned back in her chair at the *Pelican Journal* and stretched her arms. She was finally settling into a normal routine, writing her column, selling ad space, making sure Casper and the other part-time staff were following leads for next week's edition.

Georgie O'Reilly had done a stellar job of running the paper during K.C.'s week away, and after her return just one week ago, the two of them had worked day and night to break the Angels Crest story in time for this week's edition. Georgie was so exhausted—and behind on her wedding plans, she pointed out more than once—that K.C. had given her the week off.

Now she almost regretted it. Since the *Journal* had rolled off the presses and hit the streets the day before, the telephone hadn't stopped ringing. Townspeople called to congratulate her. People from as far away as San Francisco called to thank her for getting their loved ones out of the cult.

It rang again, and she frowned, expecting another such interruption.

"Hello," she almost growled into the receiver.

"K.C.!" There was no mistaking the voice.

"Hey, Marigold. What's up?" She probably needn't ask. Likely it was time for the annual live oak tape-measuring event. A reporter would be required. And a photographer, of course.

Marigold's voice was breathless with excitement. "You'll never guess what I've done."

"You're probably right, Marigold. I can never guess what you're up to. What *have* you done?"

Marigold hesitated. "Well, more about all that later. But first of all, how are you doing after all the excitement?"

She couldn't help chuckling. She figured Marigold would be talking about "the excitement" for at least the next dozen years. "That's sweet of you to ask, Marigold. I'm actually settling back into the routine of things with the *Journal*, with my home…"

"With Gav?"

Aha. This was the real reason behind the call. K.C. knew that practically everyone in their small hometown wondered about the relationship. "No," she said. "Not with Gav."

"You two aren't…ah…planning to, well, get back together?"

"No, we're not," K.C. sighed. "At least, not yet."

"Well, why not?"

"It's personal. All I can tell you is that we've decided to give ourselves some time…and space. We'll see how it goes. Besides, he's got a job to do at Sugarloaf Ridge. I've got a job to do here." She paused. "Is that why you called?"

"Oh, lands, no!" she said quickly. "Absolutely not."

"Well, then—?"

Again the breathless quality returned to the big woman's voice. "Well," she laughed. "I called *Time*."

"You mean the magazine?"

"It wasn't time and temperature."

"Marigold, why?"

"So they'd come out and do an interview."

K.C. groaned. "I don't want to talk to any more reporters, Marigold. You know that." She paused. "You even agreed that after the last hundred phone calls begging for our time, we wouldn't accept any more. None of us."

"Well, I didn't think you meant it," Marigold said, now in a huff. "Besides, I didn't do it just for you. It's for the sakes of all those poor former cult members. It means so much to them, K.C., that you're still out there telling their story."

"I doubt that they want any more attention. I've a mind to call up the *Time* people and tell them no."

Marigold let out an audible sigh. "Well, if you want to let them down—and our friends from Angels Crest—that's fine by me. I thought I was doing you and them a favor."

K.C. bit her tongue. She'd rather measure oak tree circumferences than face another interview, but she said, "Okay, give me the stats."

"The what?"

"Stats. You know, time, place. Please, don't tell me it's in my office." K.C. looked around the messy room with its stacks of papers, galleys, moldy coffee cups.

"No, no. Not your office. I knew that wouldn't do at all."

"Then where?"

"At the gazebo out by the Shorecliff Lodge. You know the place?"

"Of course, but that's a strange place for an interview."

"They wanted a small-town, seaside look in the background. You know, atmosphere."

"They asked you to set this up?"

"Well, I, ah, sort of volunteered," confessed Marigold. "This one's for you, K.C. They asked specifically for you." She sounded jealous. "That means you'll get all the good quotes."

K.C. glanced at the pile of work on her desk, knowing she could ill afford the time away. Especially with Georgie O'Reilly gone this week. But Marigold had gone to all this trouble. "Okay," she finally said. "What time?"

"Noon," Marigold said. "Noon sharp."

"I'll be there," K.C. said with a sigh. She looked at her watch. She had just enough time to swing by her condo, pick up Satinka for her grooming appointment, then drive the winding road to the Shorecliff. The *Time* folks must have picked the location for their own convenience, she decided.

331

The Shorecliff was probably providing their lodging, and they didn't want to miss one moment of the beautiful view. But no matter, it would be a refreshing drive.

K.C. headed out to the Morgan, folded back the top, and fastened it into place. Moments later, she was speeding toward her condo.

"Ah, sweet baby," she said, cuddling the little cat before gently placing her in the carrier. After her disguise at Angels Crest, she would never think of Satinka in quite the same way. For one thing, now she usually preferred to call her pet Tink.

It took only a few more minutes to deposit Tink at the vet's, then steer the Morgan back onto the highway leading out of town. The sun beat on her shoulders, and she threw back her head, relishing the fresh ocean breeze hitting her face and tumbling her hair.

An indigo sky spread above an almost emerald ocean. Below the winding road where she drove, under steep red cliffs, frothy waves rolled to shore. She breathed in the sea air and smiled at the awkward flights of the pelicans as they tumbled and dove for fish. Intermingled with them, seagulls swooped and soared, their alabaster wings backlit by the sun. And in the ocean's forest of kelp, sea otters frolicked, swimming on their backs, cracking their clamshells open with stones.

Sights that only a week ago, K.C. was certain she wouldn't see again.

Freedom never tastes more precious than after you've known life without it. Light is never brighter than when you've known darkness. And love?

Love is never sweeter, K.C. thought, than when you feared it was lost forever.

She swung the little sportster into the parking lot next to the Shorecliff Lodge. At first it struck her as odd that there were no other vehicles, then she remembered that *Time* magazine, of course, was probably sending a single journalist and perhaps a photographer. They probably were driving from their nearest office in San Francisco.

It was strange, though, that Aunt Theo, Father Max, Gav, and of course Marigold weren't there yet. They had attended all the other interviews in force. Well, K.C. thought, if she had to face this one alone, she could certainly do it.

As she walked out to the gazebo, which was located at the end of a long promontory above the cliffs, she reviewed the facts for the interview: Rance Randolph was in jail, without possibility of bail, having been charged with one count of murder—Ariel Tilman—and some twenty-seven counts of fraud. By the time he was formally arraigned, it was expected that the count would be in the hundreds.

Lawyers were scrambling to freeze his foreign assets and untangle the mass of legal red tape required for returning all funds to their rightful owners. It would be a long process, probably unsettled for years to come.

Many of the former cult members were undergoing therapy and were expected to join their families and friends within a few weeks. It would take years for the damage to be undone. Some professionals had openly wondered if the scars would ever fade completely.

K.C. had ended all interviews by telling reports of the surprising hope experienced by the former Angels of Fellowship members. Many of them had gone into the cult believing that they were unloved by family and friends. Of course, Randolph had played on their emotions, convincing them their families had turned their backs. In some cases, he'd even planted ideas of child abuse in their "cleansed" minds.

Without K.C.'s knowledge, Georgie O'Reilly had called these family members and friends into action, printing the truth about Angels Crest in her edition of the *Pelican Journal*.

By the time the group was transported to hotels and motels throughout the Napa Valley, friends and family flooded into the region from all around the country. The stunned former cult members had been overwhelmed, and the outpouring of love had done more for the healing process than any other single act.

She sighed. Yes, she was ready for the reporters, though after checking her watch again, she couldn't help but feel irritated that they were late.

K.C. had now reached the gazebo. Puzzled, she walked inside. A small, round table was set with a red-checkered cloth. A picnic basket was set to one side, and daisies, tiger lilies, and a sprig of eucalyptus had been placed in a small watering can in the center of the table.

A vehicle swung into the parking lot, and K.C. shaded her eyes and squinted into the sun, hoping it was the news crew so they could get this interview over with. Obviously the lodge had set up the gazebo for expected guests, and she didn't want to intrude.

Then she realized that the vehicle was a black-and-white, a sheriff's four-wheel drive—just like Gav's.

She blinked and looked again. It *was* Gav. Grinning ear to ear, he hurried toward her.

"Did Marigold call you, too?" She asked, still puzzled, when he'd almost reached her.

"Actually, no," he said.

K.C. frowned. "Then, how did you know—?"

He was right in front of her now and had caught up her hands in his. "I called her," he said, still grinning.

"You did?"

He nodded. "I wanted this to be a surprise." He walked to the table, plucked one of the daisies from its container, then handed it to her. "This is for you, Kace."

"There's no interview from *Time*?"

He shook his head, looking very pleased with himself. "Marigold came up with the ruse when I asked her to help me. She, of course, was delighted. Said it would give her a chance to practice her acting skills."

"Next thing we know she'll be doing Shakespeare," K.C. said, smiling into Gav's eyes. "Maybe she'll land the role of Puck again."

"Actually, I don't really care what Marigold Green will be doing," he said, his gaze locked on hers.

"You don't?" whispered K.C., feeling her heart start to dance beneath her ribs.

"Not really." He gathered her into his arms. "I only care what we're doing," he said, his voice suddenly husky. "And, my love, that we're doing it together."

She touched his face in wonder. "Really?"

"I don't ever want to be away from you again," he said, and bent his head to touch his lips to hers.

K.C. thought her knees might give way beneath her. "Oh, Gav…" she breathed, circling her arms around his neck and holding on for dear life as he thoroughly kissed her again. "Oh, Gav…" was all she could manage.

Finally, he pulled back just enough to again look in her eyes. "When I said I wanted us to be together a minute ago, I didn't mean just for right now."

"I know," she breathed.

"I mean—"

"Forever," she finished.

Gav threw back his head and laughed out loud, then, folding her into his arms, he held her tight. "Forever," he murmured into her hair.

Dear Reader:

Last summer before I began writing *Tangled Vines,* my husband and I visited the Napa and Sonoma Valleys of California where lush, green vineyards stretch for miles across the rolling hills.

As we drove along, I noticed the gardeners in the vineyards, pruning and clipping and cutting. Many of the vines were thick and gnarled, obviously decades old. Through the years they had been severely pruned. They had survived California's weather pattern of floods and droughts and searing heat. Yet here they were—beautiful, strong, and abundant with clumps of grapes!

I thought of John 15: "I am the true vine, and my Father is the gardener. He cuts off every branch in me that bears no fruit, while every branch that does bear fruit he prunes so that it will be even more fruitful…. I am the vine; you are the branches."

God's pruning can be painful. Often we find it difficult to understand why troublesome circumstances come our way. Yet James tells us that these "prunings" are occasions for joy because they test our faith and develop in us perseverance and maturity (James 1:2–4).

Joy? Oh, my. That's hard. Especially in the middle of the Gardener's pruning and cutting. I find it helps to remember, though, those strong and glorious vineyards I saw last summer. What a wonder—what joy!—to think that our Gardener is working to produce that same beauty, strength, and fruit in me—and in you!

God bless you, dear readers. I treasure you all. Though I can't always answer your letters personally, I love hearing from you. Each of you remains in my heart and prayers.

All praise and glory to Him!

Write to Diane Noble
c/o Alabaster Books
P.O. Box 1720
Sisters, Oregon 97759

THE PALISADES LINE

Look for these new releases at your local bookstore. If the title you seek is not in stock, the store may order you a copy using the ISBN listed.

Heartland Skies, Melody Carlson (March 1998)
ISBN 1-57673-264-9

Jayne Morgan moves to the small town of Paradise with the prospect of marriage, a new job, and plenty of horses to ride. But when her fiancé dumps her, she's left with loose ends. Then she wins a horse in a raffle, and the handsome rancher who boards her horse makes things look decidedly better.

Memories, Peggy Darty (May 1998)
ISBN 1-57673-171-5

In this sequel to *Promises*, Elizabeth Calloway is left with amnesia after witnessing a hit-and-run accident. Her husband, Michael, takes her on a vacation to Cancún so that she can relax and recover her memory. What they don't realize is that the killer is following them, hoping to wipe out Elizabeth's memory permanently....

Remembering the Roses, Marion Duckworth (June 1998)
ISBN 1-57673-236-3

Sammie Sternberg is trying to escape her memories of the man who betrayed her, and she ends up in a small town on the Olympic Peninsula in Washington. There she opens her dream business—an antique shop in an old Victorian—and meets a reclusive watercolor artist who helps to heal her broken heart.

Waterfalls, Robin Jones Gunn
ISBN 1-57673-221-5

In a visit to Glenbrooke, Oregon, Meredith Graham meets movie star Jacob Wilde and is sure he's the one. But when Meri puts her foot in her mouth, things fall apart. Is isn't until the two of them get thrown together working on a book-and-movie project that Jacob realizes his true feelings, and this time he's the one who's starstruck.

China Doll, Barbara Jean Hicks (June 1998)
ISBN 1-57673-262-2
Bronson Bailey is having a mid-life crisis: after years of globetrotting in his journalism career, he's feeling restless. Georgine Nichols has also reached a turning point: after years of longing for a child, she's decided to adopt. The problem is, now she's fallen in love with Bronson, and he doesn't want a child.

Angel in the Senate, Kristen Johnson Ingram (April 1998)
ISBN 1-57673-263-0
Newly elected senator Megan Likely heads to Washington with high hopes for making a difference in government. But accusations of election fraud, two shocking murders, and threats on her life make the Senate take a backseat. She needs to find answers, but she's not sure who she can trust anymore.

Irish Rogue, Annie Jones
ISBN 1-57673-189-8
Michael Shaughnessy has paid the price for stealing a pot of gold, and now he's ready to make amends to the people he's hurt. Fiona O'Dea is number one on his list. The problem is, Fiona doesn't want to let Michael near enough to hurt her again. But before she knows it, he's taken his Irish charm and worked his way back into her life...and her heart.

Forgotten, Lorena McCourtney (February 1998)
ISBN 1-57673-222-3
A woman wakes up in an Oregon hospital with no memory of who she is. When she's identified as Kat Cavanaugh, she returns

to her home in California. As Kat struggles to recover her memory, she meets a fiancé she doesn't trust and an attractive neighbor who can't believe how she's changed. She begins to wonder if she's really Kat Cavanaugh, but if she isn't, what happened to the real Kat?

The Key, Gayle Roper (April 1998)
ISBN 1-57673-223-1
On Kristie Matthews's first day living on an Amish farm, she gets bitten by a dog and is rushed to the emergency room by a handsome stranger. In the ER, an elderly man in the throes of a heart attack hands her a key and tells her to keep it safe. Suddenly odd accidents begin to happen to her, but no one's giving her any answers.

Tables on the Prairie, Joyce Valdois Smith (May 1998)
ISBN 1-57673-188-X
In the space of a few months, Elise Dumond's life has changed forever. Both her parents are dead, and her family is in danger of losing their farm. Her brother's friend Daniel comes to the rescue and suggests Elise get a job as a Harvey Girl in one of the restaurants "civilizing" the West. The best part for Elise is that she'll get to spend more time with Daniel....

— ANTHOLOGIES —

Fools for Love, Ball, Brooks, Jones (March 1998)
ISBN 1-57673-235-5
By Karen Ball: Kitty starts pet-sitting, but when her clients turn out to be more than she can handle, she enlists help from a handsome handyman.
By Jennifer Brooks: Caleb Murphy tries to acquire a book collection from a widow, but she has one condition: he must marry her granddaughter first.

By Annie Jones: A college professor who has been burned by love vows not to be fooled twice, until her ex-fiancé shows up and ruins her plans!

Heart's Delight, **Ball, Hicks, Noble**
ISBN 1-57673-220-7
By Karen Ball: Corie receives a Valentine's Day date from her sisters and thinks she's finally found the one...until she learns she went out with the wrong man.
By Barbara Jean Hicks: Carina and Reid are determined to break up their parents' romance, but when it looks like things are working, they have a change of heart.
By Diane Noble: Two elderly bird-watchers set aside their differences to try to save a park from disaster but learn they've bitten off more than they can chew.

BE SURE TO LOOK FOR ANY OF THE 1997 TITLES
YOU MAY HAVE MISSED:

Surrender, **Lynn Bulock** (ISBN 1-57673-104-9)
Single mom Cassie Neel accepts a blind date from her children for her birthday.

Wise Man's House, **Melody Carlson** (ISBN 1-57673-070-0)
A young widow buys her childhood dream house, and a mysterious stranger moves into her caretaker's cottage.

Moonglow, **Peggy Darty** (ISBN 1-57673-112-X)
Tracy Kosell comes back to Moonglow, Georgia, and investigates a case with a former schoolmate, who's now a detective.

Promises, **Peggy Darty** (ISBN 1-57673-149-9)
A Christian psychologist asks her detective husband to help her find a dangerous woman.

Texas Tender, **Sharon Gillenwater** (ISBN 1-57673-111-1)
Shelby Nolan inherits a watermelon farm and asks the sheriff for help when two elderly men begin digging holes in her fields.

Clouds, **Robin Jones Gunn** (ISBN 1-57673-113-8)
Flight attendant Shelly Graham runs into her old boyfriend, Jonathan Renfield, and learns he's engaged.

Sunsets, **Robin Jones Gunn** (ISBN 1-57673-103-0)
Alissa Benson has a run-in at work with Brad Phillips, and is more than a little upset when she finds out he's her neighbor!

Snow Swan, **Barbara Jean Hicks** (ISBN 1-57673-107-3)
Toni, an unwed mother and a recovering alcoholic, falls in love for the first time. But if Clark finds out the truth about her past, will he still love her?

Irish Eyes, **Annie Jones** (ISBN 1-57673-108-1)
Julia Reed gets drawn into a crime involving a pot of gold and has her life turned upside down by Interpol agent Cameron O'Dea.

Father by Faith, **Annie Jones** (ISBN 1-57673-117-0)
Nina Jackson buys a dude ranch and hires cowboy Clint Cooper as her foreman, but her son, Alex, thinks Clint is his new daddy!

Stardust, **Shari MacDonald** (ISBN 1-57673-109-X)
Gillian Spencer gets her dream assignment but is shocked to learn she must work with Maxwell Bishop, who once broke her heart.

Kingdom Come, **Amanda MacLean** (ISBN 1-57673-120-0)
Ivy Rose Clayborne, M.D., pairs up with the grandson of the coal baron to fight the mining company that is ravaging her town.

Dear Silver, **Lorena McCourtney** (ISBN 1-57673-110-3)
When Silver Sinclair receives a letter from Chris Bentley ending their relationship, she's shocked, since she's never met the man!

Enough! **Gayle Roper** (ISBN 1-57673-185-5)
When Molly Gregory gets fed up with her three teenaged children, she announces that she's going on strike.

A Mother's Love, **Bergren, Colson, MacLean**
(ISBN 1-57673-106-5)
Three heartwarming stories share the joy of a mother's love.

Silver Bells, **Bergren, Krause, MacDonald**
(ISBN 1-57673-119-7)
Three novellas focus on romance during Christmastime.